THE RELIGIOUS DIMENSION
OF POLITICAL BEHAVIOR

Recent Titles in
Bibliographies and Indexes in Religious Studies

Christian Voluntarism in Britain and North America: A Bibliography and Critical
Assessment
William H. Brackney

Ecology, Justice, and Christian Faith: A Critical Guide to the Literature
Peter W. Bakken, Joan Gibb Engel, and J. Ronald Engel

Modern American Popular Religion: A Critical Assessment and Annotated Bibliography
Charles H. Lippy

Reincarnation: A Selected Annotated Bibliography
Lynn Kear

Psychoanalytic Studies of Religion: A Critical Assessment and Annotated Bibliography
Benjamin Beit-Hallahmi

The Confessions of Saint Augustine: An Annotated Bibliography of Modern
Criticism, 1888–1995
Richard Severson

New Religious Movements in Western Europe: An Annotated Bibliography
Elisabeth Arweck and Peter B. Clarke

African Traditional Religion in South Africa: An Annotated Bibliography
David Chidester, Chirevo Kwenda, Robert Petty, Judy Tobler, and Darrell Wratten

The Islamic Revival Since 1988: A Critical Survey and Bibliography
Yvonne Yasbeck Haddad and John L. Esposito with Elizabeth Hiel and Hibba Abugideiri

Christianity in South Africa: An Annotated Bibliography
David Chidester, Judy Tobler, and Darrel Wratten

Islam, Hinduism, and Judaism in South Africa: An Annotated Bibliography
David Chidester, Judy Tobler, and Darrel Wratten

Consulting Spirits: A Bibliography
Joel Bjorling

THE RELIGIOUS DIMENSION OF POLITICAL BEHAVIOR

A Critical Analysis and Annotated Bibliography

Compiled by
Laura R. Olson and Ted G. Jelen

Bibliographies and Indexes in Religious Studies, Number 47
G. E. Gorman, Advisory Editor

Greenwood Press
Westport, Connecticut • London

Library of Congress Cataloging-in-Publication Data

Olson, Laura, 1967–
    The religious dimension of political behavior : a
critical analysis and annotated bibliography /
compiled by Laura R. Olson and Ted G. Jelen.
        p.   cm.—(Bibliographies and indexes in
religious studies, ISSN 0742–6836 ; no.   47)
    Includes indexes.
    ISBN 0–313–28484–9 (alk. paper)
    1. Religion and politics—United States—
Bibliography.   1. Jelen, Ted G.   11. Title.
III. Series.
Z7776.72.047   1998
[BL65.P7]
016.3205′5′0973—dc21   98–28016

British Library Cataloguing in Publication Data is available.

Copyright © 1998 by Ted G. Jelen and Laura R. Olson

Library of Congress Catalog Card Number: 98–28016
ISBN: 0–313–28484–9
ISSN: 0742–6836

First published in 1998

Greenwood Press, 88 Post Road West, Westport, CT 06881
An imprint of Greenwood Publishing Group, Inc.

Printed in the United States of America

The paper used in this book complies with the
Permanent Paper Standard issued by the National
Information Standards Organization (Z39.48–1984).

10 9 8 7 6 5 4 3 2 1

Contents

Foreword

The state is not the sphere of life in which truth, love, and holiness as such are intended. These all transcend it, even though they cannot come into existence without it. But as they cannot come into existence without it, the state participates in the holiness of that which it helps into existence, and therefore it participates in truth and love and has value through them. So that it may not take the place of the holy, the state opposes every element of hypocrisy that inevitably accompanies every alliance of political will to power and religious demand.

- Paul Tillich,
Political Expectation

The great return to roots has begun. You and I have seen only the beginning, only the first act. But even that beginning is enough to get the blood racing with exultation. Christians in America have struck free. We could once be counted on by Caesar — for the silence that kills, for bargains arrived at across the bodies of the victims, for a blessing on violence and a sanction on murder. No more of that.

- Daniel
Berrigan,
America is Hard
to Find

Paul Tillich offers us a theoretical or philosophical framework for the relation between political behavior and religion; Daniel Berrigan exemplifies the religious man as political activist. These two individuals, one an outstanding Protestant philosopher-theologian and the other a Jesuit activist and social commentator, exemplify two aspects of the creative tension between religion and political behavior in our era. But the relationship between these spheres is not unique to the second half of the twentieth century.

Indeed, in many respects the history of the Judeo-Christian tradition can be characterized as the history of interaction between religion and politics. Entire sections of the Hebrew Bible are devoted to theological musings on the political life of Israel, or to prophetic utterances on the political concerns and future of the people of Israel. And what is the New Testament, if not the political story of a man who opposed the dominant authority and, as a consequence, paid the ultimate sacrifice? The subsequent history of both Jews and Christians, as well as Muslims, is one in which politics and belief, secular and sacred, are intimately related – witness St. Augustine's *De Civitae Dei*, St. Bernard of Clairvaux on the Second Crusade, Bonhoeffer and the Nazi movement, the Dutch Reformed Church and *apartheid* in South Africa or, conversely, Martin Luther King and the civil rights movement in the United States. Every era has its examples of how religion has responded to and sought to influence political action. These examples are not historically significant figures in some far-off land, a Helder Camara or Beyers Naudé perhaps, but rather very often individuals in "our own back yard."

We are often told by politicians and other vested interests that religion should "stay out" of politics, and in the U.S. there is almost a paranoid concern about this in some circles. As a slightly personal aside, when in 1997 some government leaders in Australia criticized leading churchmen for speaking out on the issue of land rights legislation for Aboriginal people, this criticism itself was attacked by most commentators. Really it is rather late in the day for anyone to demand that religion not address issues of political importance, for it is part of the fabric of Christianity and Judaism, and of Islam as well, for religion to have a political focus. As Jelen says elsewhere in this volume, "whether the framers of the [American] Constitution were religious men or not is a moot question; the fact is that throughout American history religion has been entwined with politics." The question, then, is not whether the relationship between religion and political behavior should exist but rather how it should manifest itself.

Indeed, throughout history in most of the world, theologians and religious leaders have addressed the political issues of their time, either to legitimize or to offer a prophetic critique. Tillich, perhaps more clearly than most, has sought to bring some order to the often chaotic range of relations between religion and politics (or political cultus) by categorizing the state as "demonic", "divine" or "watchman".[1] The demonic state, a Hobbesian Leviathan, is all-powerful: "all spiritual values are subjected to it, and are permitted or excluded by it." Conversely, in the Hegelian divine state, it has become a "...bearer of all spiritual values" and identical with morality and religion. The state is the earthly God, and "all holiness is concentrated in it." The third symbol is that of the "watchman state" characteristic of liberalism and modern secularism; here the state is not consecrated but rather acts to protect religion and belief so that they can develop freely. Thus, "The state has a purely negative function. It struggles against the powers of the night which threaten the peaceful process of life."

This Tillichian paradigm is summarized here partly to show the complexity of relations that have existed between religion and political behavior (or the state in Tillich's sheme) and partly to indicate that it has been an issue of focused debate in the West at least since the seventeenth century. It is also offered as one model to help make sense of the multitude of views and approaches exemplified in the writings discussed in this annotated bibliography. Perhaps wisely, the compilers of *The Religious Dimension of Political Behavior* have not sought to impose their own bibliographic classification on the literature, allowing the introductory essay to offer a more discursive framework. Nevertheless, as the project has developed and the final selection of entries been made, the demonic-divine-"watchman" model seemed to offer suitable means of categorizing the content of most of the literature.

That the literature needs to be categorized in some way is indisputable in view of the fact that it is so all-encompassing in political, religious and social terms. In the first place, "political behavior" legitimately cannot be confined to a specific type of activity; it includes voting behavior, interest and pressure group activity, socio-political movements, the formation of public opinion. Furthermore, religious concern is not limited to a single issue or even a definable range of related issues with political import; one year it may be the abortion debate, in another year environmental issues, and perhaps capital punishment or the personal morality of politicians in a third.[2] If the range of issues is this broad, so too is the spectrum of religious groups and denominations involved in political debate. For example, in the 1960's the Jesuits, through clergy such as Daniel Berrigan, were noted for their "radical" involvement in political discussion and activism; more recently, and more conservatively, the U.S. National Conference of Catholic Bishops has continued its clear opposition to abortion. At the other end of the denominational spectrum, conservative evangelical Protestants have been mobilized on a range of direct political issues through the Moral Majority and the Christian Coalition. Almost every other religious persuasion, with the exception of the avowedly quietistic, has had its say on one issue or another in recent years.

If political behavior is interpreted so inclusively, if the issues under discussion are so all-encompassing and if the spectrum of religious groups engaged in the debate is so broad, then the literature on salient topics is unlikely to be insignificant in volume. Indeed, in the anglophone world the extent of writing on these topics in the last three decades or so has been daunting. Not only church leaders and politicians, but also social scientists and journalists, philosophers and theologians, historians, ethnicists and biblical scholars have all felt compelled to add their perspectives to the debate. Journals and publishers too numerous to count have taken an interest in the range of issues related to religion and politics, and it is unusual not to find a new book or article on the subject during weekly forays to the university library or trips across the Internet.

For these and a number of related reasons it was most gratifying to have Ted Jelen agree, back in 1990, to take on the task of preparing a volume devoted to this perennially popular area of investigation. Professor Jelen of the University of Nevada and his colleague, Dr. Laura Olson of Clemson University, possess ample measures of those qualities needed to collect and assess the literature on religious dimensions of political behavior - this much is evident from their impeccable choices of entries and the quality of annotations in the bibliography. Moreover, the introductory survey, "The Religious Dimensions of Political Behavior: Successes and Limitations," comprehensively analyzes the principal developments and themes in the field. Students new to this area of study, as well as scholars seeking to order their more extensive knowledge, will find this opening discussion immensely beneficial. Furthermore, the bibliography itself succeeds in covering the key aspects of the field, from historical and philosophical underpinnings to grassroots activities and institutional structures. In a single listing of both books and articles the compilers have thoroughly and – a key consideration in this field – objectively annotated a representative range of the most important works on the religion-politics nexus. Indeed, so thorough is their treatment (extending to some 400 items) that the bibliography will serve as a major resource not only for newcomers to the religion and politics debate, but also for those engaged in advanced study and scholarship.

Putting this volume together has been no simple task for the compilers, yet they have done so competently and professionally, thereby making my task as advisory editor exceptionally enjoyable. The result of Jelen and Olson's careful scholarship is a judicious survey of the most significant literature that is at once accessible to students and useful to scholars. *The Religious Dimension of Political Behavior: A Critical Analysis and Annotated Bibliography* is a worthy complement to Roger T. Wolcott and Dorita Bolger's earlier volume in the series, *Church and Social Action: A Critical Assessment and Bibliographical Survey* (1990), and I am pleased to welcome it as another quality addition to Bibliographies and Indexes in Religious Studies.

1.   Paul Tillich, Political Expectation. Trans. by James Luther Adams (New York: Harper and Row, 1971), pp. 100-101.
2.   It is worth pointing out that religion and environmental issues have been dealt with elsewhere in the series; see Peter W. Bakken, Joan Gibb Engel and J. Ronald Engel, *Ecology, Justice and Christian Faith: A Critical Guide to the Literature*. Bibliographies and Indexes in Religious Studies, 36 (Westport: Greenwood Press, 1995). Similarly, the matter of capital punishment is being addressed in a forthcoming volume.

Dr. G.E. Gorman FLA FRSA
Advisory Editor
Charles Stuart University
Riverina
March 1998

Preface

During the past two decades, religion has become a highly visible force in American politics. In 1979, Rev. Jerry Falwell founded an organization, known as Moral Majority, which promised (or threatened) to alter the nature and practice of political discourse in the United States. Supporters of Moral Majority regarded the mobilization of Christian conservatives as the force that would return traditional American values to a nation which had gone astray. Conversely, opponents feared that Moral Majority would usher in a new period of intolerance and repression of those who do not conform to the doctrinal and behavioral requisites of the Christian Right. Such opponents regarded Moral Majority as genuinely subversive of core American values like freedom, tolerance, and diversity.

Twenty years later, neither the hopes nor fears of observers of the Christian Right have been realized. Religious conservatives have not enacted much of their social agenda: Abortion remains legal, organized prayer in public school remains proscribed by the Courts, and the emancipation of women from traditional gender roles continues. However, religious interest groups have become entrenched in U.S. politics at all levels, and the Christian Right has become a formidable faction within the Republican Party. While religious conservatives have not dominated political life in the United States, they have gained (in Ralph Reeds words) a place at the table of American political discourse.

The increased political visibility of religion has occasioned a corresponding growth in scholarly writing in this area. Over the past twenty years or so, a large number of empirical studies on the relationship between religious belief and political behavior on the part of the mass public have been published. This book constitutes an attempt to provide guidance and interpretation of this growing literature. We have confined our attention to empirical work in the field of religion and politics in the United States. We ignore, for most purposes, ethical or normative concerns, and issues of constitutional law. While these are fascinating areas of study, they are simply beyond the scope of the present effort. Similarly, although religion is an important political force in many other nations of the world, we do not address the extensive literature on the political role of religion in comparative politics.

What follows is an interpretive essay on the religion and politics literature, an annotated bibliography, and indexes organized by title, author, and subject. In our view, the field of religion and politics has produced a number of useful empirical generalizations, but has not generated much in the way of systematic theory or scientific progress. We further argue that the lack of general theory in the religion and politics literature is the result of the substantive nature of the subject matter, and is thus not attributable to any intellectual or methodological failure of political scientists or sociologists. The shortage of generally accepted theoretical frameworks for understanding religious politics has guided the construction of the annotated bibliography, which constitutes the bulk of this volume. In writing each entry, we have chosen to focus on a relatively narrow description of the general theoretical basis, methodological approach, and empirical results of each study under consideration, and have devoted less attention to conceptual or theoretical frameworks. In our estimation, any particular empirical study may be relevant to a variety of substantive or theoretical agendas, and we have chosen to present empirical findings in as undigested a form as possible, given the limits of brevity and scope of this volume.

There are two general uses to which this book may be put. First, readers who are new to the field of religion and politics may find our introductory essay useful, in that we seek to provide thematic summaries of a variety of literatures. Students and scholars alike may wish to incorporate religious variables into their accounts of American political phenomena, but (perhaps understandably) do not wish to make such an undertaking their lives work. We hope our efforts will provide a starting point and useful summary for those approaching the subject for the first time.

Second, we are hopeful that more advanced scholars will find this book useful as a reference tool. As we have noted, there is a great deal of work being done in the field of religion and politics, and it is difficult for even sophisticated analysts to keep up with the literature. With all due modesty, we believe we have found some fascinating studies in rather unlikely places, and we believe that our efforts will help provide a common understanding of a rapidly growing corpus of scholarly writing. In compiling the bibliography, we were particularly distressed at the incredible lack of cross-citation between the disciplines of political science and sociology. In our view, the study of religion and politics is one in which it makes even less sense than usual to respect disciplinary boundaries, and we would suggest that this volume makes an interdisciplinary approach to the study of religious politics somewhat easier.

There are several people we would like to thank for their assistance along the way. Tom Gorman, Alicia Merritt and Pamela St. Clair have our eternal gratitude for their guidance, confidence, and (above all) patience. Pat Ariano, of Benedictine University, and Dawn Pomento, of the University of Nevada at Las Vegas, were quite helpful in transforming messy draft manuscripts into camera-ready copy; a task for which we are extremely grateful. Finally, we would like to thank Mary Olson, Marthe Chandler, and Booth Fowler for valuable help and support.

While each of us contributed different portions of the volume, the final result is a genuinely collaborative effort. For readers curious as to which of us wrote which entries, sections, etc., we would simply note that Jelen wrote the vowels and Olson the consonants.

The Religious Dimension of Political Behavior: Successes and Limitations

In 1976, the presidential candidacy of Jimmy Carter, an avowed born-again Christian and Southern Baptist, ushered in the first of several recent "Years of the Evangelical" (Kellstedt et al., 195). Three years later, partially in response to a White House Conference on Families (Conover, 045), Rev. Jerry Falwell founded Moral Majority, the first grassroots political organization designed to advocate the agenda of theologically conservative Protestants. Indeed, 1979 was a watershed year for American religion, especially with regard to its relationship with the political realm. In addition to the birth of Moral Majority, 1979 witnessed the coup staged by Islamic fundamentalists against the Shah of Iran as well as the subsequent seizure of the American Embassy; and the aftermath of the mass suicide of over 900 American followers of cult leader Jim Jones in Jonestown, Guyana. In the following year, the election of Ronald Reagan, along with the defeat of several veteran Senate liberals, led some observers to wonder whether the mobilization of religious conservatives had permanently altered the scope and style of American politics.

In response to the sudden reassertion of religion's public role on the world stage, some political scientists began the systemic investigation of the political significance of religion. Since the early 1980s, a great deal of scholarly attention has been devoted to the relationship between religion and politics. Many studies have been written on this topic; some have been included in the leading journals of political science and sociology. A large number of books and anthologies have also been published. A well-organized section of the American Political Science Association is itself devoted to religion and politics, and leading scholars, particularly David Leege, Kenneth Wald, and Lyman Kellstedt, have worked diligently to produce better measures of religiosity for inclusion in national surveys such as the American National Election Study and the National Opinion Research Center's General Social Survey. Many colleges and universities have also begun to offer courses in religion and politics. In short, the study of religion and politics appears to have gained strong institutional support in a relatively short amount of time.

While a good deal of progress has been made in the study of the relationship between the sacred and the secular, it seems fair to assert that, to date, the empirical study of religion and politics has largely been conducted by specialist in the subfield. Relatively few political scientists outside the area have incorporated either particular variables or theoretical insights from the realm of religion (for a prominent exception, see Verba et al. 338). In part, the relatively isolation of the study of religion in politics has resulted from what might be termed a "worldview difficulty"; that is, many academics hold beliefs which are so thoroughly secular that it seems virtually inconceivable that spiritual matters have consequences for political behavior. However, it may also be that specialists in the religion and politics subfield have not made their insights intellectually accessible to the discipline at large. For reasons which will be elaborated below, "religionists" in political science have produced neither parsimonious measurement strategies for assessing the impact of religious variables nor theoretical insights which have clear bearings on other issues within the study of political behavior in the United States.

Building from this, it is important to assess the extent to which there has been progress in the field of religion and political behavior since it began to grow rapidly in the late 1970s. There has been great success in this field in an inductive, cumulative sense. However, research in religion and political behavior has not produced much in the way of broader explanatory theory. Nor have unique covering laws been explicated. Empirical research in the area of religion and political behavior relies on the theory building of others. This fact renders the literature both sterile and chaotic, and it limits the extent to which scholars of religion and politics can make contributions to the broader literatures of political science.

Before beginning an analysis of the progress which has been made in the pursuit of knowledge regarding the relationship between religion and political behavior, it is important to define what exactly is meant by political behavior. Both masses and elites engage in political activity, and religion can and does temper the actions of both groups. The vast bulk of studies of religion and political behavior have focused on voting behavior, particularly at the presidential level. This is not surprising since the most convenient and widespread way for American citizens to engage in political action is voting. Naturally, it is necessary to understand the role played by religion on voting behavior. Another important form of conventional participation in which citizens engage is interest group activity. What is the range of religious lobby groups? What are their tactics? How influential have they been? Religio-political behavior may also take unconventional forms, particularly through social movements. It is especially important to discuss the role of churches in the civil rights movement. And what of the participation of elites? The interaction of religion and politics needs to be characterized as it regards both religious elites and political elites. To what extent are clergy involved in politics? Do they take steps to fashion themselves political leaders? Finally, it is of great importance to understand what effect, if any, religion may have on the actions taken by political elites. How religious are members of Congress, for example, and do their beliefs influence their voting records?

Religion and Public Opinion

A natural place to begin the consideration of the nexus between religion and politics in the United States is by assessing the effects of religious affiliation and religiosity on public opinion surrounding various issues. One of the most studied topics in the field of religion and political behavior has been public opinion about the issue of legal abortion. Other areas of public opinion have also provided fertile ground for research as well. The views of religious groups on issues such as the environment and capital punishment have been examined by a variety of scholars. A fair number of studies have also been conducted which address the relationship between religiosity, religious background, and tolerance.

The issue of abortion has been politicized for decades, and religious groups have been among the most vocal participants in the debate. The hierarchy of the Catholic Church, of course, has always stood in staunch opposition to abortion, and the Christian Right has also made abortion a centerpiece of its political agenda. What is the relationship between religion and opinions about legal abortion? A variety of religious variables have been shown to be related to abortion opinion, including religious background and church attendance (Ebaugh, 057; Rhodes, 279; Schmalzbauer, 284; Woodrum and Davison, 403). However, the story is not so simple. It has been shown (Jelen, 147, 150) that before the mid-1980s, the psychological basis of pro-life sentiment varied across religious groups. Catholics who opposed legal abortion tend to do so out of a general respect for life, which may be related to the "seamless garment of life" ideology taught by some Catholic leaders including the late Cardinal Joseph Bernardin (see Cleghorn, 044). Evangelicals were most likely to oppose abortion due to moral rigidity, however; they disapprove of sexual promiscuity, so they also disapprove of abortion. Similar research producing similar findings has also been conducted by Joseph Tamney and his colleagues (333) and Michael Welch and David Leege (355).

The abortion issue has served not only to divide American public opinion, but also to politicize American religious groups, which only augments the issue's legal abortion. A variety of studies have explored the rather extensive involvement of Catholic Bishops in anti-abortion activism (Byrnes, 035, 036, 037; O'Hara, 258). On balance, Catholics have been shown to be more strenuously opposed to abortion than adherents of other religions (Heimer, 114). Ironically, however, non-Catholics who happen to live in states where Catholics are numerous are more likely to hold pro-choice attitudes than other Americans (Cook et al., 047). Furthermore, Donald Granberg has reported that Catholics who convert to evangelical Protestantism are more consistently pro-life that lifelong Catholics (078). Evangelicals are undoubtedly strong opponents of abortion. In fact, in some circumstances, evangelical churches have worked side-by-side with Catholics to fight abortion (Day, 050).

There are several other issues which have historically concerned various American religious groups, and some of these have been addressed within the literature on religion and politics. Among these issues are the environment and capital punishment. James Guth and his colleagues have reported that evangelicals are unlikely to display great concern for the environment (095, 098). Reporting a similar finding, Andrew Greeley (079) advances the argument that psychological rigidity is the root source of this attitude. Conversely, Ronald Shaiko notes that environmentalists appear to be less religious than the American population at large (288). Theological conservatives are supportive of the death penalty. J. Stephen Cleghorn (044) has asserted that this attitude may stem from a "defense of society" ideology, which would not be likely to mesh well with environmentalism. The existence of such an ideology, however, would allow Stephen Johnson and Joseph Tamney (181) to grapple with the "inconsistencies" they perceive in evangelicals who favor the death penalty but oppose abortion.

Tolerance is a large theme which has been seriously addressed within the literature on religion and public opinion. The very tolerance implies openmindedness and willingness to accept diversity within American society. Stereotypical portrayals of religious groups which erect high boundaries between themselves and society often convey a strong implication of intolerance. Research has shown that these stereotypes are not entirely false. Kathleen Murphy Beatty and Oliver Walter (013) have shown that evangelicals tend to be less tolerant than mainline Protestants, and that frequent church attendance appears to increase intolerance (see also Kirkpatrick, 207). This intolerance takes a variety of forms, including anti-semitism (Lotz, 228), distaste for new religious movements (O'Donnell,

257), and discrimination against persons with AIDS. Not all intolerance of diversity, however, is directly related to religiosity or religious preference. Both Ted Jelen (146) and Christopher Ellison and Marc Musick (059) have shown, for example, that region is also an important independent variable in this complicated equation, as Southerners are generally less tolerant than Americans living in other geographical areas. Ideology also appears to have a strong independent effect on tolerance (Schmidt and Penning, 310).

Religion and Voting Behavior

The election of Ronald Reagan to the presidency in 1980, and the apparent role played by evangelical Protestants In his victory, led to a boom in the study of religion and voting behavior. In fact, there have been so many studies of the voting behavior of various groups, especially "Christian Right" identifiers, that the field of religion and politics in general comes to be characterized almost exclusively by them. Most studies have focused in particular on presidential voting behavior, but lately scholars have wisely begun to study the impact of religion on lower level elections as well.

After Ronald Reagan was elected to the presidency in 1980, scholars began in earnest to consider whether conservative Protestants – the so-called "Christian Right" – had played a significant role in his victory. Thus emerged the growth industry that is the study of the relationship between religion and presidential voting behavior. While some attention has been paid to the preferences of Catholics (Kenski and Lockwood, 201, 202; Penning, 266), Jews (Cranor, 049; Lieberman, 224; Sigelman, 293, 294), and mainline Protestants (Johnson, 176; Kellstedt et al., 195, 199; Wilcox, 379, 381) at the polls, research in this area has focused almost exclusively on the voting behavior of conservative Protestants. This fact may be attributed to the intense media scrutiny of evangelicals which was brought about by the emergence of Moral Majority, and the research program is not without merit. However, it is important to keep in mind that evangelicals constitute (at most) slightly more than one-quarter of the American population.

The most important finding to emerge from the research program about the voting behavior or evangelicals has been the discovery of a Republican realignment which has evidently occurred among evangelical voters since the 1980s (Bednar and Hertzke, 016; Kellstedt, 191; Kiecolt and Nelsen, 204; Smidt and Kellstedt, 308, 309). Before the 1980s, identification with the Republican Party and evangelicalism did not necessarily go hand in glove (Olson and Beck, 260). This changed, though, when many evangelicals felt betrayed by Jimmy Carter's presidency because he did not pursue a conservative policy agenda. Since the late 1970s, then, there has been a sea change in the aggregate partisanship of evangelicals. Lyman

Kellstedt (191) has demonstrated that generational replacement is a partial explanation for this phenomenon. It is also important to note, however, that this realignment is far from all-encompassing. To assume that all evangelicals are Republicans is folly; Corwin Smidt has provided evidence which highlights the remarkable heterogeneity of American evangelicalism (303, 304).

But does an aggregate change in partisanship result in history-changing electoral might? Scholars differ over the extent to which Ronald Reagan owed his 1980 victory to the Christina Right, but most agree that Reagan's election was the result of much more than disenchantment among evangelicals. Jerome Himmelstein and James McRae (124) have argued that the outcome of the 1980 election was much more a national expression of no confidence in Jimmy Carter than it was a Christian-led political revolution (see also Perkins et al., 269). Adding fuel to the fire are Stephen Johnson and Joseph Tamney (177), who argue that Reagan voters were most concerned about economic–not religio-moral—issues. On the other hand, Jeffrey Brudney and Gary Copeland (032) report that "hyper-religious" citizens, whom they found to make up six to ten percent of the electorate, voted overwhelmingly for Reagan.

Studies of later elections provide similarly mixed results. Some scholars have reported that religiosity and religious background were very important predictors of voting preference in 1984 (Woodrum, 401), perhaps more important than in 1980 (Johnson and Tamney, 179). Others have found that evangelicals were equally likely to vote for Ronald Reagan in 1980 as in 1984 (Smidt, 304). Furthermore, turnout among evangelicals seems to have been lower in 1984 than it had been four years earlier (Smidt, 304; Wilcox, 370).

In 1988, the bulk of the attention turned to the candidacy of Marion "Pat" Robertson. John Green and James Guth (080, 081) provide compelling evidence that the potential success Robertson's candidacy was limited by the fact that he drew support mainly from charismatic Christians, who constitute only a small fraction of the evangelical world (see also Jelen and Wilcox, 168; Smidt, 312). Scholars were also interested in his neo-populist appeal (Hertzke, 119, 120), the mobilizational opportunities he may have bungled (Johnson et al., 182; Langenbach and Green, 212; Wilcox, 379), and the discord he seems to have caused within the Republican Party (Penning, 267). It is quite interesting to note that while a few scholars discussed Jesse Jackson's highly viable 1988 presidential run as a counterpoint to that of Pat Robertson (Baker et al., 010; Hertke, 119, 120), only one, Clyde Wilcox, paid any exclusive attention to Jackson's candidacy and his supporters (376). In the end, George Bush seems to have won the election in 1988 with somewhat lukewarm support from evangelicals

(Kellstedt et al., 199). The jury is still out on the extent to which religiosity and religious background may have contributed to the election of Bill Clinton to two terms in the White House, but it is safe to assume that the Christian Right had little interest in electing a Democratic president.

Elections for other offices have been largely ignored until recent years, despite the fact that the Christian Right itself long ago learned Tip O'Neill's famous lesson that "all politics is local." A valuable recent addition to the literature which begins to fill this gap is a collection of essays, edited by Mark Rozell and Clyde Wilcox entitled *God at the Grassroots* (which includes Bednar and Hertzke, 016; Gilbert and Peterson, 076; Guth, 089; Rozell and Wilcox, 282; Wald, 342), which address the role played by the Christian Right in the historic 1994 congressional elections. This was not, however, the first treatment of religion and congressional elections. This was not, however, the first treatment of religion and congressional elections. Stephen Johnson and his colleagues (183) demonstrated in 1990 that congressional candidates who identify with the Christian Right face a serious electoral constraint in that there are often relatively few voters willing to support them, because relatively few Americans share the "Christian Right agenda." Still, an earlier study by Arthur Miller and Martin Wattenberg (239) suggested that Christian Right candidates may actually have a better chance of winning election than Christian Right presidential candidates.

Religion and Collective Political Participation

Studying the connection between religion and voting behavior is crucial, and it has been done well, particularly at the presidential level. However, voting is merely one form of political participation. Citizens participate in the American Polity in a myriad of ways, both individually and collectively. Scholars of religion and politics have been concerned primarily about collective political participation, and justifiably so, as religious groups have most frequently attempted to change American politics through collective action. Many of these groups have been successful in their efforts. It is therefore of the essence to investigate the extent to which religion bears upon forms of political participation.

Ironically, one of the most significant results of the interaction between religion and politics in American history – the civil rights movement of the 1950s and 1960s – has not been the topic of many studies in the political science literature. This due in part to the fact that the study of social movements has historically been the nearly exclusive domain of sociologists. Despite this fact, it is curious that so few political scientists have given serious consideration to the civil rights movement in light of the importance of the nexus between religion and politics for this history making movement. The few studies which have been conducted do not focus on the religious dimension of mobilization for civil rights activism. Rather, there has been a fascination among a small group of scholars with the lingering aftereffects of the civil rights movement. Nancy Tatom Ammerman (005) has reported that civil rights activism inspires clergy to take further collective political action. In a related exploration of the psychological roots of civil rights activism. Clarence Tygart (337) reports that theology and ideology combine to lead clergy either toward or away from support for the civil rights of African Americans.

Collective political action appears to have become more interesting to scholars of religion and politics when it was first embraced by white evangelicals in the form of Jerry Falwell's Moral Majority. Founded in June 1979, Moral Majority was intended to serve both as a lobby group and educational foundation representing the interests of evangelicals. Moral Majority attracted a great deal of attention from the press for a variety of reasons. First, evangelicals had largely been absent from the political realm for generations; their clergy, who had not wished to be involved in the affairs of "this world," had scrupulously avoided politics. Second, the right-wing ideological message presented by Falwell struck some as somewhat strident. In any case, scholars which fall into two principal categories: (1) the movement itself and (2) its supporters.

It is not unreasonable to argue that scholars practically exhausted the topic of Moral Majority as a collective political movement. One obvious question is how evangelicals, who were so accustomed to political disengagement, handled the rapid political mobilization which Falwell brought about. Sharon Linzey Georgianna (074; see also Wilcox et al., 388) reports that many evangelicals actually experienced cognitive dissonance when they felt they had to choose between pursuing politics and evangelizing. People who become Moral Majority activists were the few who had the capacity to perceive a connection between religion and politics, as Clyde Wilcox has shown (363). It should not be surprising, then, that Moral Majority's base of financial contributors was in fact rather small. James Guth and John Green (091) report that Moral Majority's external financial support came in large part from a very small set of conservative interest groups. It would seem that many evangelicals found Falwell's message too conservative. As it turns out, religious periodicals such as *Christianity Today* have historically presented politics in an appreciably more moderate key than did Falwell (063). The longer the organization was in existence, though, the more Falwell tempered its message, as David Snowball has demonstrated (313).

Scholars have also been keenly interested in the extent to which Americans supported the political goals and policy agenda espoused by Moral Majority. Most, including Anson Shupe and William Stacey (291, 292) have found that a large majority of Americans did not support the group, even during its height of influence and popularity. Even among people who share the organization's religious and political outlooks, Moral Majority was rather unpopular (Buell and Sigelman, 033, 034). Support for Moral Majority has been shown to stem from a variety of somewhat unexpected sources. Ted Jelen (159) has shown that antipathy toward cultural minority groups is positively related to support for Moral Majority. Furthermore, Stephen Johnson (173; Johnson and Tamney, 178) reports that people who support the organization are frequent viewers of religious television, and he speculates that the typical Moral Majority supporter is authoritarian and xenophobic.

As Matthew Moen (248) has pointed out, there have been two principal phases of Christian Right political engagement: (1) the Moral Majority and (2) its aftermath. Pat Robertson's Christian Coalition, which he founded after his 1988 presidential bid, has been the primary focus of research about the "later phase" of the Christian Right. Perhaps the first lesson which needs to be learned is that it is a mistake to assume that Christian Coalition is the monolith of the contemporary Christian Right. The Christian Right is far more diverse that this single organization, as James Guth clearly demonstrates (089). Nonetheless, Christian Coalition has often been cast as the Christian Right's great hope in the wake of the failure of Moral Majority and scandals brought about by religious broadcasters such as Jim Bakker and Jimmy Swaggart. (elen and Wilcox, 169; but see Wilcox, 382)

Lately an important concern among scholars of the collective political participation of religious groups has been whether the Christian Right is being transformed into a faction within the Republican Party. At first, the Christian Right was widely perceived as a source of tension within the party. Pat Robertson may have been to blame for some of this early dissent, but has since helped to revitalize the party (Penning, 267). In some states, such as Oklahoma (Bednar and Hertzke, 016), it has still been having difficult time even gaining a foothold. Whether the Christian Right will remain loyal to the Republican Party across the board, however, remains to be seen.

In general, far less has been written about Christian Coalition than was written about Moral Majority. That does not mean, however, that scholars have abandoned the subject of mass political participation in recent years. Rather than focusing on specific organizations, there has been a heartening trend among scholars to study the tactics of religious interest groups more generally. The chief contributions in this area of literature have been made by Allen Hertzke (117, 118) and Matthew Moen (243, 244). Hertzke's 1988 study of religious interest groups shows that religious lobbying is quite widespread across the theological spectrum, and that both religious liberals and conservatives feel threatened by political elites. These elites respond to religious interest groups by granting selective access to those with whom they are sympathetic. Moen's primary contribution comes in his 1989 study of the extent to which Christian Right organizations such as Moral Majority were able to influence Congress. His most important finding is that the Christian Right had very limited success beyond helping to shape the policy agenda. Daniel Hofrenning (125) extends these scholars' work by exploring the extent to which religious lobbyists are capable of becoming Washington insiders from both structural and philosophical perspectives. One serious deficiency in this literature is that few have studied religious interest groups' utilization of the legal system to further their political goals, which has actually increased since the 1980s (Ivers, 145).

The Political Participation of Religious Elites

From the 1950s through the 1970s, churches served as rallying points for history-making social movements. By the 1980s, previously inactive evangelical Protestants began to emerge as a potent electoral force, and in 1988, two presidential contenders were actually Protestant clergy. Most recently, politically active Christian groups have been important players in the political struggle to define American morality. It should stand to reason, then, that local clergy may often be under great pressure to play political roles. However, widely divergent views about both the desirability and scope of pastoral political involvement coexist within the world of American clergy.

It is curious, though, that so little scholarly attention has been paid to the political involvement of clergy. Even though much has been made of the political mobilization of religious people, there has been little discussion of the role of the pastor. In their studies of political mobilization in churches, Kenneth Wald and his colleagues (345, 347) discuss the "political tenor" of various religious communities at length, but they do not focus much attention on the roles clergy play in shaping political context for their congregations. This is perhaps most surprising given that religio-political activism is really an example of the broader phenomenon of political involvement among the elites of non-political social institutions. It has, however, rarely been treated as such.

Of all clergy, perhaps the most is known about the political involvement of Catholic Bishops. Particularly interesting to scholars has been the advocacy by some bishops of a political agenda deriving from Cardinal Joseph Bernardin's argument that life in all forms must be protected. This agenda led Bernardin himself to ally himself with both liberals and conservatives (Borelli, 023). At times, other bishops have found themselves publicly at odds with elected officials, as was the case with Cardinal John O'Connor of New York in his conflict with then-governor Mario Cuomo (Byrnes, 036). Catholic Bishops have also taken active roles in campaigns from time to time (Segers, 286) and agenda setting about issues other than abortion (Wald, 341). Timothy Byrnes (035) presents the most complete analysis of bishops' political involvement. He nicely illuminates the diversity within the National Conference of Catholic Bishops and the related debate over the question of whether abortion should be the centerpiece of the bishops' political agenda or just one element thereof (see also Hanna, 108).

And what of Protestant clergy? Not surprisingly, the bulk of scholarly emphasis has been placed upon evangelical pastors and their political outlooks. The seminal work in this vein was conducted by James Guth (087, 088). Guth's analysis shows that while Southern Baptist clergy frequently reported holding conservative political views, they were relatively unlikely to support Moral Majority (see also Beatty and Oliver, 014). This ambivalence among evangelical clergy about politics continued into the late 1980s, when Pat Robertson even had trouble mobilizing his fellow clergy for his 1988 presidential campaign (Lagenbach and Green, 212; Wilcox, 397). Very little work has been done on either mainline or African American Protestant clergy. Donald Luidens and Roger Nemeth (229) have investigated the so-called "clergy-laity gap" which is said to constrain mainline clergy who wish to become politically active. However, studies beyond this small piece and the work of Dean Hoge (126) are rare.

Few studies directly compare clergy from different religious traditions, but the tide may be turning on this count. The forthcoming work of James Guth and his colleagues gives much promise for the expansion of our understanding of the general phenomenon of the political involvement of clergy. Stephen Johnson and Joseph Tamney have done a bit of work comparing and contrasting liberal and conservative clergy (180); they have found that liberal clergy exhibit a higher degree of ideological constraint. Sharon Price-Bonham and her colleagues studied the variety in clergy's attitudes about abortion (274; see also Wagenaar and Bartos, 339).

Religion and American Political Culture

Religion is inextricably interwoven in the fabric that is American political culture. Whether the framers of the Constitution were religious men or not is a moot question; the fact is that throughout American history religion has been entwined with politics, as Alexis de Tocqueville observed in the nation's early days. Religion has an equally important influence, therefore, on the institutions of American government as it does on the political behavior of American citizens. Of special interest to scholars of religion and politics has been the United States Congress, and the beacon for this niche in the literature is Peter Benson and Dorothy Williams' masterful *Religion on Capitol Hill* (017). Benson and Williams report that contrary to conventional wisdom, religious beliefs are widespread among members of Congress. They also contribute a pathbreaking set of measures of religiosity. Other scholars have further investigated the bearing of religious background and religiosity on members' congressional voting records. Byron Daynes and Raymond Tatalovich (051), for example, report that liberal Protestant and Jewish members of Congress are most likely to be pro-choice.

Rarely has the connection between religion and the office of the presidency been explored. This is ironic given the president's status as the high priest, in some sense, of the American civil religion. Some have argued that Americans share an uncodified "civil religion," the central tenet of which is that the United is unique, transcendent, and untouched by the hand of God. In this sense the civil religion is non-sectarian public theology which glorifies the distinctly American form of democracy. Several studies have lent credence to the hypothesis that such a civil religion in fact exists (Funderburk, 070; Smidt, 302; Williams and Demerath, 392). Skillful presidents such as Ronald Reagan have been able to tap into such civil religious imagery to rally support for themselves (Adams, 004; Toolin, 335). Recently, the most important scholar of civil religion has been Ronald Wimberley. Wimberley has contributed a great deal to the theoretical development of the concept (Christenson and Wimberley, 041; Wimberley et al., 398) as well as to the difficult matter of its measurement (393, 394). Perhaps most important is his finding that voters who espouse civil religious beliefs are more likely to vote for Republican presidential candidates (395).

Finally, any essay on the state of the literature in religion and political behavior would be incomplete without a mention of James Davison Hunter's much-discussed "culture wars" thesis (141, 142). Hunter has argued that contemporary American politics is degenerating into war, which is really a zero-sum game, pitting the "orthodox" against the "progressive" on issues such as abortion. Meaningful discourse cannot be conducted because both sides are strident and unbending in their convictions.

Consensus, therefore, becomes an impossibility. Lately other scholars have been putting Hunter's assumptions to the test. Ted Jelen (164) has explored the extent to which voting patterns among various religious groups reflect "culture wars" themes. Both evangelical and mainline Protestants appear to have aligned themselves along the dimensions Hunter outlines, but Catholics have not. Like Hunter, they argue that social issues are most salient in the fighting of such culture wars.

Methodological Strategies

The relative success enjoyed by students of religion and politics has been accompanied by a good deal of progress in the measurement of religious phenomena. While there has perhaps been an excessive reliance on sample surveys of mass opinion, the field has moved from such simple (and often outdated) measurements of church attendance and denominational affiliation to a wide variety of measurement strategies, which appear to capture the diversity and complexity of American religion much more completely (for general overviews of methodological innovations in this areas, see Kellstedt, 192, 193; Kellstedt and Smidt, 197; Wilcox, 196; and Wald and Smidt, 350).

To begin, analysts of religion and politics have become much more sophisticated about the classifications of Protestant denominations themselves. Moving from simple categories of "Protestant, Catholic, and Jew" to elaborate distinctions between branches of Baptism, Lutheranism, and other denominations, several observers have produced quite useful groupings of denominational "families" or "traditions" (see, for example, Kellstedt and Green, 194; Kellstedt, Smidt and Kellstedt, 199). This is an important methodological consideration, since the denomination is, in some ways, the basic unit of American religious life. Increasing precision about the classification of such groups has clearly increased the explanatory power of this most basic of religious variables.

However, recent scholarship in religion and politics has shown that denominational affiliation is not sufficient to account for the political impact of religious belief. Given the stubborn decentralization of some denominations, and the individualism which characterizes the American political culture generally, analysts of the effects of religion have turned to more attitudinal variables. For example, a great deal of work has been done on attitudes toward doctrinal orthodoxy, including beliefs about the authority of the Bible (Dixon, Jones, and Lowery, 054; Jelen, 151; Jelen, Wilcox, and Smidt, 171; Kellstedt, 198; Smidt, 306). Some additional attention has been paid to religious experience (Dixon, Levy, and Lowery, 055, 056; Jelen, Smidt, and wilcox, 165; Smidt, 306), and to religious self-identification (Beatty and Wlater, 015; Jelen, 155, 156, 159; Smidt and

Penning, 312; Wilcox, 359, 363, 369; Wilcox, Jelen, and Leege, 387; and Turner and Guth, 336). The latter research appeared particularly promising, since group identification (including identification with political parties) has proven to be a very powerful variable in the study of political behavior generally. Other research efforts have focused on foundational beliefs (Leege, 218; Leege and Kellstedt, 219; Leege and Welch, 221), and on religious salience and devotionalism (Leege, Wald, and Kellstedt, 220; Wald, Kellstedt and Leege, 343).

Two general observations are possible with respect to this proliferation of methodological innovations. First, most of the scholarly effort to date has been focused on evangelical Protestantism. This concentration is not surprising, given the prominence of evangelicals in politics during the 1980s. However, relatively little progress has been made in developing items which might account for variations in the political behavior of Roman Catholics (an interesting group, given their persistent Democratic partisanship) or of Mainline Protestants. What are the analogues of religious salience or doctrinal orthodoxy which might make the attitudes and behavior of these groups more accessible?

Second, and perhaps more disturbingly, these methodological innovations have been empirically quite successful, at the apparent expense of theoretical parsimony and sophistication. In multivariate analyses in which several of these measures are included in the same model (see especially Kellstedt, 193) most or all of the measures listed above appear to have statistically significant effects on voting behavior and political participation. For example, knowing that a particular respondent is a member of an evangelical denomination increases our ability to predict that person's vote choices and partisanship. Knowing that that same person attends religious services several times a week adds to the explanatory power of the model, as does knowledge of her/his belief in the authority of Scripture, and the occurrence or non-occurrence of a "born-again" experience in that person's life. In other words, the methodological innovations which have taken place over the past two decades have not limited the range of intellectually permissible explanations of the religious basis of political attitudes and behavior, but have instead increased our collective sense of the complexity of the phenomenon. To the frustration of scholars who wish to incorporate religious variables into their analyses, but who understandably do not wish to make the measurement of religious affiliations and beliefs their life's work, there are no simple theoretical or methodological strategies which can be incorporated. If the purpose of science (perhaps especially social science) is to simplify our understanding of the world, the study of religion and politics has not been particularly successful in this regard.

Conclusion: In Lieu of General Theory

It is our contention that the lack of parsimonious measurement and general theory in the study of religion and politics does not represent a failure of the scholarly enterprise. As the levels of effort and sophistication in research on religious politics have increased, so has our appreciation of the complexity of the independent variable: religion. The apparent lack of rigor and theoretical simplicity which characterizes our collective scholarly endeavor is attributable, in our view, to the inherent complexity of American religion. Indeed, the proliferation of empirically successful measurement innovations described in the previous section represent an important substantive finding; namely, religious belief, practice, and membership in the United States are characterized by centrifugal forces which make successful theorizing (or, indeed, successful political action) quite difficult.

Recent developments in the sociology of religion provide a theory of this tendency toward disaggregation. Several scholars (Finke and Starke, 065, 067; Iannaconne, 143, 144; Stark and McCann, 317; and Warner, 351) have introduced an economic model of religious competition. In this emerging research program, religious denominations are compared to firms in an economy. In social contexts which are characterized by religious pluralism, denominational "firms" are forced to compete with one another, by responding to the needs and concerns of potential parishioners (or "customers"). The greater responsiveness of churches in pluralistic, competitive, settings is thought to increase the aggregate level of lay membership and participation in religious organizations. Since potential church members have the option of non-affiliation, religious "monopolies" are thought to lack incentives to recruit new members, and are less responsive to the desires of potential members.

Many areas of the United States are characterized by high levels of religious pluralism and (perhaps) competition. The diversity of American religion, as well as the lack of established churches, may render the United States a highly competitive religious market, and may therefore account for the relatively high level of aggregate religious membership and observance in the U.S.

A corollary of the religious competition model is that religious "firms" may need to engage in "product differentiation." That is, if the metaphor of economic competition has any force, denominations (or indeed congregations) will have strong incentives to distinguish themselves from one another. Indeed, it might be anticipated that denominations will work hardest to distance themselves from their theologically proximate competitors. Thus, Jelen (161) has shown that, among evangelical clergy, there is a strong tendency toward religious particularism. Doctrinally conservative ministers distinguish quite readily between different types of Baptists, between charismatics and non-charismatics, and (even) between charismatics and pentecostals. Similarly, a number of sophisticated empirical studies (Gilbert, 075; Jelen, 155, 158; Wald, et al., 345) have shown that the <u>congregation</u> is an irreducible element of political socialization, even after the effects of denominational affiliation, religious experience, and doctrinal orthodoxy have been taken into account.

The need for religious bodies to distinguish themselves from one another may have both political and scientific consequences. Politically, the demands of theological differentiation may be incompatible with the formation of political coalitions. Many analyses of the Christian Right in the 1980s have suggested that the movement was fragmented by the effects of religious particularism (Jelen, 155, 159; Wilcox, 365, 377; Green, 080). The inability of charismatic candidate Marion "Pat" Robertson to extend his appeal to non-charismatic evangelicals, the unwillingness of conservative Roman Catholics and evangelical Protestants to sustain an ecumenical "pro-life" coalition around the abortion issue, and the failure of Christian right organizations to recruit effectively among African-Americans may all have roots in the importance attached by religious leaders to clarifying theological differences.

From the standpoint of social science, the implications of the pluralist research program may be equally profound. Different measurement strategies reflect different theoretical approaches to the subject of religion. Is religion "really" a group membership, a set of doctrinal beliefs, a set of experiences, or participation in a sacramental tradition? To some extent, the defining characteristics of a particular of a particular religious tradition or denomination vary across religious bodies, and, indeed, are in a constant state of change and adaptation.

The implication of this insight for the study of religion and politics is that we may never achieve either theoretical sophistication nor agreement on the "correct" conceptualizations of measurements of religious phenomena. The political role of religion is a <u>variable</u>, and is crucially dependent on time, place, and circumstance. The most recent theoretical development in this area provides an account of the complexity and variability of the interplay between religion and politics, rather than plausible candidates for covering laws.

Bibliography

001 Abelman, Robert. "Why Do People Watch Religious TV? A Uses and Gratification Approach." *Review of Religious Research* 29 (1987): 199-210.
Using a sample of 210 Midwesterners to investigate the reasons for religious television viewing, Abelman makes a distinction between two frequently observed motives: habitual viewing and information seeking. However, religious television usage seems best explained by a "reactionary" motive, in which the viewer makes a conscious rejection of commercial television.

002 Abelman, Robert, and Neuendorf, Kimberly. "Themes and Topics in Religious Television Programming." *Review of Religious Research* 29 (1987): 152-174.
The authors set out to document the content of religious television programming. A content analysis of religious television reveals that specifically religious themes dominate such programming. Political content seems confined to a few specific programs, although the authors discern a tendency for the messages of televangelists to become more political over time.

003 Abramowitz, Alan; McGlennon, John; and Rapoport, Ronald. "Virginia: A Case Study of Fundamentalism in State Party Politics." In *Religion and Politics in the South: Mass and Elite Perspectives*, ed. by Tod A. Baker, Robert P. Steed, and Laurence W. Moreland, 144-160. New York: Praeger Publishers, 1983.

Surveys of participants in state party conventions in 1978 and 1980 suggest that although Christian fundamentalists were generally less "pragmatic" than their non-fundamentalist counterparts, they were otherwise not distinctive. Most were found to be experienced political activists who did not bring an uncompromising, "moralistic" style to their political participation.

004 Adams, David S. "Ronald Reagan's 'Revival': Voluntarism as a Theme in Reagan's Civil Religion." *Sociological Analysis* 48 (1987): 17-29.
The author theorizes that presidents contribute to and transform American civil religion with their rhetoric. A content analysis of Reagan's public utterances demonstrates extensive use of several themes involving the concept of "voluntarism." This concept enabled Reagan to generate a simple myth regarding sin and salvation in the United States.

005 Ammerman, Nancy T. "The Civil Rights Movement and the Clergy in a Southern Community." *Sociological Analysis* 41 (1980): 339-350.
Involvement by clergy in the Christian Right movement is hypothesized to be related to individual backgrounds and current social situations. Data from a survey of 72 clergy in Tuscaloosa, Alabama, were subjected to a non-recursive causal model. Civil rights activism occasioned a decline in localism and the formation of supportive reference groups of other clergy and denominations.

006 Ammerman, Nancy T. "Operationalizing Evangelicalism: An Amendment." *Sociological Analysis* 43 (1982): 170-172.
In this brief note, Ammerman responds to Hunter's 1981 piece, "Operationalizing Evangelicalism..." (137). She argues that a belief in an inerrant Bible may be too demanding a criterion, and suggests that a question eliciting attitudes toward the creation story in Genesis may be a more appropriate measure. Furthermore, she argues that it is necessary to distinguish evangelicals from fundamentalists rather carefully, and that Hunter's identification of evangelical cultures should be used with a good deal of caution.

007 Ammerman, Nancy T. "Southern Baptists and the New Christian Right." *Review of Religious Research* 32 (1991): 213-239.
Using samples of clergy and lay leaders, Ammerman investigates the hypothesis that there are significant religious and political divisions within the Southern Baptist Convention. Although the Southern Baptist Convention and the Christian Right have similar theological and social roots, there is very little interaction between clergy of the two. There is, however, the exists considerable overlap at the laity level. Identification with conservative Republicanism among Baptist laity is associated with conservative positions on secular rather than religious issues. Ammerman

speculates that the relationship between the Southern Baptist Convention and the Christian Right has some growth potential.

008 Baggaley, Andrew R. "Abortion Beliefs and Values: A Simpler Analysis of the Tamney, Johnson, and Burton Data." *Journal for the Scientific Study of Religion* 31 (1992): 533-534.

In this piece, Baggaley re-analyzes the correlation matrix provided in Tamney et al. (333). He suggests that the various attitudes measured by these previous authors be combined into a single "orthodoxy" scale, which would provide a simpler interpretation of the original data.

009 Baker, Tod A.; Steed, Robert P.; and Moreland, Laurence W. "Fundamentalist Beliefs and Southern Distinctiveness: A Study of the Political Attitudes of State Party Activists." In *Religion and Politics in the South: Mass and Elite Perspectives*, ed. by Tod A. Baker, Robert P. Steed, Steed, and Laurence W. Moreland, 133-143. New York: Praeger Publishers, 1983.

A survey of party activists in Virginia and South Carolina shows that while religious fundamentalism has not replaced race as the dominant cleavage in Southern politics, such beliefs are quite powerful predictors of attitudes about moral issues.

010 Baker, Tod A.; Steed, Robert P.; and Moreland, Laurence W. "Preachers and Politics: Jesse Jackson, Pat Robertson, and the 1988 Presidential Nomination Campaign in South Carolina." In *The Bible and the Ballot Box: Religion and Politics in the 1988 Election*, ed. by James L. Guth and John C. Green, 94-112. Boulder, CO: Westview Press, 1991.

In this study the authors set out to compare the characteristics of delegates representing Pat Robertson and Jesse Jackson at the 1988 South Carolina state party conventions. The analysis suggests that Jackson delegates were more likely than Robertson delegates to have been previously active in political affairs; the majority of Robertson delegates were newcomers to the political process.

011 Barrish, Gerald, and Welch, Michael R. "Student Religiosity and Discriminatory Attitudes Toward Women." *Sociological Analysis* 41 (1980): 66-73.

The authors examine the hypothesized relationship between religiosity and discriminatory attitudes about gender. Analysis of a survey of students at three universities yields no significant relationships between gender role stereotyping and a variety of religious variables. In the ensuing discussion, the authors suggest that the connection between religiosity and gender role traditionalism may be exaggerated in other accounts.

012 Bates, Vernon L. "Lobbying for the Lord: The New Christian Right Home-Schooling Movement and Grassroots Lobbying." *Review of Religious Research* 33 (1991): 3-17.
In a descriptive study of the home-school movement in Oregon, Bates uses intensive interviewing and participant observation to examine the basis for political activism on this issue. He supplements a resource mobilization perspective by examining the role of ideology and grievance in the mobilization of previously apolitical people.

013 Beatty, Kathleen Murphy, and Walter, Oliver B. "Religious Preference and Practice: Reevaluating Their Impact on Political Tolerance." *Public Opinion Quarterly* 48 (1984): 318-329.
To evaluate the relationship between religious preference and practice and tolerance, the authors analyze National Opinion Research Center data from 1972-1980. They report differences among denominations in tolerance of nonconformists, which are not captured by Protestant-Catholic distinctions, or even by distinguishing evangelical Protestants from mainline Protestants. Some groups of conservative Protestants are found to be indiscriminately intolerant of groups outside the mainstream of American politics. Church attendance depresses tolerance for all denominations, but the effects of religious observance are much stronger for some denominations than for others.

014 Beatty, Kathleen Murphy, and Walter, Oliver B. "Fundamentalists, Evangelicals and Politics." *American Politics Quarterly* 16 (1988): 43-59.
Beatty and Walter challenge the notion that the Christian Right is a homogeneous monolith. A national telephone survey of ministers reveals that religious self-identifications are powerful predictors of a variety of political attitudes. In general, self-identified fundamentalists are more conservative than self-characterized evangelicals, who in turn are more conservative than non-identifiers. Religious identification is not related to party identification.

015 Beatty, Kathleen Murphy, and Walter, Oliver B. "A Group Theory of Religion and Politics." *Western Political Quarterly* 42 (1989): 129-146.
Beatty and Walter wish to bring inter-group conflict theory to bear on religion and politics. Using a survey of clergy, they compare the effects of doctrinal orthodoxy (a "liberal-conservative" identification) with denominational affiliation on a variety of political attitudes. While orthodoxy is the stronger predictor of political ideology, denominational affiliation is more closely related to political participation, and the amount of political discussion which takes place in church.

016 Bednar, Nancy L., and Hertzke, Allen D. "Oklahoma: The Christian Right and Republican Realignment." In *God at the Grassroots: The Christian Right in the 1994 Elections*, ed. by Mark J. Rozell and Clyde Wilcox, 91-107. Lanham, MD: Rowman & Littlefield Publishers,1995.
Bednar and Hertzke are interested in the extent to which the Christian Right exercised electoral influence in the state of Oklahoma in the 1994 midterm elections. They report that many congressional races had distinctly religious overtones, and evangelicals are undergoing a realignment toward the Republican Party in Oklahoma.

017 Benson, Peter L., and Williams, Dorothy L. *Religion on Capitol Hill: Myths and Realities.* New York: Oxford University Press, 1982.
How religious are members of Congress, and to what extent do religious beliefs bear upon the legislative process? In a creative study based on a survey of a probability sample of members of Congress, Benson and Williams employ a variety of unconventional measures of religious belief. They find that religious beliefs are widespread among members of Congress, and that religious beliefs are important predictors of congressional voting behavior.

018 Berk, Marc. "Pluralist Theory and Church Policy Positions on Racial and Sexual Equality." *Sociological Analysis* 39 (1978): 338-350.
Because large denominations are thought to have heterogeneous memberships, Berk hypothesizes that large denominations will take moderate public positions on social issues. By contrast, smaller (and presumably, more homogeneous) denominations are considered likely to take either strongly discriminatory or activist positions on issues of racial and gender equality. The hypothesis is not confirmed, since content analysis shows that large denominations generally take stronger positions.

019 Billings, Dwight B. "Religion as Opposition: A Gramscian Analysis." *American Journal of Sociology* 96 (1990): 1-31.
Using Gramsci's notion of hegemony, Billings studies the circumstances under which religion leads to quiescence or opposition. A set of case studies shows the variable roles of religion in Southern labor relations. In some instances, religious leaders are found to support the status quo, while others cast religion in the role of opposition. Religion is not found to be epiphenomenal, but rather seems to be an autonomous social force.

020 Blanchard, Dallas A., and Prewitt, Terry J. *Religious Violence and Abortion: The Gideon Project.* Gainesville, FL: University Press of Florida, 1993.
The first part of this work is a description of the "Gideon Project," involving the bombing of abortion clinics in Pensacola, Florida in 1984. The second portion is devoted to an analysis of antiabortion violence, in which the

authors assert a connection between religious violence and fundamentalism. By this account, a definitional characteristic of fundamentalism is a propensity toward violence.

021 Bock, E. Wilbur; Beeghley, Leonard; and Mixon, Anthony J. "Religion, Socio-economic Status, and Sexual Morality: An Application of Reference Group Theory." *Sociological Quarterly* 24 (1983): 545-559.
Using reference group theory as their point of departure, the authors analyze National Opinion Research Center data with an eye toward the relationships among religiosity, socioeconomic status, and views on sexual morality. This study shows that generally, denominational preference and subjective religious intensity are stronger predictors of attitudes toward issues involving sexual morality than is socioeconomic status. These issues include attitudes toward birth control, abortion, pornography, and non-marital sex.

022 Bolton, S. Charles, and Ledbetter, Cal Jr. "Compulsory Bible Reading in Arkansas and the Culture of Fundamentalism." *Social Science Quarterly* 64 (1983): 670-679.
This article compares county voting in Arkansas on two referenda: an anti-evolution referendum in 1928 and a compulsory Bible reading act in 1930. At the county level, the relationship between support for each of these measures was quite weak. The authors argue that the Bible reading proposal was much less controversial and therefore resulted in a very low level of religious polarization.

023 Borrelli, MaryAnne. "The Consistent Life Ethic in State Politics: Joseph Cardinal Bernardin and the Abortion Issue in Illinois." In *The Catholic Church and the Politics of Abortion: A View From the States*, ed. by Timothy A. Byrnes and Mary C. Segers, 71-86. Boulder, CO: Westview Press, 1992.
Borrelli presents an analysis of Bernardin's role in Illinois politics, and argues that the Cardinal's insistence that abortion is but one aspect of a "consistent ethic of life" has led Bernardin to seek a coalition of liberals and conservatives. The Church in Illinois has supported a number of social welfare, "quality of life" issues in addition to its opposition to legal abortion, and such efforts have met measurable, but limited, success.

024 Breault, Kevin D. "New Evidence on Religious Pluralism, Urbanisim, and Religious Participation." *American Sociological Review* 54 (1989): 1048-1053.
This piece challenges the result reported in Finke and Stark (065). Breault attributes the Finke and Stark findings to the confounding effects of collinearity, and suggests that religious participation is greater in religiously

conservative environments.   Thus, the original results are based on sampling distributions and methodological artifacts.

025 Breault, Kevin D.   "A Reexamination of the Relationship Between Religious Diversity and Religious Adherents."   *American Sociological Review* 54 (1989): 1056-1059.
This note is a response to the response of Finke and Stark (066). Breault introduces some new evidence, which suggests that pluralism undermines religious activity. He reasserts the contention that the results reported by Finke and Stark (065) are attributable to collinearity.

026 Brinkerhoff, Merlin B.; Jacob, Jeffrey C.; and Mackie, Marlene M. "Mormonism and the Moral Majority Make Strange Bedfellows?   An Exploratory Critique." *Review of Religious Research* 28 (1987): 236-251.
In a response to Shupe and Heinerman (290), the authors argue that a Mormon-Christian coalition is extremely implausible. Although there exists broad value agreement between the two groups, analysis of survey data suggests that conservative Christians (the Christian Right constituency) hold very negative feelings about members of the LDS Church, and some regard Mormonism as a cult.

027 Brinkerhoff, Merlin B., and Mackie, Marlene M.   "Religious Denominations' Impact Upon Gender Attitudes: Some Methodological Implications." *Review of Religious Research* 25 (1984): 365-378.
A number of different classifications of denominational preference are examined in a sample of 464 Canadians with respect to their relationships with attitudes toward gender roles and abortion.   It is found that the respondent's current affiliation with a specific denomination performs better than more general denominational classifications. Furthermore, religious variables generally have stronger relationships with these dependent variables than do demographic characteristics.

028 Bruce, Steve.   *The Rise and Fall of the New Christian Right: Conservative Protestant Politics in America, 1978-1988.*   Oxford: Clarendon Press, 1988.
Bruce argues that the Christian Right in America was a passing phenomenon, but that there is a need to consider how, and in what context, Christian Right identifiers were first mobilized. He considers the sources of Christian Right strength, their activities, leadership, and agenda.   Bruce argues that the Christian Right was already a wing of the Republican Party and speculates that it may have influenced some Reagan judicial appointments. He argues, however, that the Christian Right would soon die because of the small size of its support base, socioeconomic and theological cleavages, and the strong liberal reaction against the Christian Right.

029 Bruce, Steve.   *Pray TV: Televangelism in America.*   New York:
Routledge, 1990.
Bruce presents an in-depth look at religious television broadcasting in the
United States. He is interested in the impact televangelists have on politics.
 Their political effectiveness, he concludes, is rather minimal, as evidenced
by the failure of Pat Robertson's presidential bid.

030 Bruce, Steve.   "The Inevitable Failure of the New Christian Right."
Sociology of Religion 55 (1994): 229-242.
Bruce lists a number of considerations which have limited the effectiveness
of the Christian Right.   These include a lack of consensus among
conservative Protestants, the need to form theologically inconvenient
coalitions with people outside conservative Protestantism, and the
mobilization of formidable enemies of Christian Right movements. Bruce
argues that overestimation of the power of the Christian Right seems
related to reaction to "secularization theory."

031 Bruce, Steve. "The Rapture of Politics: The Christian Right As the
United States Approaches the Year 2000."   *Sociology of Religion* 55
(1994): 223-357.
Bruce is convinced that the Christian Right has never been, and will never
be, effective politically. The Christian Right cannot point to many legislative
victories, nor can it claim many successes in securing elected or appointed
office for its supporters.

032 Brudney, Jeffrey L., and Copeland, Gary W.   "Evangelicals as a
Political Force: Reagan and the 1980 Religious Vote." *Social Science
Quarterly* 65 (1984): 1072-1079.
In an examination of the support of highly religious voters for Ronald
Reagan in 1980, the authors find a good measure of support for their
hypothesis (given a very stringent operational definition of religiosity).
"Hyperreligious" citizens, who account for between six and ten percent of
the electorate, voted overwhelmingly for Reagan.   These same voters
provided about ten percent of Reagan's electoral margin over Jimmy
Carter.

033 Buell, Emmett, and Sigelman, Lee. "An Army That Meets Every
Sunday? Popular Support for the Moral Majority in 1980." *Social Science
Quarterly* 66 (1985): 426-434.
Using feeling thermometers and proximity measures, Buell and Sigelman
estimate support for Moral Majority among American voters. They find that
the organization is relatively unpopular, even among people who share the
organization's religious and political agendas. Surprisingly, the authors
report that feminist attitudes and membership in fundamentalist churches
are not related to support for Moral Majority in a multivariate model.

034 Buell, Emmett, and Sigelman, Lee. "A Second Look at 'Popular Support for the Moral Majority: A Second Look'." *Social Science Quarterly* 68 (1987): 167-169.
In this brief note, the authors respond to the criticisms of Wilcox (362). Buell and Sigelman question the strategy of adjusting feeling thermometers for response sets, but acknowledge the possibility that some of Wilcox's methodological innovations may constitute improvements over their original design. Nevertheless, the main conclusions of the original 1985 article are not changed by altering the methods of analysis.

035 Byrnes, Timothy A. *Catholic Bishops in American Politics*. Princeton, NJ: Princeton University Press, 1991.
Byrnes traces the history of the political activity of the American Catholic Bishops, with heaviest emphasis on the most recent national elections. His basic thesis is that the politics of the bishops is generally reactive to other actors in American politics. Thus, the recent emphasis on public policy directed from Washington has occasioned a more cohesive National Conference for the bishops, from which they can address a relatively wide range of issues. Similarly, the bishops were actively involved in the presidential campaigns of 1976 and 1984, but not in 1988. These differences in involvement are described as reactions to the strategic choices of the major party candidates in each election.

036 Byrnes, Timothy A. "The Cardinal and the Governor: The Politics of Abortion in New York State." In *The Catholic Church and the Politics of Abortion: A View From the States*, ed. by Timothy A. Byrnes and Mary C. Segers, 137-151. Boulder, CO: Westview Press, 1992.
In this piece, Byrnes describes the interaction between Archbishop O'Connor and Catholic Governor Mario Cuomo over the abortion issue. The author analyzes the somewhat personal attacks which O'Connor directed at Cuomo and compares competing positions on the proper role of Catholic politicians in the abortion debate.

037 Byrnes, Timothy A. "The Politics of Abortion: The Catholic Bishops." In *The Catholic Church and the Politics of Abortion: A View From the States*, ed. by Timothy A. Byrnes and Mary C. Segers, 14-26. Boulder, CO: Westview Press, 1992.
This study is an analysis of the political activity of the American Catholic Bishops since the Supreme Court's *Webster* decision of 1989, which permitted state governments greater latitude in regulating abortion. Byrnes shows that in the aftermath of *Webster*, the bishops sharpened their discussion of the political aspects of abortion. Moreover, the bishops seemed to increase their level of agreement on the abortion issue after the 1989 decision.

038 Campbell, Keith E., and Granberg, Donald. "Religiosity and Attitudes Toward the Viet Nam War: A Research Note." *Sociological Analysis* 40 (1979): 254-256.
Campbell and Granberg briefly investigate the hypothesis that there is a positive relationship between religiosity and support for United States military intervention. Using national probability samples, the authors show no relationship between a variety of measures of religiosity and support for the war in Viet Nam. This finding contradicts other research, which shows a positive relationship among college students.

039 Chalfant, H. Paul, and Peek, Charles W. "Religious Affiliation, Religiosity, and Racial Prejudice: A New Look at Old Relationships." *Review of Religious Research* 25 (1983): 155-161.
The authors address a conventional wisdom which suggests that religiosity and religious fundamentalism are positively related to racial prejudice. After a methodological critique of previous studies, the authors show that the hypothesized relationships do not hold true for fully-specified models of representative national samples. The findings suggest that general theological categories are insufficient to account for variations in racial prejudice.

040 Chandler, Marthe A.; Cook, Elizabeth Adell; Jelen, Ted G.; and Wilcox, Clyde. "Abortion in the United States and Canada: A Comparative Study of Public Opinion." In *Abortion Politics in the United States and Canada: Studies in Public Opinion*, ed. by Ted G. Jelen and Marthe A. Chandler, 131-143. Westport, CT: Praeger Publishers, 1994. Using data from American and Canadian National Election surveys, the authors show that apparent similarities in abortion attitudes between the two countries conceal important differences. In general, religious variables are more powerful predictors of abortion attitudes in Canada, but their aggregate impact is inhibited by the relatively low levels of religious observance in Canada. By contrast, the effects of relatively high religiosity in the United States may be offset by the individualism which has characterized the American political culture. A set of "simulated regressions" supports this hypothesis. Religion is a more important predictor of abortion attitudes in the United States among members of minority groups, while the effects of religion on abortion attitudes in Canada are strongest among local religious majorities.

041 Christenson, James A., and Wimberley, Ronald C. "Who Is Civil Religious?" *Sociological Analysis* 39 (1978): 77-83.
The authors ask whether a vast majority of Americans actually share civil religious ideology. Using a survey of North Carolina residents, the authors show that tenets of American civil religion receive widespread support. Furthermore, the relationships between civil religion and other religious or demographic variables are quite weak, which suggests that civil religion is a

basic component of the American political culture and is not confined to any set of subcultures.

042 Christiano, Kevin J. "Religion and Radical Labor Unionism: American States in the 1920s." *Journal for the Scientific Study of Religion* 27 (1988): 378-388.
Christiano uses aggregate data shows a strong negative relationship between church membership and I. W. W. activity in the 1920s. The relationship persists in the face of multivariate controls. A longitudinal design shows that church membership and "Wobblie" activity were causally (and negatively) related.

043 Clapp, Spencer McCoy. "Leading the Nation After *Webster:* Connecticut's Abortion Law." In *The Catholic Church and the Politics of Abortion: A View From the States*, ed. by Timothy A. Byrnes and Mary C. Segers, 118-136. Boulder, CO: Westview Press, 1992.
Connecticut, which has a large Catholic population, passed a relatively permissive abortion law in 1990 (in the wake of the *Webster* decision). This piece analyzes the legislative politics leading up to the passage of that law, with emphasis on the lobbying activities of the Connecticut Coalition for Choice and the Pro-Life Council. The author argues that the rather liberal Connecticut law passed because of the willingness of the Coalition to compromise with its opponents.

044 Cleghorn, J. Stephen. "Respect for Life: Research Notes on Cardinal Bernardin's 'Seamless Garment'." *Review of Religious Research* 28 (1986): 129-141.
In an effort to relate Joseph Cardinal Bernardin's teachings with public opinion, Cleghorn shows that some of the issues involved in Bernardin's "consistent life ethic" (which the Cardinal presents theoretically as part of a single gestalt) form two dimensions: a personal autonomy dimension (consisting of attitudes toward euthanasia, suicide, and abortion) and a "defense of society" dimension (comprised of attitudes toward defense spending and capital punishment). Further, analysis of National Opinion Research Center data reveals that religious variables are only weakly related to either of these attitudes in the general public.

045 Conover, Pamela Johnston. "The Mobilization of the New Right: A Test of Various Hypotheses." *Western Political Quarterly* 36 (1983): 632-649.
Using a sample of attendees at a White House Conference on Families in 1980, Conover compares four theories of support for and activism in the "New Right:" psychological theory, status politics theory, mass society theory, and symbolic politics theory. The symbolic politics explanation has

the greatest empirical explanatory power. New Right support is related to traditional morality and "family values."

046 Conover, Pamela Johnston, and Gray, Virginia. *Feminism and the New Right: Conflict Over the American Family.* New York: Praeger Publishers, 1983.
This ambitious work uses both symbolic politics and resource mobilization approaches to explain the mobilization of the Christian Right and feminist activists. The authors argue that both abortion and the Equal Rights Amendment have served as "condensational symbols" which have crystallized a number of diverse concerns. This would suggest that activists on both sides hold distinctive world views; such cognitive incompatibility makes dialogue and accommodation difficult.

047 Cook, Elizabeth Adell; Jelen, Ted G.; and Wilcox, Clyde. "Catholicism and Abortion Attitudes in the American States: A Contextual Analysis." *Journal for the Scientific Study of Religion* 32 (1993): 223-230.
This piece shows that while individual Catholics are more "pro-life" than other Americans, living in a state in which Catholics are numerous exerts a significant "pro-choice" effect. The authors speculate that a strong Catholic presence in a state's politics may occasion an anti-Catholic counter-mobilization.

048 Cook, Elizabeth Adell, and Wilcox, Clyde. "Religious Orientations and Political Attitudes Among Blacks in Washington, D. C." *Polity* 22 (1990): 527-539.
What bearing do religious beliefs have on the political attitudes of African Americans? Evangelical and pentecostal doctrine are shown to be related to conservative positions on social issues among a sample of urban African Americans. Such beliefs are not, however, related to attitudes on economic or foreign policy issues.

049 Cranor, John D. "Jews, Blacks, and the Democrats, 1984." In *The Political Role of Religion in the United States,* ed. by Stephen D. Johnson and Joseph B. Tamney, 199-217. Boulder, CO: Westview Press, 1986.
Cranor analyzes the rhetoric of African Americans and Jews during the 1984 election. He finds that although religious differences were a source of divisiveness during the primary season, both groups gave Walter Mondale strong support in the general election.

050 Day, Christine. "Abortion and Religious Coalitions: The Case of Louisiana." In *The Catholic Church and the Politics of Abortion: A View From the States,* ed. by Timothy A. Byrnes and Mary C. Segers, 105-117. Boulder, CO: Westview Press, 1992.

This piece contains an analysis of the passage of Louisiana's post-*Webster* abortion law, which was among the most restrictive in the nation. Day argues that the success of the pro-life forces in Louisiana depended crucially upon the ability of the Catholic Church to coordinate its efforts with fundamentalist groups. Multivariate analysis of public opinion data suggests that affiliation with either Catholic or fundamentalist churches is related to a pro-life position on abortion, but that the religious interest groups involved took much more conservative positions than those endorsed by most of their constituents.

051 Daynes, Byron W., and Tatalovich, Raymond. "Religious Influence and Congressional Voting on Abortion." *Journal for the Scientific Study of Religion* 23 (1984): 197-200.
This study examines Congressional roll-call votes on abortion, 1973-1980. Members of Congress who identified themselves as Liberal Protestants or Jews were the most pro-choice; Catholics, Mormons, and Lutherans were the most pro-life. The positions of members from other denominations (such as Baptists) are considerably more mixed.

052 Demerath, N. J. III, and Williams, Rhys. *A Bridging of Faiths: Religion and Politics in a Northeastern City.* Princeton, NJ: Princeton University Press, 1992.
This book presents three case studies of religion-politics interactions in Springfield, Massachusetts. The authors show that despite the fact that the city's population is largely Catholic, the Catholic diocese does not dominate city politics. However, the authors find that religious groups do exercise "civil influence," and that such influence generally falls within constitutional bounds.

053 Diekema, David A. "Televangelism and the Mediated Charismatic Relationship." *Social Science Journal* 28 (1991): 143-162.
In this analysis Diekema distinguishes pure charismatic relationships from routinized and pseudo-charismatic relationships. He argues that religious television is pseudo-charismatic because the relationship between speaker and viewer is decontextualized, due to a lack of physical presence and reflexivity.

054 Dixon, Richard D.; Jones, Lloyd P.; and Lowery, Roger C. "Biblical Authority Questions: Two Choices in Identifying Conservative Christian Subcultures." *Sociological Analysis* 53 (1992): 63-72.
This study compares two questions eliciting attitudes toward the authority of Scripture: a question concerning the "literalness" of the entire Bible, and a question abut the literal truth of the Genesis creation story. Analysis of a telephone survey conducted in a Southern county shows that the creation story version yields a higher estimate of the proportion of biblical "literalists."

However, the "whole Bible" item has stronger relationships with a variety of other variables associated with conservative Christianity.

055 Dixon, Richard D.; Levy, Diane E.; and Lowery, Roger C. "Asking the 'Born-Again' Question." *Review of Religious Research* 30 (1988): 33-46.
In this study, the authors experiment with several different versions of survey items which measure "born-again" status or experiences and show that the marginal distributions of such questions vary enormously across the same population. The authors suggest that the response indicating that the respondent is not "born-again" should also include the term "Christian" to avoid a social desirability bias.

056 Dixon, Richard D.; Lowery, Roger C.; and Jones, Lloyd P. "The Fact and Form of Born-Again Religious Conversions and Socio-Political Conservatism." *Review of Religious Research* 34 (1993): 117-131.
The authors are interested in validating Gallup-style questions about born-again status. A survey of a single Southeastern county reveals that having had a "born-again" experience or status is significantly related to sociopolitical conservatism in bivariate models. However, the pace of the conversion (sudden or gradual) is not related to such conservatism. The effects of being "born-again" are not significant once subjected to multivariate controls, since other religious variables have stronger relationships with political attitudes.

057 Ebaugh, Helen Rose Fuchs. "Church Attendance and Attitudes Toward Abortion." *Journal for the Scientific Study of Religion* 17 (1978): 407-413.
The author explores the relationship between regularity of church attendance and abortion attitudes. Analysis of a national sample of adults taken in 1976 shows that church attendance is related to pro-life attitudes among people who report affiliation with a fundamentalist denomination, but attendance has no effect on abortion attitudes among members of liberal churches.

058 Ellison, Christopher G. "Identification and Separatism: Religious Involvement and Racial Orientations Among Black Americans." *Sociological Quarterly* 32 (1991): 477-494.
Ellison uses the National Survey of Black Americans to investigate the relationship between racial orientations and religious involvement. Public and private religious observance are shown to be related to racial identity among African Americans, although the relationship is much weaker for older individuals. In general, religiosity is not related to attitudes of racial separatism. Separatism is most prevalent among middle-aged African Americans who attend church frequently; Black Muslims; and those who are adherents of non-traditional religions.

059 Ellison, Christopher G., and Musick, Marc A. "Southern Intolerance: A Fundamentalist Effect?" *Social Forces* 72 (1993): 379-398.
Are Southerners less tolerant because they are more religious? An examination of regional differences in tolerance of left-wing groups in National Opinion Research Center data reveals that although religious fundamentalism is a significant predictor of intolerance, significant regional differences remain after the effects of religious variables have been controlled. The authors suggest that religious fundamentalism may have an effect on the social context of the American South.

060 Ellison, Christopher G., and Sherkat, Darren E. "Conservative Protestantism and Support for Corporal Punishment." *American Sociological Review* 58 (1993): 131-144.
Using National Opinion Research Center data, the authors investigate support among evangelicals for corporal punishment, assuming that their belief in the sinful nature of humans will allow them psychologically to support punishing children in this way. The study replicates the frequent finding that conservative Christians are more supportive of corporal punishment than other Americans. The authors show that this higher level of support is largely attributable to three doctrinal beliefs: an inerrant Bible, the reality of original sin (thus, a sinful human nature), and a belief that sin must be punished.

061 Ethridge, F. Maurice, and Feagin, Joe R. "Varieties of 'Fundamentalism': A Conceptual and Empirical Analysis of Two Protestant Denominations." *Sociological Quarterly* 20 (1979): 37-48.
The authors explore differing conceptualizations of fundamentalism. Analysis of a survey of members of the Disciples of Christ and the United Church of Christ reveals three distinct types of fundamentalism: organization, sociocultural, and theological-supernatural. They suggest that future research be directed toward denominationally-specific measures of fundamentalism.

062 Fairbanks, James David. "Religious Forces and 'Morality' Policies in the American States." *Western Political Quarterly* 30 (1977): 411-417.
Fairbanks investigates the possibility that public policy may differ in states on the basis of the comparative strength of organized religion. An analysis of state level aggregate data shows that religious variables are more powerful predictors of state policies on gambling and liquor than are sociodemographic variables. General Protestantism accounts for most variation in gambling policies, while state level fundamentalist affiliation is most strongly related to restrictive state policies concerning alcoholic beverages. Roman Catholicism is related to permissive state policies in both areas.

063 Fairbanks, James David. "Politics and the Evangelical Press, 1960-85." In *Religion and Political Behavior in the United States*, ed. by Ted G. Jelen, 243-257. New York: Praeger Publishers, 1989.
A quarter-century content analysis of *Christianity Today, Christian Herald,* and *Eternity* suggests that such evangelical publications have always addressed political issues from the standpoint of moderate conservatism. The political orientations of these periodicals are quite different from those articulated by Moral Majority or other televangelists.

064 Fairbanks, James David. "The Politics of Christianity Today:1956-1986."*In Contemporary Evangelical Political Involvement: An Analysis and Assessment*, ed. by Corwin E. Smidt, 25-43. New York: University Press of America, 1989.
Using a content analysis of an important evangelical publication, Fairbanks finds little support for the hypothesis that evangelicals experienced high levels of political mobilization in the 1980s. The coverage devoted by *Christianity Today* to politics was relatively constant over a thirty-year period.

065 Finke, Roger, and Stark, Rodney. "Religious Economies and Sacred Canopies: Religious Mobilization in American Cities, 1906." *American Sociological Review* 53 (1988): 41-49.
Do large cities facilitate or inhibit religiosity? Analyzing data from the 1906 Census of Religious Bodies, Finke and Stark show that contrary to previously held beliefs, urbanization is positively related to religious participation. The authors attribute this finding to market competition among different religious bodies.

066 Finke, Roger, and Stark, Rodney. "Evaluating the Evidence: Religious Economies and Sacred Canopies." *American Sociological Review* 54 (1989): 1054-1056.
This brief note is a response to Breault (024). The authors reassert their original conclusion that religious pluralism is positively related to religious participation, and suggest that the data on which Breault bases his contrary conclusions are limited and unrepresentative.

067 Finke, Roger, and Stark, Rodney. *The Churching of America: 1776-1990.* New Brunswick, NJ: Rutgers University Press, 1992.
Using extensive analyses of historical data, Finke and Stark show that religious involvement is positively associated with religious competition between denominations. "Low church," popular denominations with non-specialized clergy tend to thrive in religiously competitive markets, while churches with more rationalized theologies and professional clergy tend to do poorly in such environments. The authors suggest that a variant of

rational choice theory accounts for the patterns of affiliation and involvement.

068 Finley, Nancy J. "Political Activism and Feminist Spirituality." *Sociological Analysis* 52 (1991): 349-362.
In this study, neo-paganism is hypothesized to be a source of political activism. Using a sample of Dianic witches, Finley shows that membership in an unorthodox new religious movement enhances personal and political efficacy, as well as political participation.

069 Frankl, Razelle. *Televangelism: The Marketing of Popular Religion.* Carbondale, IL: Southern Illinois University Press, 1987.
Frankl provides an overview of religious television. She devotes a section to the historical roots of televangelism ("urban revivalism"), and she also considers financial and programmatic aspects of televised religion. Frankl concludes that religious programming is more varied, and the audience considerably larger, than previous research had suggested.

070 Funderburk, Charles. "Religion, Political Legitimacy, and Civil Violence: A Survey of Children and Adolescents." *Sociological Focus* 19 (1986): 289-298.
To what extent do churches serve as agents of political socialization? A survey of 736 children and adolescents reveals that religiosity is positively related to support for the political system and its symbols, and (to a lesser extent) support for political leaders. Religiosity is negatively related to approval of civil violence. These relationships vary directly with age, suggesting that the religious basis of political learning occurs throughout the pre-adult years.

071 Gaddy, Gary D. "The Power of the Religious Media: Religious Broadcast Use and the Role of Religious Organizations in Public Affairs." *Review of Religious Research* 25 (1984): 289-302.
Path analysis of national survey data is used to investigate the relationships between religious broadcast use and support for political involvement by religious groups. The results show that a belief that religious organizations should involve themselves in public affairs is related to usage of religious radio and television. However, the reverse is not the case, and usage of religiously oriented electronic media does not have a politicizing effect on the user.

072 Gamoran, Adam. "Civil Religion in American Schools." *Sociological Analysis* 51 (1990): 235-256.
Does civil religion serve to marginalize certain groups of children, such as those of immigrants? A multi-method description of civil religion in American elementary schools suggests that the use of civil religious

symbols is quite widespread. While such socialization may result in the learning of a common set of cultural meanings, it does have the effect of marginalizing members of subgroups who are unable to participate fully in the American political culture.

073 Gay, David, and Ellison, Christopher G. "Religious Subcultures and Political Tolerance: Do Denominations Still Matter?" *Review of Religious Research* 34 (1993): 311-332.
Using National Opinion Research Center data, the authors use several different methods of classifying religious denominations and examine the effects of each on attitudes toward civil liberties. They find that a scheme of religious "families" has the strongest explanatory power with respect to attitudes toward First Amendment issues. Such an approach is empirically superior to examining individual denominations.

074 Georgianna, Sharon Linzey. *The Moral Majority and Fundamentalism: Plausibility and Dissonance.* Lewiston, ME: Mellen Press, 1989.
This study addresses an apparent paradox: why do fundamentalists, who are often characterized as "separatist" or "otherworldly," engage in political activity by supporting Moral Majority? Using a mail survey of Moral Majority members in Indiana and Arkansas, the author finds that members experience some cognitive dissonance, but believe that the cause of making the United States "righteous" overrides their commitment to evangelism.

075 Gilbert, Christopher P. *The Impact of Churches on Political Behavior: An Empirical Study.* Westport, CT: Greenwood Press,1993.Based on the 1984 South Bend (Indiana) Community Study, this work compares the impact of churches to other social contexts in explaining a variety of political attitudes. Using sophisticated research designs measuring (among other things) the impact of discussion partners, Gilbert shows that churches are powerful sources of political socialization, but their precise influence is complex and varies across issues and settings.

076 Gilbert, Christopher P., and Peterson, David A. "Minnesota: Christians and Quistians in the GOP." In *God at the Grassroots: The Christian Right in the 1994 Elections*, ed. by Mark J. Rozell and Clyde Wilcox, 169-189. Lanham, MD: Rowman & Littlefield Publishers,1995.
Gilbert and Peterson are concerned with the relationship between the Christian Right and the Republican Party in Minnesota, particularly as this relationship played out in the 1994 midterm elections. They show that the media played an important role in structuring voters' opinions about Christian conservative candidates, particularly Allen Quist, who ran for governor, and that the Christian Right is surprisingly strong in progressive Minnesota.

077 Glenn, Norval, and Gotard, Erin. "The Religion of Blacks in the United States: Some Recent Trends and Current Characteristics." *American Journal of Sociology* 83 (1977): 443-451.
In this piece the authors report that membership in African American denominations is highly stable, although there has been a decline in the recruitment of African American clergy.   Furthermore, contrary to conventional wisdom, this study contains no evidence that African American religion is "escapist" or "otherworldly."

078 Granberg, Donald.   "Conformity to Religious Norms Regarding Abortion." *Sociological Quarterly* 32 (1991): 267-275.
Under what circumstances do Catholics conform to the Church's teachings about abortion?   An analysis of Catholics' current religious preference, religious preference at age 16, and spouse's denomination shows that white Catholics married to other Catholics are likely to oppose legal abortion, but non-Catholics married to Catholics are more likely to approve of abortion. Catholic converts to evangelical denominations are more "pro-life" than lifetime Catholics.   Any exposure to Judaism occasions "pro-choice" attitudes.

079 Greeley, Andrew.   "Religion and Attitudes Toward the Environment." *Journal for the Scientific Study of Religion* 32 (1993): 19-28.
A variety of religious attitudes and memberships are found to be associated with different levels of environmental concern.   Low concern for the environment is related to belief in biblical literalism, being a Christian, and expressing high confidence in the existence of God. Catholicism and belief in a gracious God are associated with high levels of environmental concern. Greeley concludes that these relationships are ultimately spurious, and that environmental concern is occasioned by psychological rigidity.

080 Green, John C. "Pat Robertson and the Latest Crusade: Religious Resources and the 1988 Presidential Campaign." *Social Science Quarterly* 74 (1993): 157-168.
This analysis of the Robertson campaign suggests that Pat Robertson drew support primarily from charismatic Christians, but that this small support group provided impressive financial resources.   Green also argues that Robertson's relatively small, but committed, base of activists was well suited for caucuses, but was not as effective in primary elections.

081 Green, John C., and Guth, James L.   "The Christian Right in the Republican Party: The Case of Pat Robertson's Supporters." *Journal of Politics* 50 (1988): 150-165.
Pat Robertson's contributors may shed light on the constituency within the Republican Party that supports the Christian Right agenda. Based on a survey of contributors to Republican presidential candidates, Green and

Guth show that Robertson's supporters were distinctive from those who contributed to other candidates. Robertson's contributors were distinctly more religious, less partisan, and less politically experienced than other contributors. Robertson contributors were also slightly more "purist" in their orientation. However, they seem sufficiently similar to other Republicans to suggest relatively easy assimilation into the party.

082 Green, John C., and Guth, James L. "The Missing Link: Political Activists and School Prayer." *Public Opinion Quarterly* 53 (1989): 41-57.
In an examination of school prayer activists, the authors present an analysis of a 1982 survey of contributors to parties and political campaigns. It reveals that unlike the mass public, members of this elite sample are sharply divided and polarized on the issue of school prayer. The authors speculate that Congress may be responding to activist opinion when measures permitting school prayer are not enacted.

083 Green, John C., and Guth, James L. "From Lambs to Sheep: Denominational Change and Political Behavior." In *Rediscovering the Religious Factor in American Politics*, ed. by David C. Leege and Lyman A. Kellstedt, 100-117. Armonk, NY: M. E. Sharpe, 1993.
This study investigates the effects of religious "switching" on political attitudes. In general, switchers engage in "anticipatory socialization," which involves adopting the political values of their new denomination. Most switching takes place between theologically similar denominations, although some respondents switch into or out of secularism. Large, pluralistic denominations experiences losses both to evangelicals and to secularism.

084 Green, John C.; Guth, James L.; and Fraser, Cleveland R. "Apostles and Apostates? Religion and Politics Among Party Activists." In *The Bible and the Ballot Box: Religion and Politics in the 1988 Election*, ed. by James L. Guth and John C. Green, 113-136. Boulder, CO: Westview Press, 1991.
A survey of financial contributors to presidential candidates reveals increasing religious polarization between and within both major political parties. In general, most orthodox and religiously observant donors contribute to the campaigns of Republicans, while the most secular contributors participate in Democratic Party politics. Both groups provide the basis for internal dissension within their respective parties as well.

085 Green, John C.; Guth, James L.; and Hill, Kevin. "Faith and Election: The Christian Right in Congressional Campaigns." *Journal of Politics* 55 (1993): 80-91.
Green et al. study the supply, demand, and allocation of resources by the Christian Right in congressional campaigns. An events data analysis of Christian Right activity in elections for the U. S. House of Representatives

suggests that Christian Right organizations target districts in affluent, rapidly growing suburban areas of the Midwest, Southwest, and Southeast. Such organizations also concentrate resources in close elections.

086 Green, John C.; Guth, James L.; Kellstedt, Lyman A.; and Smidt, Corwin E. "Uncivil Challenges: Support for Civil Liberties Among Religious Activists." *Journal of Political Science* 22 (1994): 25-49.
The authors set out to investigate the degree to which religious activists of the political left and right support civil liberties. Using a survey of such activists, they show that support for the First Amendment rights of unpopular groups is generally related to a doctrinal definition of "fundamentalism," which appears to occasion pessimism about the practices of American politics. Liberal activists typically are more optimistic about political processes, and hold narrower grievances. Such activists are therefore more supportive of civil liberties.

087 Guth, James L. "Preachers and Politics: Varieties of Activism Among Southern Baptist Ministers." In *Religion and Politics in the South: Mass and Elite Perspectives*, ed. by Tod A. Baker, Robert P. Steed, and Laurence W. Moreland, 161-183. New York: Praeger Publishers, 1983.
Although most Southern Baptist ministers take conservative positions on political issues, many report having deep reservations about Christian Right organizations. There are even some ministers who hold moderate to liberal positions. As the locus of power within the Southern Baptist Convention shifts from the South Atlantic to the Southwest and Deep South, the prospects for polarization within the Southern Baptist Convention will increase.

088 Guth, James L. "Southern Baptist Clergy: Vanguard of the Christian Right?" In *The New Christian Right: Mobilization and Legitimation*, ed. by Robert C. Lehman and Robert Wuthnow, 117-130. New York: Aldine Press, 1983.
A 1980 survey of Southern Baptist ministers reveals that Baptist clergy are about evenly divided in their evaluation of Moral Majority. Members and sympathizers are more theologically and politically conservative than opponents. They are also more likely both to see a strong connection between religious and political conservatism and to be in the process of defecting from the Democratic Party. The effects of demographic and contextual variables are also shown to be significant sources of attitudes toward Moral Majority.

089 Guth, James L. "South Carolina: The Christian Right Wins One." In *God at the Grassroots: The Christian Right in the 1994 Elections*, ed. by Mark J. Rozell and Clyde Wilcox, 133-145. Lanham, MD: Rowman & Littlefield Publishers, 1995.

Guth's analysis of the Christian Right's role in 1994 races in South Carolina illuminates several important points. First, it is a mistake to equate "the Christian Right" with the Christian Coalition. Rather, there are many other organizations which are heavily involved in politics, such as (in the case of South Carolina) individuals affiliated with the fundamentalist Bob Jones University. Also, candidates who have secured the support of the Christian Right (such as Governor David Beasley) must work to maintain that support.

090 Guth, James L., and Green, John C. "Faith and Politics: Religion and Ideology Among Political Contributors." *American Politics Quarterly* 14 (1986): 186-200.
Using survey data from a study of contributors to political groups, the authors set out to investigate the influence of religiosity on these individuals' patterns of giving. Religious contributors are found to contribute to conservative political action committees (PACs) and to the Republican Party, while secular contributors give to the Democrats and to liberal PACs. The effects of religion persist in the face of elaborate multivariate controls.

091 Guth, James L., and Green, John C. "The Moralizing Minority: Christian Right Supporters Among Political Contributors." *Social Science Quarterly* 68 (1987): 598-616.
Data from a survey of political activists suggests that Moral Majority draws support from only a small group of financial contributors. Such support is concentrated in conservative PACs, which provide resources for arenas in less public contexts.

092 Guth, James L., and Green, John C. "God and the GOP: Religion Among Republican Activists." In *Religion and Political Behavior in the United States*, ed. by Ted G. Jelen, 223-241. New York: Praeger Publishers, 1989.
A sample of Republican contributors is found to be quite religious, with all religious variables loading on a single dimension. While relatively few contributors report making donations to televangelists such as Jerry Falwell, these contributors are nonetheless found to be quite religious. Highly religious contributors are more "purist" than their less religious counterparts, and less tolerant of nonconformists as well. Supporters of the Christian Right are the most conservative, and have a distinct issue agenda.

093 Guth, James L., and Green, John C. "Politics in a New Key: Religiosity and Participation Among Political Activists." *Western Political Quarterly* 43 (1990): 153-179.
In an analysis of financial contributors to political parties and candidates designed to shed light on an increase in religio-political conflict, Guth and

Green show that religiosity is an important predictor of a variety of political attitudes. The main cleavage appears to exist between activists of higher and lower religiosity, rather than between adherents of different denominations.

094 Guth, James L., and Green, John C. "Salience: The Core Concept?" In *Rediscovering the Religious Factor in American Politics*, ed. by David C. Leege and Lyman A. Kellstedt, 157-174. Armonk, NY: M. E. Sharpe, 1993.
The authors develop a scale of religious salience based on respondents' church attendance, private devotionalism, and the extent to which they find religion to be an important source of guidance. This scale is related to a variety of political attitudes, both directly and as a conditioner of other religious variables.

095 Guth, James L.; Green, John C.; and Kellstedt, Lyman A. "Faith and the Environment: Religious Beliefs and Attitudes on Environmental Policy." *American Journal of Political Science* 39 (1995): 364-382.
The authors hypothesize that conservative Protestants will not support public policy designed to protect the environment. Using data from surveys of clergy, religious activists, party contributors, and the mass public, they find that conservative eschatology predicts non-supportive attitudes about environmental policy, especially among clergy.

096 Guth, James L.; Green, John C.; Smidt, Corwin E.; and Poloma, M. Margaret. "Pulpits and Politics: The Protestant Clergy in the 1988 Presidential Election." In *The Bible and the Ballot Box: Religion and Politics in the 1988 Election*, ed. by James L. Guth and John C. Green, 73-93. Boulder, CO: Westview Press, 1991.
Based on a mail survey of Protestant ministers, this study suggests that political polarization is occurring among the clergy, with doctrinally liberal and conservative preachers taking distinctive positions on political issues, partisanship, and candidate choices. In some instances, such polarization is inhibited by attitudes characteristic of particular denominations.

097 Guth, James L.; Jelen, Ted G.; Kellstedt, Lyman A.; Smidt, Corwin E.; and Wald, Kenneth D. "The Politics of Religion in America: Issues for Investigation." *American Politics Quarterly* 16 (1988): 357-397.
This essay reviews and synthesizes the empirical literature relating religion to political behavior, and charts an agenda for future research. A number of different research approaches are compared and analyzed, and a variety of potential research questions are discussed.

098 Guth, James L.; Kellstedt, Lyman A.; Smidt, Corwin E.; and Green, John C.   "Theological Perspectives and Environmentalism Among Religious Activists." *Journal for the Scientific Study of Religion* 32 (1993): 373-382.
An analysis of a large survey of activists in religious interest groups employs a detailed measure of fundamentalism. The measure not only includes aspects of Christian orthodoxy, but contains measures of dispensationalism and eschatological perspectives as well. This measure is strongly and negatively related to environmentalism.

099 Guth, James L.; Kellstedt, Lyman A.; Smidt, Corwin E.; and Green, John C. "Cut From the Whole Cloth: Antiabortion Mobilization Among Religious Activists." In *Abortion Politics in the United States and Canada: Studies in Public Opinion*, ed. by Ted G. Jelen and Marthe A. Chandler, 107-130. Westport, CT: Praeger Publishers, 1994.
The authors show that support for two pro-life interest groups (the National Right to Life Committee and Operation Rescue) is related to political conservatism, religious fundamentalism, doctrinal orthodoxy, and religious militancy. However, support for the direct action group Operation Rescue does not differ qualitatively from that for the National Right to Life Committee.

100 Guth, James L.; Smidt, Corwin E.; Kellstedt, Lyman A.; and Green, John C.   "The Sources of Antiabortion Attitudes: The Case of Religious Political Activists." *American Politics Quarterly* 21 (1993): 65-80.
The authors are principally interested here in the abortion attitudes of religious activists. Based on a sample of members of religious interest groups, this study shows that doctrinal orthodoxy, Roman Catholicism, and fundamentalist theological beliefs contribute to pro-life attitudes, even within a relatively homogenous sample. Moreover, religious variables are far more important than other respondent attitudes and characteristics in explaining attitudes toward legal abortion.

101 Hadden, Jeffrey K. "Religious Broadcasting and the Mobilization of the New Christian Right." *Journal for the Scientific Study of Religion* 26 (1987): 1-24.
This article offers three reasons for the burst of "televangelism" which occurred in the 1980s: a renewal of "urban revivalism," the novel domination of religious airwaves by religious conservatives, and the importance of the "Dominion creation" myth. The latter consideration refers to a belief that there exists a special relationship between God and the United States.

102 Hallum, Anne M. "Presbyterians as Political Amateurs." In *Religion in American Politics*, ed. by Charles W. Dunn, 63-73. Washington, DC: Congressional Quarterly Press, 1989.
Hallum suggests that the principal political arm of Presbyterian Church (USA) , Presbyterians for Democracy and Religious Freedom, can be characterized as amateurish due to its inflexibility.

103 Hallum, Anne M. "From Candidates to Agenda Setters: Protestant Leaders and the 1988 Presidential Campaign." In *The Bible and the Ballot Box: Religion and Politics in the 1988 Election*, ed. by James L. Guth and John C. Green, 31-41. Boulder, CO: Westview Press, 1991.
Based on interviews with national Protestant leaders, Hallum reviews the possible political roles of such people. These range from deep involvement with a specific campaign to "selective" agenda-setting to "broad" agenda setting .

104 Hammond, Phillip E.; Shibley, Mark A.; and Solow, Peter M. "Religion and Family Values In Presidential Voting." *Sociology of Religion* 55 (1994): 277-290.
The authors develop several dimensions of conservative ideology, including religion and family values. While the latter were not particularly important predictors of presidential voting in the 1980s, both were quite important in accounting for presidential vote in 1992. Family values accounted for most variance in vote choice.

105 Handberg, Roger. "Creationism, Conservatism and Ideology: Fringe Issues in American Politics." *Social Science Journal* 21 (1984): 37-51.
Based on analysis of survey data, Handberg reports that support for creationism is positively related to religious fundamentalism and negatively related to level of education. Creationists generally have few resources with which to influence public policy. Support for evolutionary theory is high among the general public, but the issue is of low salience to most Americans.

106 Hanna, Mary T. "Bishops as Political Leaders." In *Religion in American Politics*, ed. by Charles W. Dunn, 75-86. Washington, DC: Congressional Quarterly Press, 1989.
Hanna traces the history of the political involvement of Catholic Bishops. She briefly discusses some of the challenges facing bishops who wish to act as political leaders, such as the fact that they are not politically accountable to anyone.

107 Hanna, Mary T. "The Dance of Legislation: Church Style." In *Religion and Political Behavior in the United States*, ed. by Ted G. Jelen, 209-221. New York: Praeger Publishers, 1989.
In this study, Hanna describes the process by which the National Conference of Catholic Bishops wrote the 1986 Pastoral Letter on the American economy. The process appears to have been one of compromise and bargaining, more closely resembling the secular legislation than theological exegesis. The bishops themselves regard such democratic procedures as fulfilling the spirit of Vatican II, rather than as accommodation of American political culture.

108 Hanna, Mary T. "Divided, Distracted, and Disengaged: Catholic Leaders and the 1988 Presidential Campaign." In *The Bible and the Ballot Box: Religion and Politics in the 1988 Election*, ed. by James L. Guth and John C. Green, 42-54. Boulder, CO: Westview Press, 1991.
Hanna reviews the public statements of American Catholic Bishops during the 1988 presidential election campaign and comes to two main conclusions. First, there was relatively little overt participation by the bishops in 1988. Second, the bishops were divided among themselves. The main division was between those (such as Cardinal O'Connor) who wished to emphasize the abortion issue, and those (such as Cardinal Bernardin) who believed that all issues involved in the "consistent ethic of life" approach were important.

109 Harper, Charles L., and Leicht, Kevin. "Religious Awakenings and Status Politics: Sources of Support for the New Religious Right." *Sociological Analysis* 45 (1984): 339-353.
The authors compare the relative merits of status politics explanations and religious and cultural variables in examining the sources of support for the religious Right. A survey of Nebraska residents affiliated with the United Churches of Christ, Disciples of Christ, and Assemblies of God reveals that religious and cultural variables are stronger predictors of agreement with the goals of Moral Majority than are status politics explanations.

110 Harris, Fredrick C. "Something Within: Religion as a Mobilizer of African-American Political Activism." *Journal of Politics* 56 (1994): 42-69.
In an analysis of National Opinion Research Center data, Harris shows that different aspects of religiosity and religious involvement serve as organizational and psychological resources for African Americans. Church attendance and activism provide organizational resources, while "internal religiosity" is a source of psychological mobilization. Church attendance is a stronger predictor of voting turnout among whites, but church activism is more strongly related to voting turnout and collective political action among African Americans.

111 Harris, Richard J., and Mills, Edgar W. "Religion, Values, and Attitudes Toward Abortion." *Journal for the Scientific Study of Religion* 24 (1985): 137-154.
Values of "self-determination" and "respect for others" are shown to be intervening variables between religious beliefs and abortion attitudes. A longitudinal analysis suggests that these values "crystallized" between 1974 and 1982, in the sense of becoming more closely related for members of the mass public.

112 Harrison, Michael I., and Lazerwitz, Bernard. "Do Denominations Matter?" *American Journal of Sociology* 88 (1982): 356-377.
This piece contains a comparison of members of and identifiers with different "denominations" within American Judaism. In general, Reform Jews are found to be most politically liberal and involved with secular organizations, with Conservative and Orthodox Jews exhibiting lower levels of liberalism and involvement.

113 Hart, Stephen. "Christian Faith and Nuclear Weapons: Rank and File Opinions." *Journal for the Scientific Study of Religion* 26 (1987): 38-62.
Based on a survey of Lutherans, Hart finds that attitudes toward nuclear weapons are multidimensional, and identifies policy, cognitive, and ethical factors. Within a sample from a single denomination, religious variables are found to be generally weak predictors of all three dimensions.

114 Heimer, David D. "Abortion Attitudes Among Catholic University Students: A Comparative Research Note." *Sociological Analysis* 37 (1976): 255-260.
Although education is generally associated with support for legal abortion, previous research had suggested that this was not true of Catholics, due to the influence of Catholic colleges. Heimer finds that a sample of Catholic college students is indeed more "pro-life" than a sample of the general population.

115 Hertel, Bradley R., and Hendershot, Gerry E. "Military Preparedness and Religion: Methodological Problems in Using Modal Religion in Cross-Cultural Research." *Review of Religious Research* 16 (1975): 208-219.
This piece assesses the utility of using "modal" religion in aggregate level studies of nations' capacity to wage war. The authors suggest that classifying countries as "Catholic," "Islamic," etc., risks a number of methodological problems, including the fallacy of composition.

116 Hertel, Bradley R., and Hughes, Michael. "Religious Affiliation, Attendance, and Support for 'Pro-Family' Issues in the United States." *Social Forces* 65 (1987): 858-882.
Using National Opinion Research Center data, the authors analyze the relationship of religious variables to support for the so-called "pro-family" agenda. Denominational affiliation is related to conservative positions across a number of different issues relating to "family values." Religiosity serves to make people more conservative on such issues within virtually all Christian denominations.

117 Hertzke, Allen D. *Representing God in Washington: The Role of Religious Lobbies in the American Polity.* Knoxville, TN: University of Tennessee Press, 1988.
Hertzke presents a detailed study of national religious interest groups. He is most interested in investigating manifestations of pluralism through the religious example. Numerous in-depth interviews with religious lobbyists show that religious lobbying is quite widespread across the theological spectrum, and that both religious liberals and conservatives feel threatened by secular elites. Both groups of lobbyists attempt to participate in the legislative process, and may increase the political influence of previously underrepresented groups.

118 Hertzke, Allen D. "Faith and Access: Religious Constituencies and the Washington Elites." In *Religion and Political Behavior in the United States*, ed. by Ted G. Jelen, 259-274. New York: Praeger Publishers, 1989.
Interviews with congressional elites and White House staffers suggests that religious lobbyists' access to political elites is most often based on the religious preferences of the official in question. Public officials at both ends of Pennsylvania Avenue permit selective access to those with whom the officials are sympathetic. A prominent exception are representatives of Jewish organizations, who are regarded as quite effective by many elites.

119 Hertzke, Allen D. "Harvest of Discontent: Religion and Populism in the 1988 Presidential Campaign." In *The Bible and the Ballot Box: Religion and Politics in the 1988 Election*, ed. by James L. Guth and John C. Green, 3-27. Boulder, CO: Westview Press, 1991.
In this piece, Hertzke makes a series of comparisons between the 1988 presidential campaigns of Jesse Jackson and Marion "Pat" Robertson. Despite some obvious differences, Hertzke discerns a core message of populism which renders the campaigns surprisingly similar.

120 Hertzke, Allen D. *Echoes of Discontent: Jesse Jackson, Pat Robertson, and the Resurgence of Populism.* Washington, DC: Congressional Quarterly Press, 1993.
Hertzke looks at two Christian political candidates, Jesse Jackson and Pat Robertson, and argues that their success in 1988 was due in large part to their populist appeal. Jackson criticizes the exploitation of the poor by the rich, while Robertson attacks "cultural elites" undermining "family values," but both candidates appeal to people through "us vs. them" frames. Hertzke argues that both candidates tap into discontent among Americans about the laissez-faire individualism that characterizes modern society.

121 Hildreth, Anne. "The Importance of Purposes in 'Purposive' Groups: Incentives and Participation in the Sanctuary Movement." *American Journal of Political Science* 38 (1994): 447-463.
Hildreth applies incentive theory to investigate participation in the Sanctuary Movement. A survey of participants in the movement (shows that the mix of incentives for such participants was mixed and complex. The importance of purposive incentives is strongest for those most committed to the activity.

122 Himmelfarb, Harold S., and Loar, R. Michael. "National Trends in Jewish Ethnicity: A Test of the Polarization Hypothesis." *Journal for the Scientific Study of Religion* 23 (1984): 140-154.
Historically, successive generations of Jewish immigrants and their descendants have grown away from certain traditions within Judaism. Although this trend may have continued for Reform and Conservative Jews, adherence to Orthodox Judaism has leveled off after the fourth generation.

123 Himmelstein, Jerome L. "The Social Basis of Antifeminism: Religious Networks and Culture." *Journal for the Scientific Study of Religion* 25 (1986): 1-15.
Himmelstein argues that opposition to legal abortion and the Equal Rights Amendment is based on integration into religious networks, rather than on low education, social position, or the lack of an independent basis of support.

124 Himmelstein, Jerome L., and McRae, James A., Jr. "Social Conservatism, New Republicans, and the 1980 Election." *Public Opinion Quarterly* 48 (1984): 592-605.
Using an analysis of 1980 American National Election data, the authors draw a contrast between "old" and "new" Republicans, defining the latter as those who voted for Republican in 1980, but not in 1976. Contrary to popular stereotypes, new Republicans were not generally more religious, more likely to have been "born-again," or more conservative on social issues. Himmelstein and McRae conclude that the 1980 election was a

referendum on the Carter administration, and did not involve the mobilization of previously apolitical fundamentalist Christians.

125 Hofrenning, Daniel J. B. *In Washington But Not Of It: The Prophetic Politics of Religious Lobbyists.* Philadelphia: Temple University Press, 1995.
The topic of this study is the diversity of religious interest groups in Washington. Religious interest groups, Hofrenning argues, generally seek more broad-based change than secular lobbies. In fact, lobbyists for religious interest groups are less likely to be Washington insiders than are secular lobbyists.

126 Hoge, Dean R. "Theological Views of America Among Protestants." *Sociological Analysis* 37 (1976): 127-139.
Hoge endeavors to formulate a theory of mainline clergy's "theology of America," that is, their perceptions of the normative role of the United States in the world system. A 1973 survey of United Presbyterian ministers shows that mainline clergy have a "religious vision" of the United States. Such pastors are more likely to view America as an example for the rest of the world, rather than as a country with an active world mission. These ministers are generally more internationalist than their laity, and seek to apply universalistic standards to the United States. Finally, Hoge's data reveal something of a "two-party" system among mainline clergy, with internationalist clergy opposing those who are committed to anti-Communism.

127 Hood, Ralph W., and Morris, Ronald D. "Boundary Maintenance, Socio-Political Views, and Presidential Preference Among High and Low Fundamentalists." *Review of Religious Research* 27 (1985): 134-145.
Using a sample of college students, the authors make a distinction between "high" and "low" fundamentalists, with "high" fundamentalists being most doctrinally orthodox. High fundamentalists are most distinctive on what the authors term "boundary maintenance" issues, which typically involve questions of personal morality. High fundamentalists are also most likely to vote for presidential candidates with whom the respondent shared a perceived religious or moral affinity.

128 Hoover, Stewart M. "The Religious Television Audience: A Matter of Significance or Size?" *Review of Religious Research* 29 (1987): 135-151.
After reviewing the controversy concerning the size of the audience for religious programming, Hoover suggests that the important questions concern the characteristics of these viewers. Hoover suggests that the audience for religious television is stable (and small) and views religious programs for short periods. Self-reports of viewership are contaminated by the high social desirability of watching religious television.

129 Hoover, Stewart M. *Mass Media Religion: The Social Sources of the Electronic Church.* Newbury Park, CA: Sage, 1988.
This work consists of an analysis of the sources and content of "televangelism." Hoover argues that the electronic church provides cognitive support for socially isolated religious conservatives, and has a number of different effects. These include supporting theological conservatives who attend mainline churches, and suggesting the legitimacy of political activism among previously apolitical evangelical Christians. Televangelism tends to supplement, rather than replace, traditional religious observance.

130 Hougland, James G. "The State and Observations of Religious Holiday Traditions: Attitudes Toward Nativity Scenes on Government Property." *Sociological Analysis* 53 (1992): 299-308.
The study consists of an analysis of two statewide polls in Kentucky (conducted in 1988 and 1990) concerning a decision by the governor to erect a crèche in the state capitol. Hougland investigates the relationships between religiosity and support for this action. Support for the nativity scene was high in both years, and, in both years, general religious variables were related to such support. However, other correlates of support varied across the time period. In a period of high controversy (extensive media coverage) political attitudes were related to support for the crèche, while personal values and social position were stronger predictors during a period of low media attention.

131 Hougland, James G., Jr., and Billings, Dwight B. "The Instability of Support for Televangelists: Public Reactions During a Period of Embarrassment." *Review of Religious Research* 32 (1990): 56-64.
In order to investigate the determinants of support for religious broadcasters, the authors compare two surveys of Kentucky residents (taken in 1981 and 1987) about the respect respondents had for televangelists. The latter survey was taken after public embarrassments by Oral Roberts and Jim and Tammy Bakker (but before the sexual scandal of Jimmy Swaggart). Televangelists had fallen considerably in public esteem in the latter period, but retained loyal viewers within limited theological markets.

132 Hougland, James G., and Lacy, William B. "Membership in Voluntary Organizations and Support for Civil Liberties." *Sociological Focus* 14 (1981): 97-110.
Using two national samples, the authors explore the degree to which various voluntary memberships contribute to high levels of support for civil liberties. In general, participation in voluntary organizations is found to be positively related to support for the First Amendment rights of unpopular

minorities. However, membership in church (or farm) organizations is negatively related to such support.

133 Hout, Michael, and Greeley, Andrew M. "The Center Doesn't Hold: Church Attendance in the United States, 1940-1984." *American Sociological Review* 52 (1987): 325-345.
The authors report that church attendance in the United States has been quite stable over a fifty-year period. One exception to this generalization is a marked decline in Catholic attendance between 1968 and 1975, which the authors attribute to opposition to the Church's position on issues of sexual morality. This opposition rarely resulted in lay people leaving the Church.

134 Huckfeldt, Robert; Plutzer, Eric; and Sprague, John. "Alternative Contexts of Political Behavior: Churches, Neighborhoods, and Individuals." *Journal of Politics* 55 (1993): 365-381.
This article compares the simple and interactive effects of various social contexts in accounting for party identification and attitudes toward abortion. Using 1984 data from an election survey in South Bend, Indiana, the authors show that while most patterns of contextual effects are easily interpretable, some counterintuitive findings suggest the possibilities of selective avoidance and self-selection.

135 Hunt, Larry L., and Hunt, Janet H. "Black Religion as BOTH Opiate and Inspiration of Civil Rights: Putting Marx's Data to the Test." *Social Forces* 56 (1977): 1-14.
In this piece, the authors show that the negative relationship between religiosity and civil rights militancy among African Americans disappears when subjected to a variety of multivariate controls. It is suggested that religion can serve as either a source of political quiescence or mobilization, depending on the circumstances.

136 Hunter, James Davison. "The New Class and the Young Evangelicals." *Review of Religious Research* 22 (1980): 115-169.
Using data gathered from religious periodicals, Hunter analyzes the "new class" of younger evangelicals employed in "knowledge industries." He suggests that such "new class" evangelicals are considerably more "left-liberal," and less doctrinally orthodox, than other evangelical Christians.

137 Hunter, James Davison. "Operationalizing Evangelicalism: A Review, Critique, and Proposal." *Sociological Analysis* 42 (1981): 363-372.
In this piece, Hunter reviews the literature on the measurement of evangelicalism and fundamentalism. He offers an approach to the operationalization of these concepts which emphasizes biblical inerrancy, Christology, and soteriology (the requisites for salvation). Hunter argues

that evangelicalism is properly understood as a Protestant phenomenon, and identifies several denominationally-defined evangelical subcultures.

138 Hunter, James Davison. "The Perils of Idealism: A Reply." *Review of Religious Research* 24 (1983): 267-276.
In this brief response to Reese (277), Hunter argues that the evangelical left has social as well as theological roots, and that it is necessary to understand the context within which religious individuals operate to appreciate their political positions.

139 Hunter, James Davison. "Religion and Political Civility: The Coming Generation of American Evangelicals." *Journal for the Scientific Study of Religion* 23 (1984): 364-380.
Using a variety of data sources, Hunter suggests that although evangelicals are more conservative than other citizens, they are committed to the norms and values of democracy. On specific issues, such as the right of gays to teach in college, the Equal Rights Amendment, and abortion, evangelicals may have difficult mobilizing other Americans, since the evangelical position is relatively unpopular.

140 Hunter, James Davison. *Evangelicalism: The Coming Generation.* Chicago: University of Chicago Press, 1987.
Based on a survey of students at evangelical colleges and universities, Hunter shows that young evangelicals are less orthodox, more secular, and more accommodating to modern culture than the standard doctrines of evangelicalism would suggest. In his concluding section, Hunter considers the place of evangelicalism in a modern world wherein the evangelical worldview is no longer culturally dominant.

141 Hunter, James Davison. *Culture Wars: The Struggle to Define America.* New York: BasicBooks, 1991.
Using a variety of materials, Hunter argues that contemporary American politics is developing into a conflict between the "orthodox" and the "progressive," that is, between people who are religious and those who are not. Hunter carefully analyzes competing rhetoric about a variety of different issues and suggests that this "two-party system" is likely to supersede other cleavages between different religious traditions.

142 Hunter, James Davison. *Before the Shooting Begins: Searching for Democracy in America's Culture War.* New York: Free Press, 1994.
Hunter focuses on the dispute in American society over abortion. He argues that institutions which ought to help mediate in this debate themselves act as interest groups, throwing fuel on fire that they could help to douse. Hunter also argues that many Americans are unable to articulate a consistent position on the abortion issue. The inability of Americans to

engage in a meaningful political discourse about abortion may be contributing to the decline of substantive democracy in the United States.

143 Iannaconne, Laurence R. "Religious Practice: A Human Capital Approach." *Journal for the Scientific Study of Religion* 29 (1990): 297-314.
This piece uses an economic model of human capital expenditure to develop a model of religious practice. Data analysis suggests that a variety of life circumstances occasion religious participation, but all can be subsumed under a simple resource allocation theory.

144 Iannaconne, Laurence R. "Why Strict Churches are Strong." *American Journal of Sociology* 99 (1994): 1180-1211.
An economic analysis of religious participation suggests that "strict" churches (those which proscribe a wide variety of "secular" behaviors) are able to attract more active membership by reducing the "free rider" problem. A "rational choice" analysis shows that increasing the costs of membership, especially by discouraging participation in competing activities outside the church, deters less committed members and potential members.

145 Ivers, Gregg. "Religious Organizations as Constitutional Litigants." *Polity* 25 (1992): 243-266.
To what extent have religious organizations utilized the courts to pursue their political agendas? Ivers shows that religious interest groups have been using the courts as political arenas for the past twenty years, and that such activity has increased since 1980. Such groups have acted as plaintiffs, and have engaged in *amicus curiae* activity.

146 Jelen, Ted G. "Sources of Political Intolerance: The Case of the American South." In *Contemporary Southern Political Attitudes and Behavior*, ed. by Robert P. Steed, Laurence W. Moreland, and Tod A. Baker, 73-91. New York: Praeger Publishers, 1982.
This study shows that to a large extent, regional differences in tolerance of left-wing groups can be attributed to a higher level of Christian fundamentalism in the South. Southerners without religious preferences are considerably less tolerant than those in the North, suggesting that Southern fundamentalists may impart intolerant cues to other residents of the region.

147 Jelen, Ted G. "Respect for Life, Sexual Morality, and Opposition to Abortion." *Review of Religious Research* 25 (1984): 220-231.
In an exploratory study using National Opinion Research Center data, Jelen examines denominational differences in rationales for opposition to abortion. Support for abortion restrictions is generally based on respect for human life (measured as attitudes toward euthanasia) among Catholics,

but such support is based on opposition to sexual promiscuity among Protestant fundamentalists.

148 Jelen, Ted G. "Fundamentalism, Feminism, and Attitudes Toward Pornography." *Review of Religious Research* 28 (1986): 97-103.
What factors explain opposition to pornography? Using National Opinion Research Center data, Jelen shows that denominationally-defined fundamentalists and respondents who hold feminist attitudes are both rather likely to support the legal suppression of pornography, but they disagree on the rationale for such a policy. While fundamentalists tend to believe that pornography occasions a "breakdown of morals," attitudinal feminists believe that pornography leads to sexual violence against women. These findings hold for both male and female respondents.

149 Jelen, Ted G. "The Effects of Religious Separatism on White Protestants in the 1984 Presidential Election." *Sociological Analysis* 48 (1987): 30-45.
Using an attitudinal measure of religious separatism to distinguish "fundamentalists" from other "evangelicals," Jelen posits, and finds, that fundamentalists (separatists) exhibit weaker relationships between positions on moral issues and vote choice than do other evangelicals. The prevalence of religious separatism suggests that some conservative Protestants may be difficult to mobilize politically.

150 Jelen, Ted G. "Changes in the Attitudinal Correlates of Opposition to Abortion, 1977-1985." *Journal for the Scientific Study of Religion* 27 (1988): 211-228.
In this study, the relative importance of "respect for human life" and sexual conservatism in explaining opposition to legal abortion are compared across different religious groups over time. In 1977, fundamentalists who opposed abortion were more likely to do so for reasons of sexual conservatism, while Catholics tended to endorse a "life" rationale. By 1985, religious groups had converged, with the "life" variable being more important in explaining "traumatic" abortion, and the sexual conservatism index being a more powerful predictor of attitudes toward "elective" abortion.

151 Jelen, Ted G. "Biblical Literalism and Inerrancy: Does the Difference Make a Difference?" *Sociological Analysis* 49 (1989): 421-429.
This study compares the relationships between two measures of attitudes toward biblical authority with several different attitudes on political issues. The author hypothesizes that small differences in question wording will create no measurable differences in such relationships. The relationships are generally quite similar for "literalist" and "inerrannist" versions of the Bible question, suggesting that these items are generally interchangeable.

152 Jelen, Ted G. "Weaker Vessels and Helpmeets: Gender Role Stereotypes and Attitudes Toward Female Ordination." *Social Science Quarterly* 70 (1989): 579-585.

Jelen makes a distinction between "weaker vessel" stereotypes (invoking a sense of female inferiority) and "helpmeet" images (involving a belief in egalitarian gender role differences). Among most survey respondents, the weaker vessel attitude is most strongly related to approval of the ordination of women as clergy. The helpmeet stereotype is related to attitudes toward female ordination among Catholic males. The role of Mary in Catholic theology is a possible source of denominational differences.

153 Jelen, Ted G. "Aging and Boundary Maintenance Among American Evangelicals: A Comment on James Davison *Hunter's Evangelicalism: The Coming Generation*." *Review of Religious Research* 31 (1990): 268-279.

In a response to James Davison Hunter (140), this study uses longitudinal survey data to suggest that a positive relationship between age and evangelical orthodoxy is a relatively constant feature of the American religious landscape. This in turn suggests that Hunter's findings may reflect a life cycle effect, rather than the identification of distinctiveness in one generation.

154 Jelen, Ted G. "Religious Belief and Attitude Constraint." *Journal for the Scientific Study of Religion* 29 (1990): 118-125.

Despite the fact that religious elites, such as leaders of the Christian Right and American Catholic Bishops, put forth constrained issue "packages," there is little evidence of internal consistency across political attitudes on the part of various lay populations. One exception is that religiosity is related to constraint across issues of sexual morality among evangelical Christians.

155 Jelen, Ted G. *The Political Mobilization of Religious Beliefs*. New York: Praeger Publishers, 1991.

Using a mail survey of fifteen congregations in a rural Midwestern county, Jelen attempts to explain support for leaders in the Christian Right and the Republican Party. He finds that party support is primarily issue based, but that support for Christian Right leaders is based on attitudes toward certain highly visible groups. Christian Right support, unlike support for the Republican Party, is fragmented by religious particularism.

156 Jelen, Ted G. "Politicized Group Identification: The Case of Fundamentalism." *Western Political Quarterly* 44 (1991): 209-219.

In a study of group consciousness among fundamentalists, Jelen relies on surveys of rural Midwesterners; he finds that self-identification as a "fundamentalist" is strongly related to a variety of political attitudes. In contrast to other research, interaction with other group-related attitudes does not enhance the explanatory power of such identification.

157 Jelen, Ted G. "The Clergy and Abortion." *Review of Religious Research* 34 (1992): 132-151.
Using intensive interviews of local Midwestern clergy, as well as a mail survey of lay members of local congregations, this study shows that there are few differences in the content of abortion attitudes among Protestant ministers. However, evangelical ministers are much more likely to attempt to socialize their congregations in a "pro-life" direction. Analysis of the attitudes of the congregants themselves shows that such religious teaching is rather effective.

158 Jelen, Ted G. "Political Christianity: A Contextual Analysis." *American Journal of Political Science* 36 (1992): 692-714.
This study is an attempt to specify the nature of contextual influences found in local congregations. To a large extent, apparently contextual effects are in fact religious messages which have been distorted or simplified in transmission. Congregational level variables are much less powerful sources of political attitudes at lower levels of conceptualization.

159 Jelen, Ted G. "The Political Consequences of Religious Group Attitudes." *Journal of Politics* 55 (1993): 178-193.
Jelen relies on a variety of group-based attitudes about politics to frame this work, which is based on a mail survey of fifteen rural congregations. He shows that group-based attitudes are most powerful in explaining support for the Christian Right. Support for figures of the Christian Right is enhanced by antipathy toward cultural minorities, and is inhibited by religious particularism.

160 Jelen, Ted G. *The Political World of the Clergy.* Westport, CT: Praeger Publishers, 1993.
Based on participant observation and discursive interviews with a number of clergy, Jelen examines the self-images of pastors as political leaders. Most ministers are inhibited from direct political teaching for theological reasons. Evangelicals are constrained by the content of their teaching, mainline Protestants by their style. Catholic priests are limited in the political effectiveness by their minority status in American culture.

161 Jelen, Ted G. "Protestant Clergy as Political Leaders: Theological Limitations." *Review of Religious Research* 36 (1994): 23-42.
This study, which is based on long interviews with Protestant ministers in a Midwestern rural county, suggests that the potential for political leadership is limited for both evangelical and mainline clergy. Evangelical clergy are limited by the content of their beliefs, which are highly individualistic, as well

as their dedication to personal salvation. By contrast, the effectiveness of the "social gospel" message of many mainline ministers is limited by a perceived lack of theological authority.

162 Jelen, Ted G. "Religion and Foreign Policy Attitudes: Exploring the Effects of Denomination and Doctrine." *American Politics Quarterly* 22 (1994): 381-400.
Using data from the American National Election Studies, the effects of religious attitudes and affiliations on foreign policy attitudes are examined. While religion is generally a weak predictor of such attitudes, evangelical beliefs are found to render Protestants more conservative. Conversely, evangelical beliefs render Catholics more receptive to some aspects of the "just war" doctrine.

163 Jelen, Ted G. "Religion and the American Political Culture: Alternative Models for Citizenship and Discipleship." *Sociology of Religion* 56 (1995): 271-284.
Jelen considers three competing models of American political culture: consensus theories, dualistic theories, and pluralist theories. In an interpretive essay, he assesses the normative role religion plays in each formulation of democracy.

164 Jelen, Ted G. "Religion and Public Opinion in the 1990s: An Empirical Overview." In *Understanding Public Opinion*, ed. by Barbara Norrander and Clyde Wilcox, 55-68. Washington, DC: Congressional Quarterly Press, 1996.
Drawing upon the "culture wars" thesis, Jelen explores whether political parties have realigned around social issues. Using National Opinion Research Center data, he traces party identification over a twenty-year time period and finds that there has been a general drift of white Protestants toward the Republican Party. This trend began for evangelical Protestants around 1980, for mainline Protestants around 1988, but has never occurred for Catholics.

165 Jelen, Ted G.; Smidt, Corwin E.; and Wilcox, Clyde. "The Political Effects of the Born-Again Phenomenon." In *Rediscovering the Religious Factor in American Politics*, ed. by David C. Leege and Lyman A. Kellstedt, 199-215. Armonk, NY: M. E. Sharpe, 1993.
In this study, the authors consider the various senses in which the status or experience of being "born-again" may have political consequences. A survey of mass attitudes shows that two measures are generally equivalent, but a survey of religious elites suggests that highly "experiential" born-again status are the most politically consequential.

166 Jelen, Ted G., and Wilcox, Clyde. "Denominational Preference and the Dimensions of Political Tolerance." *Sociological Analysis* 51 (1990): 69-81.
The results of this study show that once controls for education have been imposed, there is a rough consensus on the dimensions of tolerance for non-conformist groups in the United States among Christians. In general, dimensions of tolerance are organized around activities, rather than on the political views of specific unpopular groups. For most denominations, tolerance toward racists forms a separate dimension.

167 Jelen, Ted G., and Wilcox, Clyde. "Religious Dogmatism Among White Christians: Causes and Effects." *Review of Religious Research* 33 (1991): 32-46.
In this study, the authors develop an index of religious dogmatism, using 1988 National Opinion Research Center data. Dogmatism is predicted by religious orthodoxy and public religious observance, and in turn is a moderately strong predictor of a variety of attitudes concerning lifestyle issues. However, doctrinal orthodoxy and religious observance retain independent effects on lifestyle issue attitudes, even when dogmatism has been controlled.

168 Jelen, Ted G., and Wilcox, Clyde. "The Effects of Religious Self-Identification on Support for the New Christian Right: An Analysis of Political Activists." *Social Science Journal* 29 (1992): 199-210.
A survey of Republican contributors to presidential campaigns reveals that both Pat Robertson and Moral Majority drew support only from relatively narrow theological traditions. Robertson was supported primarily by self-identified charismatics, while Moral Majority garnered support from fundamentalist identifiers. While religious identification was not a source of negative affect toward Christian Right objects, religious particularism seems to have limited Christian Right support in this activist sample.

169 Jelen, Ted G., and Wilcox, Clyde. "The Christian Right in the 1990s." *The Public Perspective* 4 (March/April, 1993): 10-12.
In this brief article, Jelen and Wilcox explore the reasons for the apparent failures of the Christian Right in the 1980s. Factors inhibiting the political mobilization of religious conservatives included inconsistent belief systems, the pervasive individualism of the American political culture, and religious particularism. The authors suggest that a new organization, Christian Coalition, might be able to avert the mistakes of previous Christian Right groups.

170 Jelen, Ted G., and Wilcox, Clyde. "Preaching to the Converted: The Causes and Consequences of Viewing Religious Television." In *Rediscovering the Religious Factor in American Politics*, ed. by David C. Leege and Lyman A. Kellstedt, 255-269. Armonk, NY: M. E. Sharpe, 1993.
The authors explore the effects of viewing religious television on a variety of political attitudes. In general, they find that viewing religious television affects issue positions more than partisan attitudes or general political orientations. Religious television does not appear to increase political learning. Some data suggest that the effects of religious television may be greatest among doctrinally conservative respondents who attend theologically liberal churches.

171 Jelen, Ted G.; Wilcox, Clyde; and Smidt, Corwin E. "Biblical Literalism and Inerrancy: A Methodological Investigation." *Sociological Analysis* 51 (1990): 307-313.
Jelen et al. report the results of a methodological experiment involving a sample of African Americans in Washington, DC. They were specifically interested in investigating the utility of an item about the authority of the Bible, in which respondents are offered both "literalist" and "inerrannist" alternatives. Contrary to previous research, the results suggest that this distinction is meaningful to doctrinally conservative Christians.

172 Johnson, Doyle D. "Religious Commitment, Social Distance, and Authoritarianism." *Review of Religious Research* 18 (1977): 99-113.
Doyle hypothesizes that "religious importance" and social distance and racial prejudice are inversely related. Using a sample of small-town residents, they study shows that church involvement and doctrinal orthodoxy are related to perceived social distance from minorities and authoritarianism.

173 Johnson, Stephen D. "The Christian Right in Middletown." In *The Political Role of Religion in the United States*, ed. by Stephen D. Johnson and Joseph B. Tamney, 181-198. Boulder, CO: Westview Press, 1986.
In this study Johnson examines sources of popular support for Moral Majority, using a telephone survey of respondents in "Middletown." He finds that such support is related to social factors including church involvement and exposure to religious television, and to psychological variables including Christian Right orientation and cultural fundamentalism. The latter two variables are regarded as consequences of authoritarianism.

174 Johnson, Stephen D. "The Role of the Black Church in Black Civil Rights Movements." In *The Political Role of Religion in the United States*, ed. by Stephen D. Johnson and Joseph B. Tamney, 308-324. Boulder, CO: Westview Press, 1986.

Johnson presents a summary of studies relating religious variables to civil rights activism. The summary reveals that two distinct groups have been most heavily involved in civil rights activism: African- Americans without religious commitments of any kind, and ministers and members of mainline African-American denominations.

175 Johnson, Stephen D. "Factors Related to Intolerance of AIDS Victims." *Journal for the Scientific Study of Religion* 26 (1987): 105-110.
Intolerance of AIDS victims is related to the perception that the United States has not recognized the contributions of Christian fundamentalists. Johnson considers several possible explanations for the association between "religious relative deprivation" and attitudes toward persons with AIDS.

176 Johnson, Stephen D. "What Relates to Vote for Three Religious Categories?" *Sociology of Religion* 55 (1994): 263-275.
Johnson investigates the differences in the presidential voting behavior of Catholics, mainline Protestants, and conservative Protestants. Using a sample from "Middletown," he finds that several variables (including partisanship and general ideology) were related to presidential vote for almost all religious groups in 1992. However, social class was a strong predictor of vote choice for Roman Catholics, while social issues were most important for conservative Protestants (as measured by denominational affiliation). No independent variable was found to be a unique source of vote choices among mainline Protestants.

177 Johnson, Stephen D., and Tamney, Joseph B. "The Christian Right and the 1980 Presidential Election." *Journal for the Scientific Study of Religion* 21 (1982): 123-133.
In a study of the contributions made by the Christian Right to Ronald Reagan's 1980 election to the presidency, Johnson and Tamney find that generalized support for Moral Majority was unrelated to presidential voting in 1980. Rather, Reagan drew support from traditional Republicans and voters concerned about inflation.

178 Johnson, Stephen D., and Tamney, Joseph B. "Support for the Moral Majority: A Test of a Model." *Journal for the Scientific Study of Religion* 23 (1984): 183-196.
Moral Majority support may be explained by agreement with issue positions taken by the Christian Right, authoritarianism, and xenophobia. Education, age, and exposure to religious television also have indirect influences on support for this Christian Right organization.

179 Johnson, Stephen D., and Tamney, Joseph B. "The Christian Right and the 1984 Presidential Election." *Review of Religious Research* 27 (1985): 124-133.
Johnson and Tamney hypothesize that the Christian Right played a more significant role in the presidential election of 1984 than it had in 1980. Using a survey of residents of "Middletown," the authors find that religious and moral values were more important determinants of presidential voting in 1984 than in 1980. In the latter election, Ronald Reagan drew strongest support from moderate (rather than strong) supporters of the Christian Right. Moral Majority itself was found to be a negative reference group for most voters, and the visibility of Moral Majority's support for Reagan had a modest pro-Mondale effect.

180 Johnson, Stephen D., and Tamney, Joseph B. "The Clergy and Public Issues in Middletown." In *The Political Role of Religion in the United States*, ed. by Stephen D. Johnson and Joseph B. Tamney, 45-70. Boulder, CO: Westview Press, 1986.
A survey of ministers in Middletown reveals that religious conservatives are more homogeneous than religious liberals at the church level, in that there are more religiously conservative pastors of liberal churches than vice versa. However, liberal clergy exhibit more attitude constraint across a number of political issues. Liberal ministers justify political positions using secular or universalistic ethical principles, while religious conservatives use specifically religious arguments.

181 Johnson, Stephen D., and Tamney, Joseph B. "Factors Related to Inconsistent Life-Views." *Review of Religious Research* 30 (1988): 40-46.
In this study, Tamney and Johnson address the question of why some people oppose legal abortion but favor the death penalty. Using National Opinion Research Center data, the authors suggest that fundamentalists, respondents concerned with sexual morality, and those who believe in the necessity of physical force are most likely to exhibit "inconsistent" views on these "life" issues.

182 Johnson, Stephen D.; Tamney, Joseph B.; and Burton, Ronald. "Pat Robertson: Who Supported His Candidacy for President?" *Journal for the Scientific Study of Religion* 28 (1989): 387-399.
Using a sample of senior citizens, the authors suggest that Pat Robertson failed to mobilize most of his potential supporters. Viewing the *700 Club* television program, embracing social traditionalism, expressing politically conservative views, and reporting lower levels of education were all found to be related to support for Robertson. Less well educated respondents were more affected by their immediate social environments, while respondents with higher levels of education supported Robertson for reasons of religious and political ideology.

183 Johnson, Stephen D.; Tamney, Joseph B.; and Burton, Ronald. "Factors Influencing Vote for a Christian Right Candidate." *Review of Religious Research* 31 (1990): 291-304.
An analysis of a survey concerning a U. S. House election in which one candidate was publicly identified with the Christian Right suggests that such candidates will have difficulty gaining sufficient public support to win elections. The religious candidate received some limited support from older Republican identifiers as well as from fundamentalist identifiers. While the Christian Right candidate did especially well among older fundamentalist Republicans, relatively few voters fell into this category.

184 Johnson, Stephen D.; Tamney, Joseph B.; and Burton, Ronald. "Economic Satisfaction and Moral Conservatism in the 1988 Presidential Election." *Sociological Focus* 24 (1991): 303-314.
The authors endeavor to compare the effects of economic and moral issues on presidential vote choices in 1988. Using respondents from "Middletown," they report that satisfaction with one's personal financial situation was a stronger predictor of presidential vote choice in 1988 than were positions of moral issues. Vote choice is operationalized in such a way that respondents who reported a Bush vote -- but also said that the selection of Dan Quayle was their most important consideration -- were coded as having voted for Dukakis. The location of Middletown in Quayle's home state of Indiana was the rationale for this decision.

185 Johnson, Stephen D.; Tamney, Joseph B.; and Burton, Ronald. "Not Seeing the Trees for the Forest: A Reply to Baggaley." *Journal for the Scientific Study of Religion* 31 (1992): 535-536.
In a response to Baggaley (008), the authors defend their analysis in Tamney et al. (333) and argue that the disaggregation of various attitudes permits a greater level of substantive understanding of abortion attitudes than would combining their indicators into an index of "orthodoxy."

186 Johnson, Stephen D.; Tamney, Joseph B.; and Halebsky, Sandy. "Christianity, Social Traditionalism, and Economic Conservatism." *Sociological Focus* 19 (1986): 299-314.
The purpose of this essay is to disentangle social, religious, and political conservatism. Using their "Middletown" data, the authors report that social traditionalism and economic conservatism have different bases of support. Indeed, the relationship between Christian Right orientation and support for free market capitalism is significant and negative.

187 Johnston, Michael. "The 'New Christian Right' in American Politics." In *The Political Role of Religion in the United States*, ed. by Stephen D. Johnson and Joseph B. Tamney, 125-145. Boulder, CO: Westview Press, 1986.

Johnston argues that there have been two phases of Christian Right activity, as demonstrated by Moral Majority: a relatively militant phase of mass mobilization (corresponding to the 1980 election) and a more recent, accommodating phase of interest group activity. The latter set of priorities is regarded as an attempt to maximize influence within the pluralistic ethos of American politics.

188 Kahoe, Richard D. "Intrinsic Religion and Authoritarianism: A Differentiated Relationship." *Journal for the Scientific Study of Religion* 16 (1977): 179-183.
Using a sample of Baptist college students, Kahoe shows that two aspects of "intrinsic" religiosity-"superstition stereotypy" and "conventionalism"- are both positively related to T. W. Adorno's F-scale, which measures authoritarianism as a personality trait. Both of these components of intrinsic religion are salient for traditional Baptists.

189 Kanagy, Conrad L., and Willits, Fern K. "A 'Greening' of Religion? Some Evidence From a Pennsylvania Sample." *Social Science Quarterly* 74 (1993): 674-683.
Several distinct environmentalist attitudes are found to be negatively related to membership in a Judeo-Christian denomination and to attendance at religious services. The latter finding holds up in the face of elaborate multivariate controls. When controls for environmentalist attitudes are applied, religiosity has a weak, but significant, positive relationship with environmentalist behavior.

190 Kauffman, J. Howard. "Dilemmas of Christian Pacifism Within a Historic Peace Church." *Sociological Analysis* 49 (1989): 368-385.
Kauffman explores the tension between Mennonite pacifism (traditionally based on a conservative view of the Bible) and the fact that contemporary pacifism is generally associated with the political left. A survey of Mennonites reveals that self-identified liberals are more supportive of pacifism than conservatives, but that most Mennonites identify with the Republican Party.

191 Kellstedt, Lyman A. "Evangelicals and Political Realignment." In *Contemporary Evangelical Political Involvement: An Analysis and Assessment*, ed. by Corwin E. Smidt, 99-117. New York: University Press of America, 1989.
Kellstedt's longitudinal analysis of party identification suggests that members of evangelical denominations who attend religious services regularly are becoming increasingly identified with the Republican Party. The data suggest that the principal source of this partisan change is generational replacement.

192 Kellstedt, Lyman A.   "The Meaning and Measurement of
Evangelicalism: Problems and Prospects."   In *Religion and Political
Behavior in the United States*, ed. by Ted G. Jelen, 3-21.   New York:
Praeger Publishers, 1989.
Kellstedt's study explores the many methodological issues involved in
measuring the concept of "evangelicalism."   He considers a variety of
measurement approaches and finally endorses a multiple-indicator
approach.

193 Kellstedt, Lyman A. "Religion, the Neglected Variable: An Agenda for
Future Research on Religion and Political Behavior." In *Rediscovering the
Religious Factor in American Politics*, ed. by David C. Leege and Lyman A.
Kellstedt, 273-303. Armonk, NY: M. E. Sharpe, 1993.
This piece summarizes the various ways in which religion has been
measured, and offers suggestions for future research about the
relationships between religion and political behavior. Multiple classification
analyses suggest that religious variables are slightly more important than
economic variables in explaining partisan identification and presidential
voting in 1988.

194 Kellstedt, Lyman A., and Green, John C.   "Knowing God's Many
People: Denominational Preference and Political Behavior."   In
Rediscovering the Religious Factor in American Politics, ed. by David C.
Leege and Lyman A. Kellstedt, 53-71. Armonk, NY: M. E. Sharpe, 1993.
This article examines the effects of denominational membership on a
variety of political attitudes and behaviors.   While denominational
distinctiveness persists, it is also useful to group denominations into
broader categories such as evangelical Protestant or mainline Protestant.

195 Kellstedt, Lyman A.; Green, John C.; Guth, James L.; and Smidt,
Corwin E. "Religious Voting Blocs in the 1992 Election: The Year of the
Evangelical?" *Sociology of Religion* 55 (1994): 307-326.
An analysis of the 1992 election, based on several data sources, shows
that this election solidified the attachment of evangelical Protestants to the
Republican Party. The authors suggest that such doctrinally conservative
Protestants are becoming a core constituency for the Republican Party.   A
large bloc of "seculars" is becoming a corresponding bloc for the
Democratic Party. Mainline Protestants tended to desert George Bush for
either Bill Clinton or Ross Perot, while Catholics returned to their former
Democratic allegiances.   The authors suggest that the parties may be
realigning along a "culture wars" cleavage, in which social issues are most
salient.

196 Kellstedt, Lyman A., and Noll, Mark A. "Religion, Voting for President, and Party Identification, 1948-1984." In *Religion and American Politics: From the Colonial Period to the 1980s*, ed. by Mark A. Noll, 355-377. New York: Oxford University Press, 1990.
An examination of religious voting and partisanship shows that African Americans, despite high levels of evangelicalism, have been moving toward the Democrats since the early 1960s. American Catholics have moved in a Republican direction to a slight extent, but still remain predominately Democratic, while white evangelicals have moved dramatically in a Republican direction. This tendency is most pronounced among Northern evangelicals who attend religious services regularly, and among Southerners.

197 Kellstedt, Lyman A., and Smidt, Corwin E. "Measuring Fundamentalism: An Analysis of Different Operational Strategies." *Journal for the Scientific Study of Religion* 30 (1991): 259-278.
Kellstedt and Smidt consider three separate means of measuring the concept of fundamentalism, including denominational membership, doctrinal beliefs, and self-identification. Each measure is found to be effective in explaining a variety dependent variables. The authors suggest that the validity of a given measure is a function of particular explananda.

198 Kellstedt, Lyman A., and Smidt, Corwin E. "Doctrinal Beliefs and Political Behavior: Views of the Bible." In *Rediscovering the Religious Factor in American Politics*, ed. by David C. Leege and Lyman A. Kellstedt, 177-198. Armonk, NY: M. E. Sharpe, 1993.
In this piece, the authors investigate the relationships between attitudes about the Bible, political attitudes, and political behavior. They also examine the methodological difficulties inherent in measuring survey respondents' attitudes toward the Bible. Attitudes about the Bible's authority are related to a variety of political attitudes, and these relationships are strongest among evangelical Christians.

199 Kellstedt, Lyman A.; Smidt, Corwin E.; and Kellstedt, Paul M. "Religious Tradition, Denomination, and Commitment: White Protestants and the 1988 Election." In *The Bible and the Ballot Box: Religion and Politics in the 1988 Election*, ed. by James L. Guth and John C. Green, 139-158. Boulder, CO: Westview Press, 1991.
White Protestants voted disproportionately for Bush in 1988, despite the low salience of religious issues in that race. Evangelicals supported Bush at higher levels than did mainline Protestants. Furthermore, there was substantial agreement among white Protestants on economic issues, but considerable disagreement about issues of personal morality.

200 Kelly, James R. "Learning and Teaching Consistency: Catholics and the Right to Life Movement." In *The Catholic Church and the Politics of Abortion: A View From the States*, ed. by Timothy A. Byrnes and Mary C. Segers, 152-168. Boulder, CO: Westview Press, 1992.
This piece contains an analysis of the roles of Roman Catholics and doctrinally conservative Protestants in anti-abortion politics. Kelly argues that the *Webster* decision and its electoral aftermath began the process of unraveling an alliance within the Republican Party between fiscal and social conservatives. Kelly predicts that the "consistent ethic" wing of the right to life movement will be a strong social force in the near future.

201 Kenski, Henry C., and Lockwood, William. "The Catholic Vote From 1960 to 1986: Continuity or Change?" In *Religion and Political Behavior in the United States*, ed. by Ted G. Jelen, 109-137. New York: Praeger Publishers, 1989.
While support among Catholics for the Democratic Party has eroded in the 1960s, Catholics still remain more Democratic than white Protestants in both voting behavior and party identification. Catholics are more volatile when it comes to voting at the presidential level: they are more likely to vote a split ticket.

202 Kenski, Henry C., and Lockwood, William. "Catholic Voting Behavior in 1988: A Critical Swing Vote." In *The Bible and the Ballot Box: Religion and Politics in the 1988 Election*, ed. by James L. Guth and John C. Green, 173-187. Boulder, CO: Westview Press, 1991.
This study reports the finding that Catholics remain primarily Democratic in their political behavior, while the Republicans appear to be approaching parity at the presidential level. Democratic identification and support are associated with higher levels of religiosity among Catholics.

203 Kiecolt, K. Jill, and Nelsen, Hart M. "The Structuring of Political Attitudes Among Liberal and Conservative Protestants." *Journal for the Scientific Study of Religion* 27 (1988): 48-59.
In relation to mainline Protestants, doctrinally conservative Protestants are found to exhibit lower levels of political sophistication, less attitude constraint, and more internal variation on issue attitudes. Based on elections surveys for 1972, 1980, and 1984, such religionists are also shown to be less involved in politics.

204 Kiecolt, K. Jill, and Nelsen, Hart M. "Evangelicals and Party Realignment, 1976-1988." *Social Science Quarterly* 72 (1991): 557-569.
This paper investigates the extent to which partisan realignment may have occurred in relation to religious affiliation. The authors find that both evangelicalism and church attendance are related to changes in partisanship outside the South only.

205 Kierulf, Stephen. "Belief in 'Armageddon Theology' and Willingness to Risk Nuclear War." *Journal for the Scientific Study of Religion* 30 (1991): 81-93.
Using a purposive sample of church members, this study develops a measure of "Armageddon Theology." This index is a combination of premillenial beliefs, "nuclear Armageddon" beliefs, and doctrinal orthodoxy. It is found to be related to beliefs in imminent nuclear war between the United States and the Soviet Union, and in the survivability of nuclear war.

206 Kinkel, John R. "Roman Catholic Church Structure and the Issue of Women's Ordination." *Social Science Journal* 20 (1983): 17-29.
In this piece, institutional and community models of church image are contrasted among a sample of Midwestern male members of a religious order. The community model has more support among younger members, and is more closely related to support for female ordination.

207 Kirkpatrick, Lee A. "Fundamentalism, Christian Orthodoxy, and Intrinsic Religious Orientation as Predictors of Discriminatory Attitudes." *Journal for the Scientific Study of Religion* 32 (1993): 256-268.
A survey of students at several different colleges shows that fundamentalism (defined as a "closed belief system") is a strong predictor of discriminatory attitudes against communists, women, gays, and African Americans. With the effects of "fundamentalism" controlled, Christian orthodoxy and religious orientation are not significantly related to discriminatory attitudes.

208 Klatch, Rebecca E. *Women of the New Right.* Philadelphia: Temple University Press, 1987.
Based on in-depth interviews with over thirty female conservative activists, this study shows that there are two distinct world views within contemporary conservatism: laissez-faire conservatism and social conservatism. Klatch argues that the differences between these two schools of thought on a variety of issues creates a tension between activists on America's political right.

209 Koller, Norma B., and Retzer, Joseph D. "The Sounds of Silence Revisited." *Sociological Analysis* 41 (1980): 155-161.
The authors set out to investigate whether clergy avoid addressing social and political issues. In contrast to previous research, this study shows that North Carolina clergy frequently address social and political issues. Although this tendency is common among clergy of all theological persuasions, different topics are addressed most frequently by religious liberals and conservatives.

210 Korpi, Michael F., and Kim, Kyong Liong. "The Uses and Effects Model of Televangelism: A Factorial Model of Support and Contribution." *Journal for the Scientific Study of Religion* 25 (1986): 410-423.
Korpi and Kim show that viewing religious television is related only to personal religiosity, while contributing to televangelists is related to receiving personal gratification for such usage. Some contributors regard the "electronic church" as an alternative to their local congregations.

211 Land, Kenneth C.; Deane, Glenn; and Blau, Judith R. "Religious Pluralism and Church Membership: A Spatial Diffusion Model." *American Sociological Review* 56 (1991): 237-249.
In this study, Land et al. attempt to reconcile the disparate findings of Finke and Stark (065, 066) and Breault (024, 025). The authors report that church participation is high in counties characterized by high levels of social deprivation and marginality (such as large cities). In counties in which these compositional characteristics are absent, religious diversity retards church membership, and, ultimately, religious participation.

212 Langenbach, Lisa, and Green, John C. "Hollow Core: Evangelical Clergy and the 1988 Robertson Campaign."*Polity* 25 (1992): 147-158.
Pat Robertson counted on the support of evangelical clergy in his 1988 presidential bid, but did he receive it? A survey of evangelical ministers in Pennsylvania shows that Robertson was generally unsuccessful in mobilizing fellow clergy to his campaign. Robertson's support was limited to social issue conservatives, and charismatic/pentecostal ministers. Pastors are shown to use secular criteria, such as viability and candidate quality, when evaluating political candidates.

213 Langenbach, Lisa, and Jelen, Ted G. "Ministers, Feminism, and Abortion: A Causal Analysis." *Women and Politics* 11 (1991): 33-52.
Among male evangelical ministers, doctrinal orthodoxy is the strongest predictor of both opposition to abortion and support for a Human Life Amendment. Moreover, both of these attitudes are related (directly and through the intervening effects of private feminism) to the employment status of the pastor's wife. Employed spouses pull doctrinally conservative ministers in a pro-choice direction.

214 Latus, Margaret Ann. "Ideological PACs and Political Action." In *The New Christian Right: Mobilization and Legitimation*, ed. by Robert C. Liebman and Robert Wuthnow, 75-99. New York: Aldine Press, 1983.
Based on a series of interviews with representatives of liberal, conservative, and religious political action committees (PACs), the author compares these groups' political strategies. She concludes that although the ideological orientation of particular PACs helps explain their behavior to

some extent, the tactical decisions of ideological PACs are also conditioned by their scope, internal organization, and external circumstances.

215 Lazerwitz, Bernard, and Harrison, Michael. "American Jewish Denominations: A Social and Religious Profile." *American Sociological Review* 44 (1979): 656-666.
Differences between Jewish denominations (Orthodox, Conservative, Reform) are examined in this research note. The authors find that different denominations within American Judaism retain their distinctiveness, although such memberships are no longer strongly associated with demographic characteristics. Reform Jews are found to be more politically liberal, as well as more active in secular organizations.

216 Lazerwitz, Bernard; Winter, J. Allen; and Dashefsky, Arnold. "Localism, Religiosity, Orthodoxy, and Liberalism: The Case of Jews in the United States." *Social Forces* 67 (1988): 229-242.
The authors analyze data from the national Jewish Population Survey and show that among American Jews, religiosity is related to localism, which in turn is a strong predictor of political conservatism. The authors make a distinction between "general localism" and sub-communal (in this instance, Jewish) localism, and show that the latter is a strong predictor of political attitudes.

217 Leege, David C. "Catholics and the Civic Order: Parish Participation, Politics, and Civic Participation." *Review of Politics* 50 (1988): 704-731.
Using the Notre Dame Study of Catholic Parish Life, Leege covers numerous aspects of the relationship between religious variables and political attitudes and behaviors. While standard religious variables are of limited utility in explaining the political orientations of Roman Catholics, methodologically unconventional concepts such as different images of God, devotional styles (especially evangelical style devotionalism), and communitarian/individualist beliefs are quite powerful predictors of a number of political attitudes. The article concludes with a typology of beliefs about the propriety of the involvement of religious leaders in political affairs.

218 Leege, David C. "Toward a Mental Measure of Religiosity in Research on Religion and Politics." In *Religion and Political Behavior in the United States*, ed. by Ted G. Jelen, 45-54. New York: Praeger Publishers, 1989.
In this piece Leege develops an ipsative measure of foundational religious beliefs which allows respondents to select a basic human problem, a path to salvation, and the outcome of salvation. Various paths permit the classification of respondents into individualist, communitarian, and integrated religionist categories. This measurement of foundational beliefs

is generally a stronger predictor of political attitudes than a more conventional attitudinal scale.

219 Leege, David C., and Kellstedt, Lyman A. "Religious Worldviews and Political Philosophies: Capturing Theory in the Grand Manner Through Empirical Data." In *Rediscovering the Religious Factor in American Politics*, ed. by David C. Leege and Lyman A. Kellstedt, 216-231. Armonk, NY: M. E. Sharpe, 1993.
After reviewing the literature on general conceptualizations of religion, the authors develop an idiographic measure of religious individualism-communalism. The resulting index is related to partisan attitudes, as well as attitudes toward abortion.

220 Leege, David C.; Wald, Kenneth D.; and Kellstedt, Lyman A. "The Public Dimension of Private Devotionalism." In *Rediscovering the Religious Factor in American Politics*, ed. by David C. Leege and Lyman A. Kellstedt, 139-156. Armonk, NY: M. E. Sharpe, 1993.
Perhaps surprisingly, private religious activities, such as prayer, Bible reading, and exposure to religious media have an independent effect on a variety of political attitudes. Race, too, is an important mitigating factor.

221 Leege, David C., and Welch, Michael R. "Religious Roots of Political Orientations: Variations Among American Catholic Parishioners." *Journal of Politics* 51 (1989): 137-162.
Leege and Welch rely on the Notre Dame Study of Catholic Parish Life to develop a measure of foundational religious beliefs which distinguishes religious "individualists" from "communitarians." While the measure does not account for party identification as well as more traditional structural characteristics, foundational beliefs are related to a variety of attitudinal beliefs about political issues.

222 Leege, David C.; Welch, Michael R.; and Trozzolo, Thomas A. "Religiosity, Church Social Teaching, and Sociopolitical Attitudes: A Research Note on Martial Homogamy as Social Context for U. S. Catholics." *Review of Religious Research* 28 (1986): 118-128.
Leege and his colleagues use National Opinion Research Center data to explore the hypothesis that homogamous Catholics are more supportive of church teachings than their heterogamous counterparts. The study shows that martial homogamy has no effect on acceptance of church teaching on peace and justice issues among American Catholics. There is a slight tendency toward greater consistency across these issues for Catholics who are in heterogamous marriages.

223 Lichter, S. Robert, and Rothman, Stanley. "Jews on the Left: The Student Movement Reconsidered." *Polity* 14 (1981): 347-366.
This study is based on the premise that Jewish students are heavily involved in politically liberal activism. In a survey of college students conducted between 1971 and 1973, the authors show that Jews were over-represented among those who participated in unconventional or radical political activity, and that a disproportionate share of student radical leaders were themselves Jewish. The differential effects of religiosity and family upbringing are discussed.

224 Lieberman, Carl. "Jewish Community Leaders and the 1988 Presidential Campaign." In *The Bible and the Ballot Box: Religion and Politics in the 1988 Election*, ed. by James L. Guth and John C. Green, 55-69. Boulder, CO: Westview Press, 1991.
This study suggests that the leaders of national Jewish organizations were not involved actively in the 1988 presidential campaign. Reasons for this lack of involvement include the fear of anti-Semitic backlash, fear for the tax-exempt status of their organizations, and recognition of the diversity of Jewish voters.

225 Litman, Barry R., and Bain, Elizabeth. "The Viewership of Religious Television Programming: A Multidisciplinary Analysis of Televangelism." *Review of Religious Research* 30 (1989): 329-343.
In an analysis of competing theories explaining religious television viewing, Litman and Bain rely on surveys of Midwesterners. They find that while there is no statistically significant relationship between use of televangelism and church attendance, a positive relationship does exist between viewership and general religiosity. Despite ecumenical claims made by televangelists, viewers of specific programs are drawn from very narrowly defined religious populations.

226 Lopatto, Paul. *Religion and the Presidential Election*. New York: Praeger Publishers, 1985.
This study consists of a longitudinal analysis of the effects of religion on presidential voting. Lopatto's data suggest that liberal and conservative Protestants had become "polarized" in the 1960s, that Catholics had lurched in a pro-Republican direction in response to the McGovern candidacy in 1972, and that religion was not an important sort-term force in 1976 or 1980. Lopatto concludes that religion is an important variable in presidential voting, but that its precise impact will depend on the nature of alternatives that voters are offered.

227 Lorentzen, Louise J. "Evangelical Life Style Concerns Expressed in Political Activism." *Sociological Analysis* 41 (1980): 144-155.
Using the theory of status politics, Lorentzen investigates the impetus behind the mobilization of certain evangelical Christians. Discursive interviews with supporters of an evangelical candidate for the U. S. Senate reveal that concerns over lifestyle issues constitute the main rationale for their activism. Supporters sought to restore "high moral standards," and enhance the influence of Christians in government.

228 Lotz, Roy. "Another Look at the Orthodoxy-Anti-Semitism Nexus." *Review of Religious Research* 18 (1977): 126-133.
This piece suggests that the indirect links between doctrinal orthodoxy and anti-semitism first reported by Stark and Glock are largely attributable to measurement error. Re-analysis of the original Stark-Glock data suggests that the relationship (direct or indirect) between orthodoxy and anti-semitism is extremely limited.

229 Luidens, Donald A., and Nemeth, Roger J. "After the Storm: Closing the Clergy-Laity Gap." *Review of Religious Research* 31 (1989): 183-195.
An examination of the Reformed Church of America suggests that the gap between liberal clergy and conservative parishioners may be narrowing. While Reformed ministers remain more politically liberal than lay people, the clergy are more conservative on theological issues. Further, divisions within the ranks of clergy and laity may supersede any possible clergy-laity polarization.

230 Lupfer, Michael B.; Hopkinson, Patricia L.; and Kelley, Patricia. "An Exploration of the Attributional Styles of Christian Fundamentalists and Authoritarians." *Journal for the Scientific Study of Religion* 27 (1988): 389-398.
Using an experimental design, the authors contrast "dispositional" and "situational" attributional styles, and hypothesize that both fundamentalists and authoritarians are less likely to embrace a situational ethics than other subjects. Contrary to expectations, there were no differences between fundamentalists and others, while authoritarians were less likely to exhibit a dispositional attributional style.

231 Lupfer, Michael, and Wald, Kenneth D. "An Exploration of Adults' Religious Orientation and Their Philosophies of Human Nature." *Journal for the Scientific Study of Religion* 24 (1985): 293-304.
Doctrinal orthodoxy is shown to be related to a benevolent view of human nature, as well as a belief in the complexity of human behavior and the assumption that most humans are externally controlled. Religious activism is associated with a belief in the uniformity of human nature. Apparent anomalies in the data are discussed.

232 Macaluso, Theodore, and Wanat, John.   "Voting Turnout and Religiosity." *Polity* 12 (1979): 158-169.
To investigate the relationship between voter turnout and religiosity, the authors analyze American National Election Study data.   Religious involvement is shown to be positively related to voter turnout.   This relationship is stronger for "high church," liturgical denominations than for "low church," pietistic denominations.

233 MacIver, Martha Abele.   "Mirror Images?   Concepts of God and Political Duty on the Left and Right of the Evangelical Spectrum." *Sociological Analysis* 51 (1990): 287-295.
A content analysis of evangelical publications reveals that left-wing and right-wing periodicals have differing images of God.   However, of somewhat greater importance are differences in the linkages made between religion and politics. These distinctions are in turn occasioned by differing attitudes toward defense, conceptions of the Kingdom of God, and eschatology.

234 Martin, Alfred R., and Jelen, Ted G.   "Knowledge and Attitudes of Catholic College Students Regarding the Creation/Evolution Controversy." In *Religion and Political Behavior in the United States*, ed. by Ted G. Jelen, 83-92. New York: Praeger Publishers, 1989.
A sample of Catholic college students is shown to be relatively ignorant of central tenets of creationism and evolution, and to be supportive of measures mandating "equal time" for these theories of the origins of the world.   Many students exhibited a tendency to compartmentalize knowledge into "religious" and "scientific" categories, and to experience little cognitive dissonance over apparently inconsistent beliefs.

235 Martinson, Oscar B.; Wilkening, E. A.; and Buttel, F. H. "Religion and Community-Oriented Attitudes." *Journal for the Scientific Study of Religion* 21 (1982): 48-58.
The authors show a positive relationship between Christian religious affiliation and attachment to one's local community, but not between religious affiliation and community satisfaction. These findings suggest that religion promotes active integration with community life, rather than passive acceptance.

236 McFarland, Sam G.   "Religious Orientations and the Targets of Discrimination." *Journal for the Scientific Study of Religion* 28 (1989): 324-336.
In this study, fundamentalism (defined primarily in terms of a closed belief system, with high boundary maintenance), is shown to be associated with a general tendency to discriminate, as well as with discriminatory attitudes

toward a variety of target groups. Different aspects of extrinsic religiosity are related to discriminatory attitudes for men and women, respectively.

237 McIntosh, William Alex; Alston, Letitia T.; and Alston, Jon P. "The Differential Impact of Religious Preference and Church Attendance on Attitudes Toward Abortion." *Review of Religious Research* 20 (1979): 195-213.
The authors explore the relationship of church attendance to abortion attitudes. Using an analysis of National Opinion Research Center data, they show that church attendance is negatively related to approval of legal abortion, regardless of denominational preference.

238 McMurry, Martha. "Religion and Women's Sex Role Traditionalism." *Sociological Focus* 11 (1978): 81-91.
Denominational affiliation is found to be related to support for traditional gender roles among women. Baptists, Catholics, and Protestant fundamentalists are found to be most conservative on these issues, with mainline Protestants, Jews, and religious "nones" taking more "feminist" positions. These relationships persist in the face of multivariate controls.

239 Miller, Arthur H., and Wattenberg, Martin P. "Politics From the Pulpit: Religiosity and the 1980 Election." *Public Opinion Quarterly* 48 (1984): 301-317.
The authors show that religiosity generally has a unidimensional structure, with Moral Majority support occupying an extreme position on this dimension. There existed a very small group of highly polarized religious voters in 1980. Religiosity was found to be related to voting in elections for the U. S. House and Senate in 1980, but not for president.

240 Miller, Wesley E. "Comment on 'Evangelical Politics and Status Issues'." *Journal for the Scientific Study of Religion* 28 (1989): 372-373.
This note criticizes Wald et al. (348) on the grounds that the authors' research design cannot account for the timing of the emergence of the Christian Right.

241 Mobley, G. Melton. "The Political Influence of Television Ministers." *Review of Religious Research* 25 (1985): 314-320.
Using an elaborate multivariate model, the author shows that viewing "televangelists" has little effect on support for church involvement in politics or presidential vote choice. This relationship persists across different levels of doctrinal orthodoxy among viewers.

242 Moen, Matthew C. "School Prayer and the Politics of Life-Style Concern." *Social Science Quarterly* 65 (1984): 1065-1071.
Using a survey of residents of Oklahoma City, Moen reports that support for school prayer is related to a belief that holders of traditional values have lost prestige and cultural dominance. Support for organized prayer in public schools is negatively related to "psychological modernity" and positively related to the perception of value threat.

243 Moen, Matthew C. "Status Politics and the Political Agenda of the Christian Right." *Sociological Quarterly* 29 (1988): 429-437.
Moen undertakes both participant observation and discursive interviews with leaders of Christian Right organizations to study the treatment of religious issues in Congress. His study shows that there is little support for status discontent as an explanation for Christian Right activity.

244 Moen, Matthew C. *The Christian Right and Congress.* Tuscaloosa, AL: University of Alabama Press, 1989.
Moen's study, based on a small number of discursive interviews with a number of Christian Right representatives, congressional staff, and members of the executive branch, shows that the Christian Right was generally quite successful as an interest group in the early 1980s. The influence of the Christian Right declined as the result of election results, co-optation by the Reagan administration, and a number of tactical errors.

245 Moen, Matthew C. "Ronald Reagan and the Social Issues: Rhetorical Support for the 'Christian Right'." *Social Science Journal* 27 (1990): 199-207.
A content analysis of Reagan's State of the Union addresses suggests that Reagan's support for the social issue agenda of the Christian Right was, at best, lukewarm. Reagan devoted little attention to these issues, confining most of his attention to traditional values, abortion, and school prayer. The vocabulary Reagan used in supporting this agenda was quite restrained.

246 Moen, Matthew C. "The Christian Right in the United States." In *The Religious Challenge to the State*, ed. by Matthew C. Moen and Lowell S. Gustafson, 75-101. Philadelphia: Temple University Press, 1992.
In this piece, Moen traces the evolution of the political tactics of the Christian Right through the decade of the 1980s. He shows that at the level of organized interest groups, the Christian Right has become less sectarian and more sophisticated. However, this accommodation to the norms of secular politics may have compromised the ideological basis of the Christian Right, and reduced its effectiveness.

247 Moen, Matthew C. *The Transformation of the Christian Right.* Tuscaloosa, AL: University of Alabama Press, 1992.
In light of many highly visible setbacks in the late 1980s, many had predicted the demise of the Christian Right as a force in American politics. Moen takes a contrary view, arguing that some Christian Right representatives have adapted to a new set of political circumstances, and are well-positioned to exercise political influence into the 1990s. New tactics of the religious Right include adopting the rhetoric of individual freedom, de-emphasizing divisive religious doctrine, and concentrating efforts on the sub-national level.

248 Moen, Matthew C. "From Revolution to Evolution: The Changing Nature of the Christian Right." *Sociology of Religion* 55 (1994): 345-357.
Moen argues that during the most recent period of Christian Right activity, the movement went through two phases: an "expansionist" period, which lasted from 1978 through approximately 1987 and an "institutionalized" phase, lasting from 1987 to the present. During the latter period, the movement has been much more tolerant, ecumenical, and less particularistic. Movement spokespersons have increasingly used the language of "rights" to place religious issue positions within the broader individualist American political culture.

249 Moore, Helen A., and Whitt, Hugh P. "Multiple Dimensions of the Moral Majority Platform: Shifting Interest Group Coalitions." *Sociological Quarterly* 27 (1986): 423-439.
What predicts support for Moral Majority? A survey of Nebraska residents shows that support for Moral Majority is quite limited, and is predicted best by membership in a fundamentalist sect and an attitude of biblical literalism. Moreover, issues on which Moral Majority has taken positions have diverse bases in public opinion. Religious variables account for conservative positions on issues relating to public education (school prayer and creationism), while issues of defense, fund control, abortion, and pornography are best explained by gender.

250 Mueller, Carol. "In Search of a Constituency for the 'New Religious Right'." *Public Opinion Quarterly* 47 (1983): 213-229.
In this piece, Mueller denies that the Christian Right has had a measurable effect on public opinion. Using National Opinion Research Center data from 1972-1980, she shows that the marginal distributions on feminist issues did not change much between 1974 and 1977, and that religious differences on these issues had actually decreased slightly during the same time period.

251 Neitz, Mary Jo. "Family, State, and God: Ideologies of the Right to Life Movement." *Sociological Analysis* 42 (1981): 265-276.
The purpose of this article is to contrast elite and mass ideologies of Catholic abortion opponents. Using ethnographic materials, the author shows that people who oppose abortion use one of two different ideologies: a "pro-life" ideology characterizes elites, while a "pro-family" perspective is utilized by mass members of anti-abortion organizations. Despite having different contents, this mass belief system is as sophisticated and coherent as the elite.

252 Nelsen, Hart M., and Baxter, Sandra. "Ministers Speak on Watergate: Effects of Clergy Roles During a Political Crisis." *Review of Religious Research* 23 (1982): 150-166.
The authors are interested in studying the theological and political orientations of clergy who preached about Watergate. A panel study of ministers shows that although doctrinally conservative ministers were less likely to give political sermons than were theologically liberal pastors, the tendency for conservative pastors to deliver sermons with political themes increased between 1972 and 1974. The tendency of liberals to give political sermons declined during the same period.

253 Nelsen, Hart M.; Madron, Thomas W.; and Yokely, Raytha "Black Religion's Promethean Motif: Orthodoxy and Militancy." *American Journal of Sociology* 81 (1975): 139-149.
Civil rights militancy is found to be positively related to religious orthodoxy, but negatively related to sectarian attitudes. Orthodoxy in turn is related to religious participation, but sectarian attitudes are not.

254 Nemeth, Roger J., and Luidens, Donald A. "The New Christian Right and Mainline Protestantism: The Case of the Reformed Church of America." *Sociological Analysis* 49 (1989): 343-352.
The authors set out to explore the degree to which the Christian Right's agenda has permeated into mainline Protestant denominations. A survey of members of the Reformed Church in America shows that support for the Christian Right is quite limited within the denomination, and is not confined to particular subgroups. Such support is most strongly related to religious devotionalism, doctrinal orthodoxy, and exposure to religious television.

255 Neuendorf, Kimberly, and Abelman, Robert. "An Interaction Analysis of Religious Television Programming." *Review of Religious Research* 29 (1987): 175-198.
Neuendorf and Abelman undertake an "interaction analysis" of religious television. The authors content analyze entertainment programming on religious television is directed toward the sorts of interactions characters have with each other. Children and elderly characters are found to have

unidimensional relationships with other characters, with older characters tending toward conflict-producing behavior. Fictional decision-making tends to be male-dominated.

256 Norr, James L. "Religion and Nation-Building: The American Case." *Sociological Focus* 11 (1978): 255-269.
Using a variety of historical materials, Norr suggests that the building of the American nation in the seventeenth and eighteenth centuries was accompanied by a decline in religious observance and institutionalization. Norr attributes most of the observed religious and political changes to the effects of increasing urbanization.

257 O'Donnell, John P. "Predicting Tolerance of New Religious Movements: A Multivariate Analysis." *Journal for the Scientific Study of Religion* 32 (1993): 356-365.
This study used the Williamsburg Survey on Church-State attitudes for mass publics and elites, and attempts to account for tolerance toward "new religious movements." These are defined in this study as Hare Krishnas, Satanists, "Moonies," and "cults." Among elites, academics are most supportive of the free exercise rights of such groups, Christian clergy (ministers and priests) least supportive. Mass tolerance toward new religious movements is predicted by education, religiosity, and having been "born-again."

258 O'Hara, Thomas J. "The Abortion Control Act of 1989: The Pennsylvania Catholics." In *The Catholic Church and the Politics of Abortion: A View From the States*, ed. by Timothy A. Byrnes and Mary C. Segers, 87-104. Boulder, CO: Westview Press, 1992.
In this piece, the passage of Pennsylvania's relatively restrictive abortion law is examined. While the Pennsylvania Catholic Bishops were not directly active in the controversy, the Pro-Life Federation (a non-denominational anti-abortion lobby) was quite effective. O'Hara suggests that the ability of Roman Catholics and Protestant fundamentalists to work together was a key factor in the bill's passage.

259 Olson, Daniel V. A., and Carroll, Jackson W. "Religiously-Based Politics: Religious Elites and the Public." *Social Forces* 70 (1992): 765-786.
Among religious elites (seminary students), the authors show that there are two political agendas: one liberal, and one conservative. However, these elite agendas (both of which are related to religious values) are not necessarily opposed. Analysis of data from the mass public shows the existence of the same two agendas, but only the socio-moral conservative agenda is related to religion. The authors predict that religion will not become a major axis of political conflict in the United States.

260 Olson, John Kevin, and Beck, Ann C. "Religion and Political Realignment in the Rocky Mountain States." *Journal for the Scientific Study of Religion* 29 (1990): 198-209.
Using county level data for the states of Montana, Idaho, Wyoming, and Colorado, the authors show that conservative Protestantism was related to support for the Republican Party in the 1980s, but not in the 1950s. Roman Catholicism was related to Democratic support in both years.

261 Page, Ann L., and Clelland, Donald A. "The Kanawha County Textbook Controversy: A Study in the Politics of Life Style Concern." *Social Forces* 57 (1978): 265-281.
The authors show that protesters of "modern" textbooks were adherents of a threatened lifestyle. The textbook controversy was ultimately about control of the "means of production" of lifestyles. The authors suggest that the notion of "status politics" be modified to include concerns over lifestyle issues.

262 Peek, Charles W. "Different Methods or Different Data? Another Interpretation of Divergent Findings on Fundamentalism and Political Sexism: Response to Powell and Steelman." *Social Forces* 60 (1982): 1159-1167.
This is a response to the response offered by Powell and Steelman (273). Peek suggests that the discrepancy between the findings of Peek et al. (263) and those of Powell and Steelman were not due to differences in method, but rather to differences in data. Powell and Steelman use more years of the National Opinion Research Center's General Social Survey, and Peek suggests that during this time span a societal change in the relationship between fundamentalism and sexism took place. The relationship between religion and sex-role stereotyping appears to have become stronger over time.

263 Peek, Charles W., and Brown, Sharon. "Sex Prejudice Among White Protestants: Like or Unlike Ethnic Prejudice?" *Social Forces* 59 (1980): 169-185.
The authors suggest that the relationship between religion and gender prejudice is substantially different than that shown in previous work between religion and racism. In the case of gender prejudice, neither fundamentalism nor religiosity is strongly related to sexism. It is suggested that religiously-based sexism may have a biblical basis.

264 Peek, Charles W.; Lowe, George D.; and Williams, L. Susan. "Gender and God's Word: Another Look at Religious Fundamentalism and Sexism." *Social Forces* 69 (1991): 1205-1221.
Using National Opinion Research Center data, the authors show that different aspects of fundamentalism are related to sexism among men and

women. For men, gender prejudice is related to affiliation with a fundamentalist denomination. For fundamentalist women, sexism is occasioned by adherence to orthodox doctrinal beliefs.

265 Penning, James M. "Changing Partisanship and Issue Stands Among American Catholics." *Sociological Analysis* 47 (1986): 29-49.
Penning investigates the hypothesis that American Catholics have grown more conservative. A longitudinal analysis of American Catholics shows that they demonstrate increasing conservatism and Republicanism over a ten-year period. However, these changes cannot be attributed to increased social status or suburbanization of Catholics. Catholics remain more liberal and Democratic than white Protestants.

266 Penning, James M. "The Political Behavior of American Catholics: An Assessment of Group Integration and Group Identification." *Western Political Quarterly* 41 (1988): 289-308.
Penning assesses group identification and integration among Catholics using American National Election Studies data. Religious "integration" (operationally defined as church attendance) is distinguished from group "identification" (measured by a "feeling thermometer"). Among Catholics, integration is a much stronger predictor of presidential vote.

267 Penning, James M. "Pat Robertson and the GOP: 1988 and Beyond." *Sociology of Religion* 55 (1994): 327-344.
Penning is interested in the degree to which Pat Robertson may have caused discord in the Republican Party. A comparison of delegates to three state Republican conventions in 1988 (Michigan, Maine, and South Carolina) shows Robertson delegates to have been considerably more "amateurish," "purist," and less committed to the party than Bush delegates. Penning analyzes Robertson's activities since then, and shows that Christian Coalition was quite active in the 1992 election at a number of different levels. Penning suggests that Christian Coalition might revitalize the Republican Party by attracting committed new adherents.

268 Perkins, Jerry. "The Moral Majority as a Political Reference Group in the 1980 and 1984 Elections." In *Religion and Political Behavior in the United States*, ed. by Ted G. Jelen, 157-168. New York: Praeger Publishers, 1989.
In this study, Perkins finds that any link between evangelical religious beliefs and vote choice is mediated by affect toward Moral Majority, and that the effects of Moral Majority affect on presidential voting are very weak but statistically significant.

269 Perkins, Jerry; Fairchild, Donald; and Havens, Murray. "The Effects of Evangelicalism on Southern Black and White Attitudes and Voting Behavior." In *Religion and Politics in the South: Mass and Elite Perspectives*, ed. by Tod A. Baker, Robert P. Steed, and Laurence W. Moreland, 57-83. New York: Praeger Publishers, 1983.
Religion is not found to be a source of division on political attitudes or voting behavior among either black or white voters in 1980. Rather, the authors interpret the election as a referendum on the Carter administration.

270 Petersen, Larry R., and Mauss, Armand L. "Religion and the 'Right to Life': Correlates of Opposition to Abortion." *Sociological Analysis* 37 (1976): 243-254.
Using a nationwide sample of National Opinion Research Center data, they report that education, church attendance, and religious liberalism-conservatism (defined by denominational membership) are the strongest predictors of attitudes toward abortion.

271 Petersen, Larry R., and Takayama, K. Peter. "Religious Commitment and Conservatism: Toward Understanding an Elusive Relationship." *Sociological Analysis* 45 (1984): 355-371.
Using a survey of Tennessee Catholics, the authors show that religious salience is a stronger and more consistent predictor of conservatism than Mass attendance, doctrinal orthodoxy, or subjective importance of church membership.

272 Peterson, Steven A. "Church Participation and Political Participation: The Spillover Effect." *American Politics Quarterly* 20 (1992): 123-139.
Peterson investigates whether religious participation leads to greater political participation. Using National Opinion Research Center data, he shows that active involvement with organized religious bodies leads to greater involvement in political affairs, as well as greater conservatism. These effects are strongest for whites and for fundamentalists, and vary between men and women.

273 Powell, Brian, and Steelman, Lala Carr. "Fundamentalism and Sexism: A Reanalysis of Peek and Brown." *Social Forces* 60 (1982): 1154-1158.
This article is a critique of a piece by Peek and Brown (263). The authors suggest that the earlier operationalization of sexism is invalid, and that the Peek and Brown measurement of fundamentalism is flawed by the inclusion of Baptists (a very diverse denomination). Using several years of National Opinion Research Center data, Powell and Steelman show that the relationship between fundamentalist denomination (excluding Baptists) and sexism is significant, and varies between men and women.

274 Price-Bonham, Sharon; Santee, Barbara; and Bonham, John M. "An Analysis of Clergymen: Attitudes Toward Abortion." *Review of Religious Research* 17 (1975): 15-27.
The authors hypothesize that clergy's abortion attitudes will be related to their demographic characteristics and selected "sociopolitical attitudes." The effects of several theological and attitudinal variables on attitudes toward abortion were examined among a sample of 94 clergy. Attitudes toward sexual morality and women were the strongest predictors of abortion attitudes.

275 Ragsdale, J. Donald, and Durham, Kenneth R. "Audience Response to Religious Fear Appeals." *Review of Religious Research* 28 (1986): 40-50.
The authors hypothesize that several psychological and demographic variables are related to the ways in which individuals evaluate and retain messages in religious speeches and sermons. An experiment using college students, shows that "high fear" religious messages about crime, morality, and race relations are more effective than similar, "low fear" messages. The acceptance of high fear religious messages is especially pronounced among subjects who are themselves highly religious. Women retain more information from high fear messages.

276 Raymond, Paul, and Norrander, Barbara. "Religion and Attitudes Toward Anti-Abortion Protest." *Review of Religious Research* 32 (1990): 151-156.
The authors hypothesize that Catholics and born-again Christians will be more tolerant of the pro-life movement than secular individuals. A multivariate analysis of Kentucky survey data concerning tolerance toward anti-abortion protesters shows that Catholics, fundamentalists, and secularists are all generally supportive of the First Amendment Rights of such people. This finding persists even when affect toward anti-abortion protesters has been controlled. The role of religion in inculcating democratic values is also discussed.

277 Reese, Boyd. "The New Class and the Young Evangelicals: Second Thoughts." *Review of Religious Research* 24 (1983): 261-266.
This piece criticizes the analysis of the "new class" of young evangelicals provided by James Davison Hunter (136). Reese argues that Hunter gives short shrift to the theological sources of evangelical liberalism, and suggests that Hunter's analysis does not explain why members of the "new class" adopt particular ideologies.

278 Reese, Laura A., and Brown, Ronald E. "The Effects of Religious Messages on Racial Identity and System Blame Among African Americans." *Journal of Politics* 57 (1995): 24-43.
Reese and Brown investigate the interrelationships among racial identity, system blame, and religiosity among African Americans. Drawing upon data from the 1984 National Black Election Study, they relate demographics to religiosity, religious messages, and several measures of racial identity. There is an important difference between two types of messages people may receive in church; some churches emphasize civic awareness while others stress political activity. Quiescence appears to be diminished most in churches where political activity is stressed.

279 Rhodes, A. Lewis. "Religion and Opposition to Abortion Reconsidered." *Review of Religious Research* 27 (1985): 158-168.
Rhodes sets out to challenge the results of previous studies of religion and abortion attitudes by utilizing a very large sample and a wide variety of variables. Using surveys of first-year college students, he shows that the relationship between denominational preference and abortion attitudes is not spurious, but interacts with church attendance, region, and mother's education.

280 Richardson, James T., and Fox, Sandie Wightman. "Religion and Voting on Abortion Reform: A Follow-up Study." *Journal for the Scientific Study of Religion* 14 (1975): 159-164.
An analysis of abortion voting in a Western state legislature prior to the *Roe* decision shows that religious affiliation is the strongest predictor of abortion voting. Both Catholics and Mormons (both numerous in this state) are significantly more pro-life than other members of the legislature.

281 Rothenberg, Stuart, and Newport, Frank. *The Evangelical Voter: Religion and Politics in America.* Washington, DC: Free Congress Research and Education Foundation, 1984.
This study shows that the potential of evangelical Christians to act as an identifiable voting bloc is simultaneously formidable and limited. Based on the authors' own nationwide telephone survey of evangelicals, the study suggests that evangelical distinctiveness is primarily limited to issues of personal morality, and that the effects of Christian Right leaders to offer a more comprehensive political agenda have been generally unsuccessful. The authors emphasize the political heterogeneity of evangelicalism.

282 Rozell, Mark J., and Wilcox, Clyde. "Virginia: God, Guns, and Oliver North." In *God at the Grassroots: The Christian Right in the 1994 Elections*, ed. by Mark J. Rozell and Clyde Wilcox, 109-131. Lanham, MD: Rowman & Littlefield Publishers, 1995.

Rozell and Wilcox are concerned with the role played by the Christian Right in the 1994 elections in Virginia, particularly the U. S. Senate race between Oliver North and Charles Robb. They find that voters are able to distinguish between candidates who are themselves Christian Right activists and those who are merely supported by the Christian Right.

283 Salokar, Rebecca M. "The First Test of *Webster's* Effect: The Florida Church." In *The Catholic Church and Abortion Politics: A View From the States*, ed. by Timothy A. Byrnes and Mary C. Segers, 48-70. Boulder, CO: Westview Press, 1992.
Salokar argues that anticipation of the *Webster* decision in 1989 led to pro-life mobilization on the part of Roman Catholics in the state of Florida. Although the special session called by Gov. Bob Martinez in later 1989 did not result in pro-life legislation, pro-life forces did register some gains in the 1990 midterm elections.

284 Schmalzbauer, John. "Evangelicals in the New Class: Class Versus Subcultural Predictors of Ideology." *Journal for the Scientific Study of Religion* 32 (1993): 330-342.
Religious subculture (defined operationally as denominational affiliation) and social class (defined by occupation) are strongly related to attitudes about sexual mores, abortion, gender roles, and civil liberties. Evangelical "new class" workers are resistant to the liberalizing effects of class on sexual mores, but are less resistant to liberal attitudes on the other issues under consideration.

285 Schoenfeld, Eugen. "Religion and Loyalty to the Political Elite: The Case of the Presidency." *Review of Religious Research* 27 (1985): 178-188.
Departing from Marx and Durkheim, Schoenfeld hypothesizes that those who frequently attend church services will exhibit greater loyalty to the president. Using a sample of college students, he shows that ritual involvement in religion is associated with high levels of support for the president, but that private prayer has a negative association with presidential support. While bearing in mind the homogeneity of his sample, the author speculates that different roles of religion ("church-priestly" versus "private-prophetic") may be operative with respect to explaining support for political elites.

286 Segers, Mary C. "Abortion Politics Post-*Webster*: The New Jersey Bishops." In *The Catholic Church and the Politics of Abortion: A View From the States*, ed. by Timothy A. Byrnes and Mary C. Segers, 27-47. Boulder, CO: Westview Press, 1992.
This piece analyzes the role of the abortion issue in the 1989 New Jersey gubernatorial race, in which pro-choice Democrat Jim Florio defeated

Republican Jim Courter. Courter had shifted from a strong pro-life stance to one of moderate pro-choice support. Despite important efforts by the New Jersey Bishops to mobilize pro-life support among the public, their campaign had little effect on public opinion. Indeed, Segers suggests that the efforts of the Church resulted in pro-choice counter-mobilization among non-Catholics in New Jersey.

287 Segers, Mary C. "The Loyal Opposition: Catholics for a Free Choice."
In *The Catholic Church and the Politics of Abortion: A View From the States*, ed. by Timothy A. Byrnes and Mary C. Segers, 169-184. Boulder, CO: Westview Press, 1992.
Segers describes the formation, history, organization, and tactics of the group Catholics for a Free Choice. Segers argues that the efforts of CFFC have forced the National Conference of Catholic Bishops to take feminist concerns into account when formulating policy, and that CFFC has also served to reduce the anti-Catholicism of the pro-choice movement.

288 Shaiko, Ronald G. "Religion, Politics, and Environmental Concern: A Powerful Mix of Passions." *Social Science Quarterly* 68 (1987): 244-262.
Based on a mail survey of members of environmentalist and conservationist groups, this study shows that environmentalists are somewhat less religious than the general population. The Judeo-Christian belief in "dominion over nature" is more characteristic of Protestants than Catholics, but the overall weak relationship between this religious value and environmentalism suggests the utility of a "stewardship" approach to the relationship between humanity and nature.

289 Sherkat, Darren E., and Ellison, Christopher G. "The Politics of Black Religious Change: Disaffection From Black Mainline Denominations." *Social Forces* 70 (1991): 431-454.
This article examines the reasons for religious apostasy among African-Americans, and considers the possibility that such religious switching may result from dissatisfaction with the political role of African-American mainline churches. The authors show that African-American switchers are most politically discontent, but are somewhat less politically active, than other African-Americans.

290 Shupe, Anson, and Heinerman, John. "Mormonism and the New Christian Right: An Emerging Coalition?" *Review of Religious Research* 27 (1985): 146-157.
This study documents a relationship between one Mormon institution (the Freeman Institute) and the Christian Right. The authors describe the incentives for an LDS-Moral Majority alliance, as well as the obstacles to such cooperation. The article concludes with a suggestion that despite

serious doctrinal disagreements, some degree of ecumenical political cooperation may be possible.

291 Shupe, Anson, and Stacey, William A. *Born-Again Politics and the Moral Majority: What Social Surveys Really Show.* New York: Edwin Mellen Press, 1982.
Based on a survey of the Dallas-Ft. Worth area in 1981, this study shows that Moral Majority was relatively unpopular, even among doctrinally conservative Protestants and people who share the organization's issue positions. The authors also suggest that the contribution of the Christian Right to Ronald Reagan's election in 1980 was quite limited.

292 Shupe, Anson, and Stacey, William A. "The Moral Majority Constituency." In *The New Christian Right: Mobilization and Legitimation,* ed. by Robert C. Liebman and Robert Wuthnow, 103-116. New York: Aldine Press, 1983.
An analysis of Moral Majority support in Dallas-Ft. Worth suggests that the Moral Majority is relatively unpopular among mass publics. Even among sympathizers, there is little agreement on issues on which the organization has taken a position. Contrary to Falwell's ecumenical claims, most support is drawn from fundamentalist Protestants.

293 Sigelman, Lee. "'If You Prick Us, Do We Not Bleed? If You Tickle Us, Do We Not Laugh?' Jews and Pocketbook Voting." *Journal of Politics* 53 (1991): 976-992.
Sigelman develops an index of retrospective evaluations of one's personal economic situation. This measure is as strongly related to presidential voting for Jews as it is for Christians. Jews are therefore shown not to be immune to "pocketbook voting," all stereotypes aside.

294 Sigelman, Lee. "Jews and the 1988 Election: More of the Same?" In *The Bible and the Ballot Box: Religion and Politics in the 1988 Election,* ed. by James L. Guth and John C. Green, 188-203. Boulder, CO: Westview Press, 1991.
Despite tensions between Jews and African Americans, and despite Republican support for Israel, Michael Dukakis received a large majority of the Jewish vote in 1988. Political differences within American Judaism are also discussed.

295 Sigelman, Lee, and Presser, Stanley. "Measuring Public Support for the New Christian Right: The Perils of Point Estimation." *Public Opinion Quarterly* 52 (1988): 325-337.
The piece suggests that Simpson's (297) estimate of support for the Moral Majority platform is much too high. Sigelman and Presser criticize Simpson for arbitrary and overly lenient cutting points, the assignment of "don't

know" responses, and using old data. The revised estimate of support for the Moral Majority platform is about five percent.

296 Sigelman, Lee; Wilcox, Clyde; and Buell, Emmett. "An Unchanging Minority: Support for the Moral Majority, 1980 and 1984." *Social Science Quarterly* 68 (1987): 876-884.
Contrary to elite perceptions of a decline in the status of Moral Majority, the authors find that support for the organization was quite stable between 1980 and 1984. In both years, support for the organization was quite low, but did not diminish over time.

297 Simpson, John H. "Moral Issues and Status Politics." In *The New Christian Right: Mobilization and Legitimation*, ed. by Robert C. Liebman and Robert Wuthnow, 187-205. New York: Aldine Press, 1983.
Analyzing support for positions taken by Moral Majority in 1977, Simpson finds that approximately 30 percent of the American people agree with Moral Majority positions on the issues of school prayer, abortion, homosexuality, and the role of women. Another 42 percent are generally sympathetic, and are characterized as "fellow traveling conservatives." Support for these positions is related to religiosity, non-mainline Protestantism, rural and Southern residence.

298 Simpson, John H.   "Socio-Moral Issues in Recent Presidential Elections." *Review of Religious Research* 27 (1985): 115-123.
Simpson tests the assertion that the Christian Right had little effect on the elections of Ronald Reagan by analyzing separate voter surveys from 1980 and 1984. The study shows that presidential vote decisions in 1980 and 1984 were strongly influenced by attitudes toward social issues, to the benefit of Ronald Reagan in both years. Simpson speculates that this relationship may be unstable, due to the difference between the economic interests of some of Reagan's social issue supporters and Republican economic policy.

299 Simpson, John H. "Status Inconsistency and Moral Issues." *Journal for the Scientific Study of Religion* 24 (1985): 155-162.
The hypothesis that status inconsistency leads to support for positions taken by the Christian Right is not generally confirmed. However, high status persons within evangelical churches are thought to provide crucial political resources.

300 Simpson, John H. "A Reply to 'Measuring Public Support for the New Christian Right': The Perils of Point Estimation." *Public Opinion Quarterly* 52 (1988): 338-342.
This is a response to the criticisms of Sigelman and Presser (295). In part, Simpson defends his cutting points, since he asserts that direction is much

more important than intensity in analyzing issue attitudes. He also argues that his use of data gathered in 1977 provides a useful baseline with which to compare subsequent "mobilized" public opinion.

301 Simpson, John H. "The Mood of America in the 1980s: Some Further Observations on Sociomoral Issues." *Sociology of Religion* 55 (1994): 291-305.
Simpson develops a typology of political "arenas" and suggests that the United States falls into a category of "quasi-ideological politics." This means that both elites and mass publics display a high level of constraint across a limited number of (social) issues. Simpson's analysis of National Opinion Research Center data suggests that there are three major groups in the United States with respect to "moral" issues: liberals (who have remained a relatively constant proportion of Americans throughout the 1980s), ambivalents (whose numbers have declined), and conservatives (whose proportion of the population increased during the 1980s).

302 Smidt, Corwin E. "Civil Religious Orientations Among Elementary School Children." *Sociological Analysis* 41 (1980): 25-40.
The author endeavors to explore children's socialization into civil religion. By assessing attitudes among elementary schoolchildren in downstate Illinois, Smidt shows that civil religious orientations are learned in childhood, and are held by both public and parochial school students. Furthermore, such orientations are related to the ways in which children conceptualize and evaluate the political system.

303 Smidt, Corwin E. "Born-Again Politics: The Political Behavior of Evangelical Christians in the South and Non-South." In *Religion and Politics in the South: Mass and Elite Perspectives*, ed. by Tod A. Baker, Robert P. Steed, and Laurence W. Moreland, 27-56. New York: Praeger Publishers, 1983.
The results of this study suggest that the political mobilization of evangelical Christians in the South is quite incomplete. Despite Republican successes in attracting the votes of Southern evangelicals in 1980, such people do not share a uniformly conservative ideology, and are religiously and politically rather heterogeneous.

304 Smidt, Corwin E. "Evangelicals and the 1984 Election: Continuity or Change?" *American Politics Quarterly* 15 (1987): 419-333.
This study involves a comparison of the behavior of white evangelicals in the presidential elections of 1980 and 1984. In both years, evangelicals were slightly more likely to vote for Reagan than the rest of the population. In 1984, evangelicals were slightly more likely to identify with the Republican Party, and somewhat less likely to vote than in 1980.

305 Smidt, Corwin E.   "Evangelicals and the New Christian Right: Coherence Versus Diversity in the Issue Stands of American Evangelicals." In *Contemporary Evangelical Political Involvement: An Analysis and Assessment*, ed. by Corwin E. Smidt, 75-97. New York: University Press of America, 1989.
Smidt examines the attitudes of evangelical Christians on two issues: abortion and the nuclear freeze movement. He finds that evangelicals are just as likely to adopt the perspective of the group JustLife as they are of the Christian Right, suggesting that evangelical beliefs on these issues are not monolithic.

306 Smidt, Corwin E. "Identifying Evangelical Respondents: An Analysis of 'Born-Again' and Bible Questions Used Across Different Surveys." In *Religion and Political Behavior in the United States*, ed. by Ted G. Jelen, 23-43. New York: Praeger Publishers, 1989.
As the title indicates, this study compares different versions of survey questions measuring "born-again" status and experiences, and different versions of items measuring personal beliefs about the Bible. Despite some important limitations, different versions of these questions appear to tap the same general set of respondents.

307 Smidt, Corwin E. "'Praise the Lord' Politics: A Comparative Analysis of the Social Characteristics and Political Views of American Evangelical and Charismatic Christians." *Sociological Analysis* 50 (1989): 53-72.
In this study, doctrinally-defined evangelicals and self-identified charismatics are compared across a number of different religious, demographic, and political variables. There is some overlap between the two, and evangelical charismatics are found to be generally more conservative than other respondents. The social and political differences between the two groups seem likely to render political coalitions rather problematic.

308 Smidt, Corwin E., and Kellstedt, Lyman A. "Evangelicalism and Survey Research: Interpretive Problems and Substantive Findings." In *The Bible, Politics, and Democracy*, ed. by Richard John Neuhaus, 81-102. Grand Rapids, MI: Eerdmans, 1987.
Using a variety of data sets, this study investigates changes in the political attitudes of evangelicals over time. The authors suggest that a realignment is underway, with evangelicals becoming more Republican, and provide a number of methodological suggestions for future research.

309 Smidt, Corwin E., and Kellstedt, Paul M. "Evangelicals in the Post-Reagan Era: An Analysis of Evangelical Voters in the 1988 Presidential Election." *Journal for the Scientific Study of Religion* 31 (1992): 330-338.
The authors report that white evangelicals have become steadily more Republican during the 1980s, and that these Republican gains solidified during the second Reagan term. Evangelicals are more likely to identify with the Republican Party and to participate in politics. Southern evangelicals have recently become somewhat more Republican than their non-evangelical counterparts.

310 Smidt, Corwin E., and Penning, James M. "Religious Commitment, Political Conservatism, and Political and Social Tolerance in the United States." *Sociological Analysis* 43 (1982): 231-246.
Smidt and Penning set out to disaggregate the concepts of conservatism, religious commitment, and intolerance. Using National Opinion Research Center data, they show that ideological self-placement and religiosity have independent effects on political tolerance, as well as attitudes toward other lifestyle issues (interracial marriage and abortion). The effects of each of these independent predictors varies over time in complex ways.

311 Smidt, Corwin E., and Penning, James M. "A Party Divided: A Comparison of Robertson and Bush Delegates to the 1988 Michigan Republican State Convention." *Polity* 23 (1990): 127-138.
Pat Robertson's delegates to the 1988 Michigan Republican convention displayed an "amateur" orientation in that they were more motivated by issue concerns, less partisan, and more conservative than supporters of George Bush. The relative conservatism of Robertson supporters is greatest on issues involving personal morality. The authors argue that the distinctiveness of the Robertson forces is not likely to create divisiveness for the Republican Party in the long term.

312 Smidt, Corwin E., and Penning, James M. "Religious Self-Identification and Support for Robertson: An Analysis of Delegates to the 1988 Michigan Republican State Convention." *Review of Religious Research* 32 (1991): 321-336.
This study is designed to assess the religious identifications of Pat Robertson's supporters. Using a survey of Republican activists, the authors find that various self-identifications are powerful predictors of support for Robertson. Multiple identifications (born-again, charismatic, fundamentalist, evangelical, etc.) are quite common, although the effects of these on support for Robertson do differ. Evangelical charismatics provide Robertson with his highest level of support (among conservative Christian delegates), while non-charismatic fundamentalists are considerably less supportive.

313 Snowball, David. *Continuity and Change in the Rhetoric of the Moral Majority.* New York: Praeger Publishers, 1991.
This study traces Moral Majority rhetoric from its inception in 1979 to its subsumption into the "Liberty Federation" in 1991. Snowball shows that the pronouncements of Falwell and others became less strident and combative, and more accommodation as the organization evolved. Despite its brief life span, Moral Majority may have served as an important "safety valve," providing representation for previously underrepresented people.

314 Stacey, William A., and Shupe, Anson. "Correlates of Support for the Electronic Church." *Journal for the Scientific Study of Religion* 21 (1982): 291-303.
Among fundamentalists, usage of religious television is related to church religiosity, while moderate and conservative Christians exhibit a positive relationship between viewership and doctrinal orthodoxy. Viewers of televangelists derive religious, rather than political, gratification for their media usage.

315 Stacey, William A., and Shupe, Anson. "Religious Values and Religiosity in the Textbook Adoption Controversy in Texas, 1981." *Review of Religious Research* 25 (1984): 321-333.
Texas' textbook adoption controversy is the subject of Stacey and Shupe's study. Using a survey of white urban Texans, as well as transcripts from hearings held by the Texas State Education Agency's Textbook Committee, the authors show that despite widespread perceptions to the contrary, there was only mixed support for Christian Right values during the textbook controversy of 1981. Their multi-method approach shows that in fact there was no consensus on conservative values at all during this period.

316 Stark, Rodney, and Christiano, Kevin J. "Support for the American Left, 1920-1924: The Opiate Thesis Reconsidered." *Journal for the Scientific Study of Religion* 31 (1992): 62-75.
This piece is a test of the Marxian hypothesis that religion represses class-based political activity. Using ecological data, the authors report a strong negative relationship between church membership and "leftism" (presidential voting and I. W. W. activity), but that this relationship disappears when controls are imposed for the proportion of Scandinavians in particular counties. Thus, the religion-leftism relationship is spurious.

317 Stark, Rodney, and McCann, James C. "Market Forces and Catholic Commitment: Exploring the New Paradigm." *Journal for the Scientific Study of Religion* 32 (1993): 111-124.
The authors describe a "new paradigm" of religious involvement, which entails the assumption that competition among multiple religious

denominations enhances religious participation. This new framework supersedes the "traditional" paradigm, which emphasized the importance of religious monopolies. The authors test the theory with ecological data, relating measures of Catholic involvement and ordination to Catholic concentrations. The hypothesis is strongly confirmed.

318 Steed, Robert P.; Moreland, Laurence W.; and Baker, Tod A. "Religion and Party Activists: Fundamentalism and Politics in Regional Perspective." In *Religion and Politics in the South: Mass and Elite Perspectives*, ed. by Tod A. Baker, Robert P. Steed, and Laurence W. Moreland, 105-132. New York: Praeger Publishers, 1983.
In a survey of party activists from several with a caucus-convention system for selecting delegates to national nominating conventions, the authors find few differences between Southern and non-Southern convention delegates. While Southerners are generally more conservative, this difference reflects regional, rather than religious, distinctions.

319 Stempien, Richard, and Coleman, Sarah. "Process of Persuasion: The Case of Creation Science." *Review of Religious Research* 27 (1985): 169-177.
The authors employ a "sociology of belief" perspective to analyze the debate over creationism. A content analysis of public debates between "Scientific Creationists" and evolutionists suggests that the apparent rhetorical success of the former is attributable to the form, rather than the content, of their arguments. Creationists tend to use tactics designed to appeal to ordinary people, while evolutionists tend to employ a more academic, scientific, style.

320 Stockton, Ronald R. "The Evangelical Phenomenon: A Falwell-Graham Typology." In *Contemporary Evangelical Political Involvement: An Analysis and Assessment*, ed. by Corwin E. Smidt, 45-74. New York: University Press of America, 1989.
Stockton compares the political platforms of evangelical leaders Jerry Falwell and Billy Graham. He finds supporters of Falwell to be politically quite distinctive across a variety of issues.

321 Storr, Jerold M. "Religious Preference, Religiosity, and Opposition to War." *Sociological Analysis* 36 (1975): 323-334.
Storr takes on what he describes as a controversial subject: the relationships between religious preferences, religiosity, and opposition to war. A study of first-year college students shows that students without religious preferences are most likely to oppose warfare, with Jews close behind. Catholics and Protestants are quite similar to each other with respect to attitudes toward warfare. Church attendance has no effect, suggesting that religiosity does not evoke outgroup hostility.

322 Stump, Roger W. "Regional Contrasts Within Black Protestantism: A Research Note." *Social Forces* 66 (1987): 143-151.
This study examines regional differences in African American religiosity. Stump shows that church attendance is related to social factors in the South and to religious factors in the North. The relationship between moral asceticism and church attendance is considerably stronger in the North.

323 Swatos, William H. "Picketing Satan Enfleshed at 7-Eleven: A Research Note." *Review of Religious Research* 30 (1988): 73-82.
This study, which is based on a survey of activists who supported anti-pornography picketing of 7-11 convenience stores, is primarily descriptive. Swatos finds no evidence of status inadequacy or discontent, but locates motivation for such activism in cultural fundamentalism. Interestingly, virtually all respondents (96 percent) believe in a literal, interventionist Devil, who is thought to animate sinful lifestyles.

324 Tamney, Joseph B. "Religion and the Abortion Issue." In *The Political Role of Religion in the United States*, ed. by Stephen D. Johnson and Joseph B. Tamney, 159-180. Boulder, CO: Westview Press, 1986.
Tamney suggests that antiabortion attitudes appear to have two major sources: antifeminism and religious socialization. Pro-choice attitudes are occasioned by the value of free choice, and an ideology of self-realization.

325 Tamney, Joseph B. "Social Class Composition of Congregations and Pastoral Support for Liberal Activism." *Review of Religious Research* 33 (1991): 18-31.
Using Marxist theory as a point of departure, Tamney tests several hypotheses about pastors' support for liberal political activism. A survey of clergy shows that church type, religious subculture (theological liberalism or conservatism) and social class composition of lay leadership are all independently related to clergy support for liberal activism (specifically, support for an ecumenical Christian organization).

326 Tamney, Joseph B.; Burton, Ronald; and Johnson, Stephen. "Christianity, Social Class, and the Catholic Bishops' Economic Policy." *Sociological Analysis* 49 (1988): 78S-96S.
In this study, the authors measure reaction among a random sample of Middletown residents to the American Catholic Bishops' pastoral letter on the economy. As a result of factor analysis, the authors find that support for "economic restructuring" is greatest among non-fundamentalist Catholics and Protestant fundamentalists. This last finding is surprising given the economically conservative positions taken by fundamentalist elites.

327 Tamney, Joseph B.; Burton, Ronald; and Johnson, Stephen D. "Fundamentalism and Economic Restructuring." In *Religion and Political Behavior in the United States*, ed. by Ted G. Jelen, 67-82. New York: Praeger Publishers, 1989.
Attitudes favoring the "restructuring" of American capitalism (toward a more egalitarian economy) are found to be related to fundamentalism (defined as a belief in biblical literalism, the second coming, and Christian particularism). Contrary to some of the pronouncements of Christian Right elites, various forms of doctrinal orthodoxy are related to modifications in the "free enterprise" system.

328 Tamney, Joseph B., and Johnson, Stephen D. "The Moral Majority in Middletown." *Journal for the Scientific Study of Religion* 22 (1983): 145-158.
Support for Moral Majority is reported to be very low, and related to usage of religious television, cultural fundamentalism, and adherence to positions taken by Christian Right leaders.

329 Tamney, Joseph B., and Johnson, Stephen D. "Religious Television in Middletown." *Review of Religious Research* 25 (1984): 303-313.
Using their "Middletown" data base, the authors investigate the frequency of viewing religious television. The authors show that usage of religious television in general is predicted by a variety of religious and demographic variables. However, viewership of theologically conservative televangelists is related only to support for issue positions advanced by the Christian Right and religious fundamentalism.

330 Tamney, Joseph B., and Johnson, Stephen D. "Christianity and the Nuclear Issue." *Sociological Analysis* 46 (1985): 321-238.
The authors hypothesize that exposure to conservative Christian culture decreases support for nuclear disarmament. A survey of residents of "Middletown" is used to evaluate support for a mutual freeze on nuclear weapons. Catholics are shown to be more supportive of a freeze than Protestants, as are religionists who are aware of church leaders' support for such a policy. These findings are not affected by controls for non-religious variables.

331 Tamney, Joseph B., and Johnson, Stephen D. "Church-State Relations in the Eighties." *Sociological Analysis* 48 (1987): 1-16.
The authors hypothesize that Catholics and conservative Protestants would be most likely to favor state support for religion. In the study, they attempt to explain public approval of government support for religion. A survey of residents of "Middletown" shows that such approval is generally based on religious fundamentalism, support for issue positions advanced by the Christian Right, and exposure to religious television.

332 Tamney, Joseph B., and Johnson, Stephen D. "Religious Diversity and Ecumenical Social Action." *Review of Religious Research* 32 (1990): 16-26. Will clergy be supportive of ecumenical efforts? A survey of clergy in "Middletown" concerning attitudes toward an ecumenical Christian agency shows that theological liberals and conservatives are willing to support quite different ecumenical programs. The authors discuss the potential and difficulty of interfaith coalitions in the public sphere.

333 Tamney, Joseph B.; Johnson, Stephen D.; and Burton, Ronald. "The Abortion Controversy: Conflicting Beliefs and Values in American Society." *Journal for the Scientific Study of Religion* 31 (1992): 32-46.
Abortion attitudes are shown to be based on a variety of beliefs, including attitudes toward privacy, beliefs about the point at which life begins, social traditionalism, and church influence. The authors suggest that traditionalism predicts abortion attitudes only for Protestants, and that other "life issues" are generally unrelated to attitudes concerning legal abortion.

334 Thorn, William J., and Garrison, Bruce. "Institutional Stress: Journalistic Norms in the Catholic Press." *Review of Religious Research* 25 (1983): 49-62.
The authors investigate the roles of Catholic diocesan press editors using a survey of such editors and their bishop-publishers. The study shows that increased professionalism of the editors of diocesan newspapers leads them to view their roles as more adversarial; this renders them less devoted to institutional communication and religious socialization. Bishops and editors view the role of the diocesan press much differently, which occasions stress and tension between the various functions of religious newspapers.

335 Toolin, Cynthia. "American Civil Religion from 1798 to 1981: A Content Analysis of Presidential Inaugural Addresses." *Review of Religious Research* 25 (1983): 39-48.
To what extent do presidents allude to civil religious imagery in their inaugural addresses? A content analysis of Inaugural addresses reveals that virtually all of them contain allusions to American civil religion. Themes most frequently employed include those of Exodus, sacrifice, national destiny, and international example. Civil religion is thought to perform an important function of legitimation.

336 Turner, Helen Lee, and Guth, James L. "The Politics of Armageddon: Dispensationalism Among Southern Baptist Ministers." In *Religion and Political Behavior in the United States*, ed. by Ted G. Jelen, 187-207. New York: Praeger Publishers, 1989.
The authors describe dispensationalism as an extreme form of premillenialism, in which human history is divided into seven eras, or

different covenants between God and humanity. Baptist ministers who identify as dispensationalists seem to be considerably more conservative politically than other Baptist clergy across a variety of issues. The authors raise the problem of explaining political activity among a group of ministers who hold premillenial beliefs.

337 Tygart, Clarence E. "The Role of Theology Among Other 'Belief' Variables for Clergy Civil Rights Activism." *Review of Religious Research* 18 (1977): 271-278.
Tygart sets out to investigate the impetus behind civil rights activism among clergy. In particular, he analyzes moral autonomy, authoritarianism, and efficacy in a national sample of clergy. He shows that theological beliefs affect civil rights activism among clergy through the intervening effects of political ideology.

338 Verba, Sidney; Schlozman, Kay Lehman; Brady, Henry; and Nie, Norman H. "Race, Ethnicity, and Political Resources: Participation in the United States." *British Journal of Political Science* 23 (1993): 453-497.
Verba and his colleagues argue that individuals who participate in politics are those who possess the resources (time, money, and civic skills) to do so. They make a particularly strong case for religious organizations as being a source of these important political resources, particularly the development of civic skills: the communication and organization skills necessary to facilitate effective political participation.

339 Wagenaar, Theodore C., and Bartos, Patricia E. "Orthodoxy and Attitudes of Clergymen Towards Homosexuality and Abortion." *Review of Religious Research* 18 (1977): 114-125.
The authors utilize data from a survey of Columbus, Ohio clergy regarding their attitudes about homosexuality and abortion. Doctrinal orthodoxy is shown to be negatively related to acceptance of homosexuality and legal abortion. Permissive attitudes toward these two lifestyle issues are also related to the tendency of some clergy to compartmentalize "religious" and "secular" attitudes.

340 Wald, Kenneth D. "Assessing the Religious Factor in Electoral Behavior." In *Religion in American Politics*, ed. by Charles W. Dunn, 105-121. Washington, DC: Congressional Quarterly Press, 1989.
Wald presents a general discussion of the relevance of religion for voting behavior as well as a case study which draws on National Opinion Research Center data. He reports that religious preference acted as a powerful predictor of support for Ronald Reagan.

341 Wald, Kenneth D. "Religious Elites and Public Opinion: The Impact of the Bishops' Peace Pastoral." *Review of Politics* 54 (1992): 112-147.
This piece examines the impact of the Catholic Bishops' pastoral letter, *The Challenge of Peace*, on lay Catholic attitudes toward defense spending. Using National Opinion Research Center data, Wald finds that the pastoral resulted in a sharp, but short-lived, decline in Catholic support for military appropriations. The article concludes with a discussion of factors relating to receptivity and acceptance of political messages from religious leaders.

342 Wald, Kenneth D. "Florida: Running Globally and Winning Locally." In *God at the Grassroots: The Christian Right in the 1994 Elections*, ed. by Mark J. Rozell and Clyde Wilcox, 19-46. Lanham, MD: Rowman & Littlefield Publishers, 1995.
Wald reports that despite the Christian Right's strategic importance to Florida's Republican Party, it is hardly a juggernaut poised to claim control of the party.

343 Wald, Kenneth D.; Kellstedt, Lyman A.; and Leege, David C. "Church Involvement and Political Behavior." In *Rediscovering the Religious Factor in American Politics*, ed. by David C. Leege and Lyman A. Kellstedt, 121-138. Armonk, NY: M. E. Sharpe, 1993.
Church involvement interacts with denominational membership to increase acceptance of church teachings. Religious involvement is extremely useful in explaining intradenominational differences on political issues.

344 Wald, Kenneth D., and Lupfer, Michael B. "Religion and Political Attitudes in the Urban South." In *Religion and Politics in the South: Mass and Elite Perspectives*, ed. by Tod A. Baker, Robert P. Steed, and Laurence W. Moreland, 84-100. New York: Praeger Publishers, 1983.
Religious orthodoxy is a strong general contributor to conservative outlooks in a survey of one Southern city. However, orthodoxy was not related to racial conservatism, party identification, or vote choice, and was a relatively weak predictor of general conservatism.

345 Wald, Kenneth D.; Owen, Dennis E.; and Hill, Samuel S. "Churches as Political Communities." *American Political Science Review* 82 (1988): 531-548.
The authors wish to portray churches as political communities. Theological environments are very important sources of political attitudes. Attending a church in which doctrinal conservatism is common is a stronger predictor of moral conservatism than the respondent's own doctrinal orthodoxy.

346 Wald, Kenneth D.; Owen, Dennis E.; and Hill, Samuel S. "Evangelical Politics and Status Issues." *Journal for the Scientific Study of Religion* 28 (1989): 1-16.
Using subjective measures of status discontent, the authors show a strong relationship between such discontent and support for the Christian Right. This relationship persists in the fact of controls for alternative explanations.

347 Wald, Kenneth D.; Owen, Dennis E.; and Hill, Samuel S. "Habits of the Mind? The Problem of Authority in the New Christian Right." In *Religion and Political Behavior in the United States*, ed. by Ted G. Jelen, 93-108. New York: Praeger Publishers, 1989.
The authors develop a measure of "authority-mindedness," which they distinguish from "authoritarianism." In the case of the former, some respondents feel that deference to legitimate authority is an important principle, and the authors argue that this attitude may not indicate psychological pathology. Authority-mindedness is found to be a much stronger source of support for the Christian Right than authoritarianism.

348 Wald, Kenneth D.; Owen, Dennis E.; and Hill, Samuel S. "Reply to Miller." *Journal for the Scientific Study of Religion* 28 (1989): 374.
The authors respond to the critique of Miller (240). Status discontent is acknowledged to be a necessary, but not sufficient, condition for the rise of the Christian Right.

349 Wald, Kenneth D.; Owen, Dennis E.; and Hill, Samuel S. "Political Cohesion in Churches." *Journal of Politics* 52 (1990): 197-215.
Using a sample drawn from twenty-one congregations in a Southern community, the authors develop a measure of "strong congregations," consisting of religious certainty, strong faith mission, religious certainty, and high levels of public and private religious worship. Such congregational "strength" is positively related to a lack of lay dissent on moral issues.

350 Wald, Kenneth D., and Smidt, Corwin E. "Measurement Strategies in the Study of Religion and Politics." In *Rediscovering the Religious Factor in American Politics*, ed. by David C. Leege and Lyman A. Kellstedt, 26-49. Armonk, NY: M. E. Sharpe, 1993.
This article contains an overview of the various means by which religion can be conceptualized and measured. Doctrinal, denomination, personality, and group-based strategies are considered.

351 Warner, R. Stephen. "Work in Progress Toward a New Paradigm for the Sociological Study of Religion in the United States." *American Journal of Sociology* 98 (1993): 1044-1093.
Warner reviews a growing literature, which suggests that organized religion in the United States flourishes in an environment of open, "market"

competition. This new approach is contrasted to older theories of religious "monopoly."

352 Welch, Michael R.; Johnson, C. Lincoln; and Pilgrim, David. "Tuning in the Spirit: Exposure to Types of Religious TV Programming Among American Catholic Parishioners." *Journal for the Scientific Study of Religion* 29 (1990): 198-197.
This study suggests that among Catholics, greater integration into parish life leads to more frequent usage of religious television. There is little evidence that Catholics use religious television as a substitute for more traditional forms of religious participation. Watching specifically Protestant programs is generally attributable to childhood socialization, not marital heterogamy or familial dynamics.

353 Welch, Michael R., and Leege, David C. "Religious Predictors of Catholic Parishioners' Sociopolitical Attitudes: Devotional Style, Closeness to God, Imagery, and Agentic/Communal Religious Identity." *Journal for the Scientific Study of Religion* 27 (1988): 536-552.
A number of different religious variables are used to predict a variety of political attitudes. In general, the most powerful religious attitudes are image of God and devotional style (evangelical vs. liturgical).

354 Welch, Michael R., and Leege, David C. "Dual Reference Groups and Political Orientations: An Examination of Evangelically-Oriented Catholics." *American Journal of Political Science* 35 (1991): 28-56.
Welch and Leege develop an index of "evangelical-style" devotionalism, which includes Bible reading, group prayer, and seeking to recruit new members. When this measure is used to explain the political attitudes of Catholics, evangelical devotionalism is positively related to acceptance of Catholic teaching on issues for which the Church has taken a clear position. Where there is no identifiably "Catholic" position, evangelical devotion is associated with positions taken by leaders of the Christian Right.

355 Welch, Michael R.; Leege, David C.; and Cavendish, James C. "Attitudes Toward Abortion Among U. S. Catholics: Another Case of Symbolic Politics?" *Social Science Quarterly* 76 (1995): 142-157.
Using data from the Notre Dame Study of Catholic Parish Life, the authors examine the reasons for some Catholics' opposition to abortion. Catholics who oppose abortion have their opinions on this issue structured by both their orientations toward sex and sexual morality as well as by their religious beliefs.

356 Welch, Michael R.; Leege, David C.; Wald, Kenneth D.; and Kellstedt, Lyman A. "Are the Sheep Hearing the Shepherds? Cue Perceptions, Congregational Responses, and Political Communication Processes." In *Rediscovering the Religious Factor in American Politics*, ed. by David C. Leege and Lyman A. Kellstedt, 235-254. Armonk, NY: M. E. Sharpe, 1993.
The effects of pastoral political cues on the political attitudes of the laity are examined. In general, pastoral cues are more efficacious for evangelicals than for mainline Protestants or Catholics. The effects of Catholic pastoral teachings appear to be limited to "pelvic politics": church teachings on abortion and sexual behavior.

357 White, O. Kendall, Jr. "A Review and Commentary on the Prospects of a Mormon New Christian Right Coalition." *Review of Religious Research* 28 (1986): 180-188.
In a response to Shupe and Heinerman (290), White suggests that there exists a strong possibility of a coalition between the LDS Church and Moral Majority, but argues that Shupe and Heinerman place far too much emphasis on the Freeman Institute. Rather, White suggests that the most plausible basis for such an ecumenical coalition lies with opposition to the Equal Rights Amendment.

358 Whitt, Hugh P., and Nelsen, Hart M. "Residence, Moral Traditionalism, and Tolerance of Atheists." *Social Forces* 54 (1975): 328-340.
How tolerant are atheists? This study shows that the relationship between place of residence and political tolerance remains significant, even after the imposition of controls for religious and social class variables. The authors suggest that the relationship between religiosity and intolerance may be spurious.

359 Wilcox, Clyde. "Evangelicals and Fundamentalists in the New Christian Right: Religious Differences in the Ohio Moral Majority." *Journal for the Scientific Study of Religion* 25 (1986): 355-363.
The effects of self-identification as "evangelical" or "fundamentalist" are examined for a sample of religious activists. Self-described fundamentalists are critical of evangelicals, which is not reciprocally true. Fundamentalists are less active politically, and are more conservative on some issues. Evangelicals who perceive some connection between religion and politics are somewhat more liberal than those who do not, while the reverse is reported for fundamentalists.

360 Wilcox, Clyde. "Fundamentalists and Politics: An Analysis of the Effects of Differing Operational Definitions." *Journal of Politics* 48 (1986): 1041-1051.
Denominational and doctrinal measurements of fundamentalism are compared using American National Election Studies data. "Doctrinal"

fundamentalists typically have higher socioeconomic status, and are less Southern and more urban than those who are classified by denominational affiliation. Doctrinal fundamentalists are also more politically active, and more Republican in their partisan self-identification.

361 Wilcox, Clyde. "America's Radical Right Revisited: A Comparison of the Activists in Christian Right Organizations From the 1960s and the 1980s." *Sociological Analysis* 48 (1987): 46-57.
This study compares the characteristics of the Christian Anti-Communist Crusade (using a survey of CAC members taken in 1962) with the Ohio Moral Majority (using a 1982 survey of that organization). The author finds impressive continuity between the two groups. Both were comprised of activist, affluent, conservative Republicans, and neither organization did much in the way of mobilizing previously apolitical people. Membership in Moral Majority was found to be more explicitly religious than in the CAC.

362 Wilcox, Clyde. "Popular Support for the Moral Majority in 1980: A Second Look." *Social Science Quarterly* 68 (1987): 157-166.
This piece is a methodological critique of Buell and Sigelman (033). Wilcox argues that feeling thermometers must be adjusted for response sets, and that such an adjustment changes some of the substantive results reported in the earlier article. Using the revised measure, Moral Majority support is negatively related to generalized support for government. Doctrinal fundamentalism is positively related to Moral Majority support.

363 Wilcox, Clyde. "Religious Attitudes and Anti-Feminism: An Analysis of the Ohio Moral Majority." *Women and Politics* 7 (1987): 59-78.
The results of this study show that among religious activists, two religious variables account for a number of political attitudes: (1) A perceived connection between religion and politics, and (2) self-identification as an evangelical or fundamentalist. Fundamentalists are generally more conservative than evangelicals across a number of different issue. These results are robust after the imposition of multivariate controls.

364 Wilcox, Clyde. "Religious Orientations and Political Attitudes: Variations Within the New Christian Right." *American Politics Quarterly* 15 (1987): 274-299.
To what extent do religious beliefs structure political attitudes? Based on a survey of activists in the Ohio Moral Majority, this study shows that there is substantial variation in the political attitudes of Christian Right supporters, despite the relative homogeneity of the sample. Denominational affiliation, church attendance, religious self-identification all make independent contributions to political attitudes, as does a belief that religion and politics are connected.

365 Wilcox, Clyde. "The Christian Right in Twentieth-Century America: Continuity and Change." *Review of Politics* 50 (1988): 659-681.
An analysis of political activity on the part of doctrinally conservative Protestants reveals there have been three waves of such participation in the twentieth-century: the 1920s, 1950s, and 1980s. Wilcox traces similarities and differences between the various movements, and pays particular attention to the Christian Right in the most recent historical period. Wilcox argues that a wave of pentecostal activism has greater potential for ecumenical political coalitions than does the fundamentalist wing of the Christian Right.

366 Wilcox, Clyde. "Political Action Committees of the New Christian Right: A Longitudinal Analysis." *Journal for the Scientific Study of Religion* 27 (1988): 60-71.
Christian Right political action committees (PACs) are found to raise large sums of money, but devote relatively little of it to congressional candidates. Christian Right PACs generally contribute to Republicans, and to non-incumbents. However, recent trends have suggested that these PACs are increasingly likely to contribute to the campaigns of incumbents, and to contribute to candidates involved in close races.

367 Wilcox, Clyde. "Seeing the Connection: Religion and Politics in the Ohio Moral Majority." *Review of Religious Research* 30 (1988): 47-58.
How do political activists connect their religious beliefs to their political views? Wilcox shows that a question which directly elicits perceptions of such a connection varies greatly, even within a sample of Christian Right activists. A close cognitive connection between religion and politics is related to gender, self-identified fundamentalism, and church attendance.

368 Wilcox, Clyde. "Feminism and Anti-Feminism Among Evangelical Women." *Western Political Quarterly* 42 (1989): 147-160.
Using data from a national survey of evangelicals, Wilcox examines the extent to which evangelical women embrace feminism. Evangelical women are about equally divided on issues of gender equality. Given a lack of liberal-conservative "constraint" among such women, neither group is considered "mobilizable" into more general, ideological political organizations.

369 Wilcox, Clyde. "The Fundamentalist Voter: Politicized Religious Identity and Political Attitudes and Behavior." *Review of Religious Research* 31 (1989): 54-67.
Wilcox contrasts fundamentalists with other evangelicals with regard to their political attitudes and behaviors, using data from the 1983 Evangelical Voter Study. The effects of fundamentalist self-identification on a variety of political variables is examined. The data show that such identification is

related to political attitudes and behavior only in interaction with religious-political elites, such as televangelists. Without exposure to elite messages, identification as a fundamentalist is not politically meaningful.

370 Wilcox, Clyde. "The New Christian Right and the Mobilization of the Evangelicals." In *Religion and Political Behavior in the United States*, ed. by Ted G. Jelen, 139-156. New York: Praeger Publishers, 1989.
Wilcox shows that the voting turnout of evangelical Protestants has increased since 1972, but that this mobilization was not attributable to the efforts of the Christian Right. Rather, the candidacy of evangelical Jimmy Carter appears to have attracted doctrinally conservative Christians into the political arena. In 1984, without Carter as a candidate, evangelical turnout declined, but not to its pre-1976 levels.

371 Wilcox, Clyde. "Popular Support for the New Christian Right." *Social Science Journal* 26 (1989): 55-63.
Using survey data, Wilcox distinguishes "rational" from "non-rational" sources of support for the Christian Right. A multivariate analysis suggests that rational bases of Christian Right support predominate.

372 Wilcox, Clyde. "Support for the Christian Right Old and New: A Comparison of Supporters of the Christian Anti-Communism Crusade and Moral Majority." *Sociological Focus* 22 (1989): 87-97.
Wilcox wishes to place Moral Majority into historical context by comparing it with the Christian Anti-Communism Crusade of the 1960s. Using American National Election Survey data from 1964 and 1984, he shows that the Crusade attracted a core of secular supporters, and that the religious supporters of the Crusade were politically rather moderate. By contrast, Moral Majority attracted virtually no secular support, and its religious supporters were consistently conservative.

373 Wilcox, Clyde. "Blacks and the New Christian Right: Support for the Moral Majority and Pat Robertson Among Washington, D. C. Blacks." *Review of Religious Research* 32 (1990): 43-55.
In this study, which is based on a telephone survey of Washington, DC area African Americans, it is suggested that there is surprising support among African Americans for two central Christian Right objects: Moral Majority and Pat Robertson. However, the bases of African American support differ for each. Support for Moral Majority is primarily derived from conservative attitudes on political issues, while Robertson's African American support is based on religious attitudes.

374 Wilcox, Clyde. "Religion and Politics Among White Evangelicals: The Impact of Religious Variables on Political Attitudes." *Review of Religious Research* 32 (1990): 27-42.
Might religious belief bring about attitude constraint (of the sort introduced by Philip Converse)? Wilcox shows that religious variables are important predictors of political attitudes, even among a very homogeneous sample of white evangelicals. Different aspects of religion affect different political attitudes. Attitude constraint is best explained by exposure to the messages of religious elites.

375 Wilcox, Clyde. "Religious Sources of Politicization Among Blacks in Washington, D. C." *Journal for the Scientific Study of Religion* 29 (1990): 387-394.
African American churches are found to be important sources of political socialization. Attendance at churches in which the pastor conveys explicitly political messages, and pentecostalism, render African Americans in Washington, DC more supportive of collective action, more likely to participate in politics, and more supportive of Jesse Jackson.

376 Wilcox, Clyde. "Religion and Electoral Politics Among Black Americans in 1988." In *The Bible and the Ballot Box: Religion and Politics in the 1988 Election*, ed. by James L. Guth and John C. Green, 159-172. Boulder, CO: Westview Press, 1991.
Although African Americans were virtually unanimous in their support for Jesse Jackson in the 1988 presidential primaries, religion had several subtle effects on the political behavior of African Americans. Frequent attendees of charismatic churches were more enthusiastic about their support for Jackson, and both religious orthodoxy and frequent church attendance increased primary turnout. In the general election, having been "born-again" was associated with support for Dukakis among African American voters.

377 Wilcox, Clyde. *God's Warriors: The Christian Right in Twentieth Century America*. Baltimore: Johns Hopkins University Press, 1992.
Beginning with an historical overview of political activity on the part of conservative Protestants, Wilcox shows that there have been three main periods of evangelical activism in this century: the 1920s, the 1950s, and the 1980s. Wilcox shows that support for the Christian Right is not generally based on social pathologies such as authoritarianism, but can be explained as the mobilization of previously underrepresented groups in response to the perception of a politically threatening environment.

378 Wilcox, Clyde. "Race, Religion, and Abortion Attitudes." *Sociological Analysis* 53 (1992): 97-105.
A number of studies have shown that African Americans are significantly less supportive of legal abortion than are whites. Wilcox shows that racial differences in religiosity and doctrinal orthodoxy account for a large portion of this difference.

379 Wilcox, Clyde. "Religion and the Preacher Vote in the South: Sources of Support for Jackson and Robertson in Southern Primaries." *Sociological Analysis* 53 (1992): 323-331.
In an exploration based on the American National Election Study Super Tuesday Survey for 1988, Wilcox shows that Pat Robertson drew strong support from charismatics and pentecostals, but much weaker support from fundamentalists. This suggests that Robertson was unable to broaden a relatively narrow religious base. Among whites, Jackson drew strong support from doctrinally conservative members of mainline denominations, and very weak support from members of evangelical denominations who did not hold evangelical beliefs.

380 Wilcox, Clyde. "The Dimensionality of Public Attitudes Toward Church-State Establishment Issues." *Journal for the Scientific Study of Religion* 32 (1993): 169-176.
Using the 1987 Williamsburg Survey on attitudes toward church-state relations, Wilcox shows that most Americans value church-state separationism in the abstract, but are rather "accommodationist" regarding concrete applications of the Establishment Clause. Nevertheless, the data show substantial "vertical" constraint (connections between abstract principles and concrete applications) and "horizontal" constraint (strong relationships between several concrete applications). Structurally, the data support a one-dimensional solution and a three-dimensional solution about equally well.

381 Wilcox, Clyde. "Evangelicalism, Social Identity, and Gender Attitudes Among Women." *American Politics Quarterly* 19 (1993): 353-363.
Wilcox uses American National Election Studies data to investigate the social identities of evangelical women vis-à-vis those of non-evangelical women. The effects of paid employment on gender role attitudes are weaker for evangelical women than for their non-evangelical counterparts. This finding is explained in part by the fact that evangelical women tend to identify themselves as housewives and mothers. The effects of labor force participation for all groups of women appears to be mediated by social identification.

382 Wilcox, Clyde. "Premillenialists at the Millenium: Some Reflections on the New Christian Right in the Twenty-First Century." *Sociology of Religion* 55 (1994): 243-261.
In this piece, Wilcox offers a brief history of the Christian Right in the twentieth century and offers some reasons for the its failures in the 1980s. These include the saturation of direct-mail fundraising and the intolerance of ministers associated with the Bible Baptist Fellowship (who comprised most of the leadership of the organization). Wilcox argues that a newer organization, Christian Coalition, stands at a crossroads and must choose between strategies of mobilization and accommodation. Wilcox predicts that Christian Coalition will not succeed in dominating or substantially altering politics in the Republican Party.

383 Wilcox, Clyde, and Cook, Elizabeth Adell. "Evangelical Women and Feminism: Some Additional Evidence." *Women and Politics* 9 (1989): 27-56.
While evangelical women are generally more supportive of gender role traditionalism than other women, the authors find substantial support for gender equality among female evangelicals. Approximately one such woman in six exhibits a politicized feminist consciousness. However, support for the feminist movement is very weak among feminist evangelical women.

384 Wilcox, Clyde, and Gomez, Leopoldo. "The Christian Right and the Pro-Life Movement: An Analysis of the Sources of Political Support." *Review of Religious Research* 31 (1990): 380-398.
An examination of support for the Moral Majority and pro-life movement (as measured by feeling thermometers in a national survey) suggests that these two movements draw support from different populations. Evangelical Protestants tend to support Moral Majority, while Catholics tend to support anti-abortion movements. Evangelicals who attend religious services frequently tend to support both organizations, while irregularly attending evangelicals tend to support only Moral Majority. Supporters of pro-life organizations tend to be more moderate on other issues than Moral Majority supporters, while respondents who support both organizations tend to be quite conservative.

385 Wilcox, Clyde, and Gomez, Leopoldo. "Religion, Group Identification, and Politics Among American Blacks." *Sociological Analysis* 51 (1990): 271-285.
This study, based on a national survey of African Americans, shows that religion is an important source of black identification, but is only weakly related to attitudes toward collective action. Public religious observance is shown to be related to higher levels of political participation, and religion

generally increases satisfaction with the status quo among older African Americans.

386 Wilcox, Clyde, and Jelen, Ted G.   "Evangelicals and Political Tolerance." *American Politics Quarterly* 18 (1990): 25-46.
The authors use National Opinion Research Center data to investigate the perception that evangelical Christians are less tolerant than other Americans. Evangelicals are found to be less tolerant of nonconformists than other respondents, with fundamentalists and pentecostals being less tolerant than other evangelicals. This result is not explainable in terms of either the demographic characteristics of evangelicals, nor by group affect. Evangelicals are shown to be intolerant of unpopular groups associated with both the political "left" and "right."

387 Wilcox, Clyde; Jelen, Ted G.; and Leege, David C. "Religious Group Identifications: Toward a Cognitive Theory of Religious Mobilization." In *Rediscovering the Religious Factor in American Politics*, ed. by David C. Leege and Lyman A. Kellstedt, 72-99. Armonk, NY: M. E. Sharpe, 1993.
This study shows that religious self-identifications are important sources of political attitudes, which are arguably superior operationalizations to more denominational, doctrinal, or experiential measures. The analysis also suggests that a model of multiple identifications (including evangelical, fundamentalist, charismatic, etc.) is more plausible than grouping conservative Protestants into a broader, "evangelical" category.

388 Wilcox, Clyde; Linzey, Sharon; and Jelen, Ted G. "Reluctant Warriors: Premillenialism and Politics in the Moral Majority." *Journal for the Scientific Study of Religion* 30 (1991): 245-258.
Based on a survey of Moral Majority members in Indiana and Arkansas, this study addresses an apparent paradox: why should premillenialists, who believe that the Second Coming will result from societal crises, engage in political activity? The data suggest that Moral Majority members indeed experience considerable cognitive dissonance over the apparent inconsistency between their eschatological beliefs and their political activities.   Support for political action is increased by belief in an interventionist Devil, and the perception that one is carrying out an inevitable struggle between God and Satan.

389 Wilcox, Clyde, and Thomas, Sue. "Religion and Feminist Attitudes Among African-American Women: A View From the Nation's Capitol." *Women and Politics* 12 (1992): 19-37.
A survey of African Americans in Washington, DC shows that religiosity and doctrinal orthodoxy are related to "pro-life" attitudes on abortion, but are not associated with inegalitarian attitudes on gender role issues.

Indeed, some religious variables (associated with gender role conservatism among whites) occasion increased support for organized feminism.

390 Will, Jeffry, and Williams, Rhys. "Political Ideology and Political Activism in the New Christian Right." *Sociological Analysis* 47 (1986): 160-168.
Re-analyzing data originally gathered by Tamney and Johnson, the authors attempt to improve the explanatory power of religious television viewership on support for the Christian Right by distinguishing between viewership of political and nonpolitical programming. This strategy, however, does not strengthen the relationship between usage of religious television and Christian Right support.

391 Williams, Dorie Giles. "Religious Beliefs About Human Life and the Abortion Decision." *Review of Religious Research* 24 (1982): 40-48.
Williams investigates five hypotheses about the sources of anti-abortion attitudes among women. Among a sample of pregnant women, some of whom had made a decision to have abortions, the most important predictor of choosing an abortion was the woman's belief about the point at which human life begins.

392 Williams, Rhys, and Demerath, N. J. III. "Religion and Political Process in an American City." *American Sociological Review* 56 (1991): 417-431.
A case study of the relation between religion and politics in Springfield, Massachusetts, this article examines the tension between "civil religion" and the "separation of church and state." The authors describe three types of resolutions: "majoritarian," in which widely-held religious beliefs are regarded as "civil," rather than sectarian; "selective," in which church-state conflict is defined out of existence by very narrow definitions of both "religion" and "politics"; and "contingent," a category which applies to cases in which religious activists use religious symbols to enhance the legitimacy of their positions.

393 Wimberley, Ronald C. "Testing the Civil Religion Hypothesis." *Sociological Analysis* 37 (1976): 341-352.
In an effort to test Bellah's hypothesis of the existence of a distinct civil religion, the author develops multiple questions measuring civil religion. Factor and cluster analyses show that civil religious attitudes are in fact unidimensional, and are empirically distinct from the values of "church" religion.

394 Wimberley, Ronald C. "Continuity in the Measurement of Civil Religion." *Sociological Analysis* 40 (1979): 59-62.
Wimberley compares older empirical measures of civil religion with more contemporary items measuring such orientations. When both sets of measures are administered to a single sample, the items load on one dimension with a very high reliability. This finding strongly suggests that earlier and later measurement strategies in fact tap the same concept.

395 Wimberley, Ronald C. "Civil Religion and the Choice for President: Nixon in 1972." *Social Forces* 59 (1980): 44-61.
Wimberley's working hypothesis is that voters who espouse civil religious beliefs will be more likely to vote Republican. A survey of residents of North Carolina shows that adherence to civil religion was a very strong predictor of presidential vote choice in 1972. Wimberley provides an analysis of the role of the office of the presidency in American civil religion.

396 Wimberley, Ronald C., and Christenson, James A. " Civil Religion and Church and State." *Sociological Quarterly* 21 (1980): 35-40.
What is the relationship between civil religious attitudes and attitudes about the separation of church and state? A factor analysis of items measuring civil religiosity and general attitudes toward church-state separation in a survey of 3000 North Carolinians shows that civil religion is empirically independent of attitudes toward the religion clauses of the First Amendment. Apparently, separationist beliefs can coexist rather easily with high levels of support for civil religion.

397 Wimberley, Ronald C., and Christenson, James A. "Civil Religion and Other Religious Identities." *Sociological Analysis* 42 (1981): 91-100.
Wimberley hypothesizes that civil religious beliefs are homogeneous across religious preferences. A mail survey of North Carolina residents reveals that adherence to the tenets of civil religion are widespread, and generally unaffected by social characteristics. However, such beliefs are less common among Jews, Unitarians, and people with no religious preference. The results of this study thus suggest limits to the universality of civil religion in the United States.

398 Wimberley, Ronald C.; Clelland, Donald A.; Hood, Thomas C.; and Lipsey, C. M. "The Civil Religious Dimension: Is It There?" *Social Forces* 54 (1976): 890-899.
Here the authors attempt to operationalize the concept of civil religion. The results of a mail survey of participants in a Billy Graham Crusade show that civil religious sentiments are empirically distinct from other measures of religious commitment. Moreover, such attitudes appear unidimensional.

399 Woodard, J. David. "Evangelicals and the Media." In *Contemporary Evangelical Political Involvement: An Analysis and Assessment*, ed. by Corwin E. Smidt, 119-131. New York: University Press of America, 1989.
Woodard compares mass attitudes of fundamentalists and non-fundamentalists from survey data, and contrasts the empirical findings with what he takes to be a "dialectical" format imposed by the news media. He finds that the attitudes of both fundamentalists and humanists are far more diverse than the "simplistic" structure imposed by the media.

400 Woodrum, Eric. "Determinants of Moral Attitudes." *Journal for the Scientific Study of Religion* 27 (1988): 553-573.
An index of moral attitudes, ranging from "liberal-relativist" to "conservative absolutist," is found to be approximately normally distributed for a sample in a large Southern city. Church membership, denominational type, church attendance, exposure to religious programming, and political self-identification are found to be related to moral conservatism.

401 Woodrum, Eric. "Moral Conservatism and the 1984 Presidential Election." *Journal for the Scientific Study of Religion* 27 (1988): 192-210.
Using a survey taken in Raleigh, North Carolina, Woodrum shows that moral conservatism (an index of attitudes toward a variety of lifestyle issues) was a strong predictor of presidential vote in 1984. While less important than race, moral conservatism was substantially more powerful than gender in accounting for individual vote decisions.

402 Woodrum, Eric, and Bell, Arnold. "Race, Politics, and Religion in Civil Religion Among Blacks." *Sociological Analysis* 49 (1989): 353-367.
The authors explore the acceptance of civil religion by African Americans. An insignificant relationship between race and adherence to the tenets of civil religion becomes significant with the imposition of multivariate controls. Controls for socioeconomic status reveal African Americans to be less civil religious than whites. Black identity also exhibits a negative relationship with civil religiosity.

403 Woodrum, Eric, and Davison, Beth L. "Reexamination of Religious Influences on Abortion Attitudes." *Review of Religious Research* 33 (1992): 229-243.
This study, which is based on a survey of North Carolinians, shows that religious variables are quite important in accounting for attitudes toward legal abortion, and that the most important predictor of "pro-life" attitudes is sexual moralism. The power of religion is derived from the fact that there is no societal consensus on the abortion issue. Further, the public, unlike activists, do not seem polarized on this issue.

404 Woodrum, Eric, and Hoban, Thomas. "Support for Prayer in Schools and Creationism." *Sociological Analysis* 53 (1992): 309-321.
A telephone poll of eight North Carolina counties shows that there exists widespread support for the teaching of creationism and school prayer. Attitudes toward both issues are predicted by education, religious salience, and political conservatism. Beyond this, there are important differences in the bases of support for these two education issues. Support for the teaching of creationism is related to biblical literalism, while the base of support for school prayer is much more heterogeneous.

405 Woodrum, Eric, and Hoban, Thomas. "Theology and Religiosity Effects on Environmentalism." *Review of Religious Research* 35 (1994): 193-206.
The authors address the question of whether Christianity occasions conservative positions on environmental issues by engendering "dominion beliefs." Using data collected from telephone interviews in North Carolina, they show that a belief that God gave humankind dominion over the earth are relatively widespread, but that such attitudes are not significantly related to conventional measures of religiosity, such as religious salience or church attendance. It is thus unlikely that religion has strong political effects on the outcomes of environmental controversies.

406 Wuthnow, Robert. "The Social Significance of Religious Television." *Review of Religious Research* 29 (1987): 125-134.
Does religious television contribute to the "privatization" of American religion? The author's analysis of the results of a Gallup Poll suggests that religious television does not cause the privatization of religion; rather, viewing religious television reinforces pre-existing social and religious cleavages.

407 Yinger, J. Milton, and Cutler, Stephen J. "The Moral Majority Viewed Sociologically." *Sociological Focus* 15 (1982): 289-305.
This article is an effort to characterize supporters of Moral Majority. Using National Opinion Research Center data, the authors show that public support for positions taken by the Moral Majority were generally stable during the period 1973-1980, and whatever changes did take place decreased support for positions taken by the organization. Religiosity (measured by church attendance), age, and education were the best predictors of support for Moral Majority issue positions.

408 Young, Robert L. "Religious Orientation, Race, and Support for the Death Penalty." *Journal for the Scientific Study of Religion* 31 (1992): 76-87.
Different aspects of religion are related to attitudes toward capital punishment. Evangelism is related to opposition to the death penalty, while

fundamentalism is associated with support for capital punishment for whites.

409 Zwier, Robert. "Coalition Strategies of Religious Interest Groups." In *Religion and Political Behavior in the United States*, ed. by Ted G. Jelen, 171-186. New York: Praeger Publishers, 1989.
Interviews with religious lobbyists in Washington show that many such groups enter into political coalitions to accomplish political goals. Moreover, since such groups are rarely motivated by material incentives, the "costs" of coalition participation are rarely considered by religious activists.

Title Index

"An Exploration of the Attributional Styles of Christian Fundamentalists and Authoritarians," 230

"The Fact and Form of Born-Again Religious Conversions and Socio-Political Conservatism," 056

"Factors Influencing Vote for a Christian Right Candidate," 183

"Factors Related to Inconsistent Life-Views," 181

"Factors Related to Intolerance of AIDS Victims," 175

"Faith and Access: Religious Constituencies and the Washington Elites," 118

"Faith and Election: The Christian Right in Congressional Campaigns," 085

"Faith and the Environment: Religious Beliefs and Attitudes on Environmental Policy," 095

"Faith and Politics: Religion and Ideology Among Political Contributors," 090

"Family, State, and God: Ideologies of the Right to Life Movement," 251

"Feminism and Anti-Feminism Among Evangelical Women," 368

Feminism and the New Right: Conflict Over the American Family, 046

"The First Test of *Webster's* Effects: The Florida Church," 283

"Florida: Running Globally and Winning Locally," 342

"From Candidates to Agenda Setters: Protestant Leaders and the 1988 Presidential Campaign," 103

"From Lambs to Sheep: Denominational Change and Political Behavior," 083

"From Revolution to Evolution: The Changing Nature of the Christian Right," 248

"Fundamentalism and Economic Restructuring," 327

"Fundamentalism and Sexism: A Reanalysis of Peek and Brown," 273

"Fundamentalism, Christian Orthodoxy, and Intrinsic Religious Orientation as Predictors of Discriminatory Attitudes," 207

"The Importance of Purposes in 'Purposive' Groups: Incentives and Participation in the Sanctuary Movement," 121

"In Search of a Constituency for the 'New Religious Right'," 250

In Washington But Not Of It: The Prophetic Politics of Religious Lobby Groups, 125

"The Inevitable Failure of the New Christian Right," 030

"The Instability of Support for Televangelists: Public Reactions During a Period of Embarrassment," 131

"Institutional Stress: Journalistic Norms in the Catholic Press," 334

"An Interaction Analysis of Religious Television Programming," 255

"Intrinsic Religion and Authoritarianism: A Differentiated Relationship," 188

"Jewish Community Leaders and the 1988 Presidential Campaign," 224

"Jews and the 1988 Election: More of the Same?" 294

"Jews, Blacks, and the Democrats, 1984," 049

"Jews on the Left: The Student Movement Reconsidered," 223

Journal for the Scientific Study of Religion, 008, 042, 047, 051, 057, 079, 098, 101, 111, 113, 122, 123, 139, 143, 150, 154, 175, 177, 178, 182, 185, 188, 197, 203, 205, 207, 210, 230, 231, 235, 236, 240, 257, 260, 280, 284, 299, 309, 314, 316, 317, 328, 333, 346, 348, 352, 353, 359, 366, 375, 380, 388, 400, 401, 408

Journal of Political Science, 086

Journal of Politics, 081, 085, 110, 134, 159, 221, 278, 293, 349, 360

"The Kanawha County Textbook Controversy: A Study in the Politics of Life Style Concern," 261

"Knowing God's Many People: Denominational Preference and Political Behavior," 194

"Knowledge and Attitudes of Catholic College Students Regarding the Creation/Evolution Controversy," 234

Name Index

Subject Index

About the Compilers

LAURA R. OLSON is an Assistant Professor of Political Science at Clemson University. She received her Ph.D. in political science from the University of Wisconsin-Madison.

TED G. JELEN is Professor and Chair of Political Science at the University of Nevada at Las Vegas. His recent books include *The Political Mobilization of Religious Beliefs* (Praeger, 1991) and *The Political World of the Clergy* (Praeger, 1993). He is also the editor of *Religion and Political Behavior in the United States* (Praeger, 1989), *Perspectives on the Politics of Abortion* (Praeger, 1995), and co-editor of *Abortion Politics in the United States and Canada: Studies in Public Opinion* (Praeger, 1994).

William J. Fellner

William J. Fellner

A BIO-BIBLIOGRAPHY

James N. Marshall

Bio-Bibliographies in Economics, Number 1

GREENWOOD PRESS
Westport, Connecticut • London

Library of Congress Cataloging-in-Publication Data

Marshall, James N.
    William J. Fellner : a bio-bibliography / James N. Marshall.
      p. cm.—(Bio-bibliographies in economics, ISSN
  1063-3197 ; no. 1)
    Includes bibliographical references and index.
    ISBN 0-313-25856-2 (alk. paper)
    1. Fellner, William John, 1905- . 2. Economists—United States—
  Biography. 3. Economics—United States—Bio-bibliography.
  I. Title. II. Series.
  HB119.F45M37 1992
  330'.092—dc20   92-15462
  [B]

British Library Cataloguing in Publication Data is available.

Library of Congress Catalog Card Number: 92-15462
ISBN: 0-313-25856-2
ISSN: 1063-3197

First published in 1992

Greenwood Press, 88 Post Road West, Westport, CT 06881
An imprint of Greenwood Publishing Group, Inc.

The paper used in this book complies with the
Permanent Paper Standard issued by the National
Information Standards Organization (Z39.48-1984).

10 9 8 7 6 5 4 3 2 1

dedicated to Valerie Korek Fellner,
whose kindness and assistance were invaluable

Contents

Preface

William J. Fellner had a very remarkable life. He compressed much into one lifetime. He was a respected academic economist, a policy adviser, and a highly regarded member of the public policy research establishment. Any one of these three roles would have been sufficient for a lesser man. Throughout every phase of his career, Fellner wrote, and wrote. The volume of his work is enormous, and its range vast. It is a sobering and formidable task to review Fellner's work. Daunting though the challenge was, I believe that I have successfully captured his life and work in this book. In writing it, I have kept two considerations uppermost in my mind. The first is that this book be useful to the professional economist, and the second that it be accessible to the non-specialist, and I am convinced that I have succeeded on both counts. Any interested reader, of whatever background and training, will benefit from an examination of Fellner's work. Contained within it is the full sweep of contemporary economic thought. Furthermore, the student of his work, whether it be the technical aspects of the theory of economic growth or the political economy of the Keynesian Revolution, will find him at all times instructive.

This book is made up of three main chapters, the first of which is a biography of Fellner. Following a brief introduction, this biographical chapter is divided into five sections: his early life and education, the years at Berkeley, those at Yale, his service on the Council of Economic Advisers, and his work with the American Enterprise Institute.

The second chapter is an annotated bibliography of Fellner's published works, and is divided into four numbered sections. The first section covers his eight books, one of which he co-authored; the second his prodigious output of articles and essays. The third covers the books he either edited or co-edited. The fourth section presents the remarks he made in a variety of public forums, including speeches, interviews, and testimony before the Senate. Within each numbered section, his works are presented chronologically. Other ways of ordering the presentation were considered (they could, for example, have been arranged by subject). While approaches other than that taken in this book have merit, it was felt that a chronological presentation has the important advantage of affording the reader great ease in locating specific works as the biographical portion of the book is read.

My coverage of Fellner's work is almost, but not quite, exhaustive. Nearly every work by Fellner is contained within the second chapter; every work of major consequence is included. Dr. Fellner wrote in many languages. Some of his articles and essays written in foreign languages are available in English, and others I have been able to translate. But the press of time made it impossible to translate others, written mainly in German. These include one very early journal article, and a few more recent pieces written for current periodicals in Germany. Aside from these, and they are quite small in number in relation to his total output, the annotated bibliography of the second chapter is comprehensive indeed.

The third and final chapter of this book is an annotated bibliography of works that are either about Fellner or about his ideas. In this latter category, for example, would fall journal articles by economists who drew their inspiration from some aspect of Fellner's work. No major works on Fellner exist. This book is unique in that sense. Before the publication of this book, only the bare essentials of Fellner's life were available. These are to be found in his obituaries, memorials published at the time of his death, Irma Adelman's entry in *The New Palgrave*, and my own biographical essay, all of which are reviewed in the third chapter of this book. This chapter also comprises those accounts found in the popular press which make reference to Fellner. He became a man of affairs after his appointment to the Council of Economic Advisers, and was very much in the public eye. This celebrity is reflected in the frequent mention he received in the major newspapers and weekly news magazines beginning in late 1973. The ordering of citations in this chapter is also chronological. Consideration was given to an alphabetical arrangement by author. But again, for the same reason noted above, a chronological ordering seemed best.

There is much to be admired in William J. Fellner's life. While he made no secret of his conservative orientation, his was never an unthinking conservatism. On the contrary, he was undogmatic and never ideological. His arguments were always respectful of evidence and based on reason. His views, though generally conservative, were at times unpredictable and not susceptible to easy categorization. An examination of his life's work demonstrates that the controversies that sometimes divide economists can be quite subtle and often elusive. To understand Fellner's work is to come to the realization that economists share far more in common than what is at times suggested by their public debate.

Acknowledgments

I have incurred many debts in writing this book. Two of those debts deserve mention here. The first is owed to Mrs. Valerie Korek Fellner. She has maintained a personal library of her late husband's works. Many of these would have proven very difficult, others impossible, for me to obtain. She has also taken care to preserve much of Dr. Fellner's correspondence. She granted me complete access to these materials, and for this I shall be forever grateful. One unexpected pleasure that arose from my work on this book has been my visits with Mrs. Fellner in Washington, D.C. While my study of Dr. Fellner's formal writing has given me a sense of him as a professional economist, it was his correspondence, and most especially, my conversations with Mrs. Fellner that allowed me to develop a fuller appreciation for the man. My discussions with her have provided me with many details of his life which would have been otherwise unobtainable. Her generous cooperation has made it possible for me to offer a far richer portrait of a very accomplished man.

My other large debt is to Dr. Robert Wind, Professor of Classics and Chair of that department at Muhlenberg College. He is greatly beloved by his colleagues for his wit and wisdom, and also highly regarded for his complete and utter mastery of word processing. I have profited much from his wit and wisdom over many years, but it is to his wizardry as word processor that I must pay homage here. Eternally in his debt, I know full well that these words would never have met a single reader's eyes without his cheerful and patient assistance.

Chronology

1905	Born May 31, 1905 in Budapest, Hungary.
1926	Left his law studies at the University of Budapest to undertake technical study in Zurich.
1927	Earned a diploma in chemical engineering from the Federal Institute of Technology in Zurich.
1928	Made his first visit to the United States.
1929	Completed his Ph.D. in economics with high honors at the University of Berlin.
1929-38	Engaged as a partner in the family manufacturing enterprises in Hungary.
1934	A second visit to the United States deepens his impression that it affords great opportunity.
1936	Married Valerie Korek in Budapest.
1938	Left Hungary to settle in California.
1939	Joined the faculty of the University of California at Berkeley as a lecturer in economics.
1942	First book published, *A Treatise on War Inflation*.
1944	Became a citizen of the United States.
1946	*Monetary Policies and Full Employment* published.
1947	Promoted to rank of Full Professor at Berkeley.
1950-51	Spent academic year as Visiting Professor at Harvard University.
1952	Left Berkeley to join faculty at Yale University; made honorary member of Phi Beta Kappa.
1956	*Trends and Cycles in Economic Activity* published.
1957-58	Spent academic year as Alfred Marshall Lecturer at Cambridge University.
1959	Named Sterling Professor of Economics at Yale.

1959-60	Appointed and participated as member of the Group of Independent Experts on Rising Prices for the Organization for European Economic Cooperation.
1962-64	Served as economics department chair at Yale.
1964	Began participation as original member of the Bellagio Group.
1969	Elected President of the American Economic Association.
1970	Began his formal association with the AEI as an Adjunct Scholar.
1971	Returned to his native Hungary for the first time since 1938.
1973	Retired from Yale as Sterling professor emeritus in July and began as an AEI Resident Scholar; took leave of absence from the AEI upon nomination and confirmation as member of the Council of Economic Advisers (CEA); oath of office administered on October 31.
1974	On September 24 announced plans to leave the CEA.
1975	Resigned from the CEA on February 25; rejoined the AEI as a Resident Scholar.
1976	Conceived and began direction of the AEI's annual *Contemporary Economic Problems* series; *Towards a Reconstruction of Macroeconomics* published.
1977	Festschrift published in his honor.
1979	Awarded the Commander's Cross of the Order of Merit of the Federal Republic of Germany on January 8.
1982	Received the Bernhard-Harms Prize of the Institute of World Economics at the University of Kiel, West Germany on June 26.
1983	Died on September 15 in Washington, D.C.

CHAPTER I
Fellner Biography

INTRODUCTION

William Fellner was a man of accomplishment at every level open to the professional economist. As an academic economist, he was a prolific author, with a mountain of professional articles and books to his credit. The breadth of his interest was also vast, and he has left his imprint in several major areas of the economics discipline: macroeconomic theory, oligopoly theory, economic growth, decision theory, and macroeconomic policy, to name a few. Some of his work has found, and will continue to find, a permanent place in the economics literature. Perhaps the greatest tribute to the enduring importance of his scholarship is that new work by a new generation of scholars continues to make reference to and be informed by his output.

Fellner received the ultimate accolade that his American peers can bestow. In recognition of his many and varied contributions to the profession, he was elected president of the American Economic Association in 1969. But in a sense his career had hardly begun. Much more was to follow, and by the end, the only major honor to elude him was the Nobel Prize. At an age when most people retire, Fellner left the academic world, only to begin a new career. In 1973, at the age of sixty-eight, he accepted appointment to the Council of Economic Advisers (CEA) at a time when policy advisers in the executive branch needed to re-establish their credibility with the public. It was a testament to the respect which Fellner was accorded by fellow economists that in this time of need he was chosen. "Blunt," "independent" and "outspoken" were the words used to describe him. Although he was clearly conservative, his nomination was universally praised within the community of academic economists. Some claimed him to be the most distinguished economist ever appointed to the Council. His role from the beginning of his tenure was unusual. His was a very public, a very visible role, at times bordering on celebrity. This was all the more unusual given that he was but a member of the Council, not its chair.

At the time of his selection for the Council, Fellner had just retired from Yale University, and was looking forward to his participation as a Resident Scholar at the American Enterprise Institute for Public Policy Research (AEI). After his resignation from the Council in 1975, he was finally able to devote his full energies to the work of the AEI, and begin yet another career. Here he spent the rest of his life in the public arena engaged in open debate over the course of macroeconomic policy. The issue of the day was inflation. In the public discourse, he led his colleagues at the AEI in offering in friendly competition a conservative counterpoint to the views of the more liberal Brookings Institution.

Fellner's public service went beyond his tenure on the Council. He was a regular consultant with the Treasury Department for twenty-five years, and frequently advised the Board of Governors of the Federal Reserve System and the Congressional Budget Office. By the end of his life, he had no enemies. All who had known him, including those who had profoundly disagreed with him, felt that they had lost a dear friend. Though surely remembered for his intellectual brilliance and prodigious scholarly output, his special place in the minds of those who knew him well was assured by the respect and fairness he accorded to the ideas of others, whether he was in agreement with them or not. To him the outcome of the economic debate mattered, but the manner in which that debate was conducted was also important.

LIFE IN HUNGARY: EDUCATION AND EARLY CAREER

William John Fellner was born the youngest of four brothers and one sister, into a wealthy and successful manufacturing family on May 31, 1905 in Budapest, Hungary. The various family enterprises were founded by his grandfather in the 1860's, and included manufacturing businesses in the sugar, alcohol and paper industries.

Following a custom widely practiced among prominent Jewish families in the Central Europe of that day, William was baptized a Christian. This was undoubtedly an attempt to provide some protection to young William against the ravages of anti-Semitism so common in that time, and in no way implied a serious religious commitment. Fellner attended a Lutheran Gymnasium, and received a classical education. His studies emphasized Latin, mathematics, history and the sciences.

Upon his graduation, he spent one year working in one of the family-owned factories.

Fellner entered the University of Budapest to study law, remaining there but one year. Given the technical nature of the businesses run by the family, his father had prevailed upon him to undertake the study of engineering. In 1926 he withdrew from the University of Budapest, and took up study at the famous Federal Institute of Technology in Zurich. He earned a diploma in chemical engineering from the Institute in 1927.

The time spent in Zurich had an important influence on Fellner, largely as a result of two very close friendships with fellow Hungarians who were also in attendance at the Institute. He befriended Emery Reves, at whose insistence he was convinced to attend his first economics lecture at the Federal Institute. His other friendship, one that dated back to his high school years in Budapest, was with John von Neumann, the famed mathematician and economic theoretician. Fellner was immediately drawn to economics. Upon the completion of his engineering studies, he sought family permission to do advanced study in economics at the University of Berlin. There was some family reluctance to accede to this request, since the firm expectation for all four sons was a career in the family businesses. The agreement struck was that he could continue his studies at Berlin but would resume his role as a partner in the family enterprise when those studies were completed.

Fellner was accompanied to Berlin by his two friends. Reves had accepted employment with a Berlin newspaper, and in the immediate prewar years was to become a journalist of some renown. He became best known for his profiles and interviews of leading European political figures. Von Neumann had also enrolled at the University of Berlin to study mathematics. In 1929 Fellner received a Ph.D. in economics with high honors. He completed his degree with distinction and dispatch, at a time when the University of Berlin was an institution of worldwide reputation in many fields, including economics. Contemporaneous with Fellner's time there, the University could boast an economics faculty that included Werner Sombart, the noted economic historian and pampleteer, and Ladislaus von Bortkiewicz, a pioneer in the application of mathematics and statistics to economic analysis. One year before Fellner received his degree, the University of Berlin awarded a Ph.D. in economics to twenty-two year old Wassily W. Leontief, a future Nobel Laureate in economics who, like Fellner, left for America in the 1930's.

Fellner's dissertation examined the economic effects of Prohibition in the United States. This topic in applied microeconomics was in Fellner's mind a source of some embarassment in later years, though well-crafted, and partly to credit for his receipt of high honors. He was susceptible to the standards and pressures of a profession that holds in highest esteem those who engage in theoretical work. Whatever inadequacy he may have felt, Fellner surely was to make up for this imagined deficiency over the course of his career. However, his topic did have its agreeable side, since it necessitated his first trip to the United States in order to collect materials needed for the completion of his dissertation.

Having completed his Ph.D., William Fellner, as he had promised, rejoined his brothers as a partner in the family manufacturing enterprises in 1929. Willy, as he was called, was much younger than his three brothers, Paul, Alfred and George. He was especially close to Paul, the oldest, who had emerged as the leader within the family. Paul had some success in prewar Hungarian politics, winning election as a member of the Hungarian Parliament. After World War II, Fellner was instrumental in seeing that each of his three brothers was safely resettled in California. In Paul's case, this involved a dramatic escape by freightcar from Communist Hungary overseen by Willy.

These were good years for Fellner, who, as a bachelor, was able to indulge himself with his impressive collection of Hungarian art, and fluent in several languages, was able to travel widely. In 1934 he made his second visit to the United States, mainly for vacation purposes, and was treated to some of the grimmer realities of American life. One lasting recollection was the segregated black ghettoes he observed during a tour of Detroit. But this in no way dissuaded him from his very favorable impression of the United States as the land of opportunity, especially for young economists seeking academic careers. However, the demands of the family business increased in 1934 when his father died, and each of the brothers had to assume added responsibilities. Whatever plans he may have harbored for an academic career suffered a temporary derailment.

In January, 1936 Fellner married Valerie Korek in Budapest. She was learned in her own right, having earned a doctorate in philosophy, and was employed at the Budapest Public Library. She has maintained a lifelong interest in Hungarian poetry and literature with activities that include the editing of periodicals and reviews. The city of Budapest is divided by the Danube into the ancient twin cities of Buda and Pest. Valerie Korek was from the Buda side, the refined cultural center. The Fellners were from the Pest side of the Danube, the industrial, commercial side. And so this marriage represented the union of the industrious with the cultivated, a symbolism pointed out on occasion over the course of a long and happy marriage. In late 1936 a daughter, Anna, was born in Budapest.

Fellner remained very active in the affairs of the family business from 1929-38. The experiences and events of that period surely colored his later views. His distaste for government intervention in the economic sphere may in part have sprung from the abrupt takeover of one of the Fellner family businesses by Hungarian authorities. Both Paul Samuelson and Irma Adelman have suggested that

Fellner's unyielding opposition to any policy that carries the risk of inflation stemmed from his first-hand experience with the great German hyper-inflations. He did maintain a continuing interest in economics, which was pursued largely in informal ways. He had two business associates who shared his interest in economics, and they had regular weekly meetings which were devoted to discussion and debate. While his days were occupied almost exclusively with business matters, Fellner spent long evenings, often extending into the late hours, devoted to reading economics, primarily the academic journals. On occasion he was able to attend a professional economics conference. Gottfried Haberler has related that he first met Fellner in 1934 at a conference in Stresa, Italy, at which a youthful Friedrich A. von Hayek was also in attendance. Perhaps the single most important indication of the seriousness of Fellner's interest in an academic career was the fact that he had begun to be published in some leading journals. In 1937 he had an article published in *Zeitschrift fur National-okonomie*, an important European journal, and by early 1938 he had had an article accepted for publication in the *Review of Economic Statistics*, published by Harvard University.

Fellner never gave up his dream of becoming an academic economist. For him it was simply a matter of waiting for the most opportune time, determined mainly by the circumstances of the family business. By the late 1930's he was ready to make his move. This period coincided with a great exodus of European scholars, many of them Jewish, from the Continent as the onset of war appeared more likely. Fellner's plans seem to have been little influenced by this larger migration. He had long been intent on an academic career, and he was fully convinced that the future direction of the economics discipline would be dominated by British, and more especially, American economists. His two visits to the United States had led him to conclude that it would afford him the greatest opportunity.

THE BERKELEY YEARS: BUILDING A REPUTATION

Believing that American economists were going to lead the way in the economics profession, the Fellners left Hungary in 1938 to settle in California and establish an academic career for William. They were not to return to their native homeland until 1971. In 1939, he joined the faculty of the University of California at Berkeley as a lecturer in economics. The Fellners very quickly acclimated to their new life, although Valerie Fellner recalls that her husband did retain some of his Continental ways, including the routine of a leisurely lunch at home followed by a nap.

The time Fellner spent at Berkeley was very productive. He began to establish himself as a first-rate scholar, and entered into a rewarding collaboration with two colleagues in the economics department at Berkeley, Harold S. Ellis and Howard M. Somers. Fellner's writing during this period reflects a wide variety of interests. There were early technical articles on the theory of the interest rate. His work also addressed some of the issues that arose out of the development of Keynesian economics. This took the form of works which confronted questions of broad import, such as the susceptibility of advanced market economies to mass stagnation, and narrower technical issues, such as the plausibility of the Keynesian notion of the speculative demand for money. A theme repeated throughout the body of Fellner's work emerged at this early point. He was not willing to concede much to Keynes. He agreed that deep depressions do require the strong intervention of government. But such experiences are thankfully rare, and when they do occur, it is largely the result of the ineptitude of policymakers. Beyond some modest concessions, Fellner either held fast to views contrary to those espoused by Keynes, or where he saw merit in the Keynesian view, questioned its originality by finding equivalent insights in the work of others.

The decade of the 1940's was one of enormous personal and professional growth for Fellner. By 1941 he had become an assistant professor, rising rapidly through the academic ranks to attain the rank of full professor by 1947. In 1944 he had gained United States citizenship. His scholarly output continued to reflect his eclectic interests. His published works covered topics as diverse as external economies, bilateral monopoly, pricing behavior in the face of uncertainty, and oligopolistic collusion, and continued to reflect his strong interest in macroeconomic theory.

In July, 1941 the University of California organized its Bureau of Business and Economic Research to promote and assist research in the business and economics fields by university faculty. In late 1942 the first book published under the auspices of the Bureau appeared, and it was also assistant professor Fellner's first book, *A Treatise on War Inflation*. The book addressed a topic of immediate and obvious concern, gaining some recognition for Fellner with a few well-placed reviews expressing moderate enthusiasm. This first book treats the reader to the distinctive Fellner writing style, one that informed his written word throughout his career. To some, his style was heavy, convoluted, at times tedious, bordering on pedantic formality. Haberler has remarked that in curious contrast to his elegant and lucid speaking style, his writing was complex and involved. He prefers to attribute this to Fellner's acute awareness of the complicated nature of most economic problems and his aversion to oversimplification. While manifestly intricate, Fellner's writing style has a precision and rhythm that the interested reader quickly comes to appreciate.

It was Fellner's next book that distinguished him as a young economist to be reckoned with, one whose ideas deserved a national audience. By the time the Bureau of Business and Economic Research published his *Monetary Policies and Full Employment* in 1946, he was himself a member of the Bureau's governing committee. This book was widely reviewed in the best journals, and the response was very favorable. Fellner sounds some very familiar themes, ones that up until that point in time remained scattered in various of his journal articles, and ones that he was to repeat consistently throughout his career. The genesis of many of his most important ideas, expressed years later, can be found in this book. He again expresses his reservations about the Keynesian preoccupation with mass stagnation, a situation that he sees arising only in the company of gross incompetence on the part of government policymakers. With that said, Fellner does state that he is prepared to grant an enlarged role to government, presumably freed from its error, on those rare occasions when a genuine catastrophe befalls market capitalism. He firmly opposes a rigid full employment guarantee. If government were to make that kind of commitment, monopoly elements within the economy, labor unions and firms with some degree of market influence, would surely exploit their market power in such a setting. Wage and price setting behavior would become inflationary, and the guarantee could be preserved without inflation only if direct controls were imposed. This, to Fellner, is the ultimate disaster: a regimented society in which government bureaucrats decide the allocation of resources through their control over wages and prices, and radical institutional changes to a system that has served the Western democracies well, both economically and politically. This refrain may be the one most frequently sounded over the course of Fellner's long career. In *Monetary Policies and Full Employment* he offers a compromise solution to this dilemma: absent a deep depression, government should act to assure an "acceptable" level of employment with price stability by an appropriately stimulative monetary and fiscal policy. This stimulus would be applied at the first sign of the onset of a business contraction, and withdrawn when either investment spending revives or inflationary pressures develop. By avoiding a rigidly defined full employment guarantee, policymakers have room to maneuver should inflation become a problem. Inflation can be restrained without suffering the political discomfort of having to reverse policy against publicly announced employment targets. Perhaps more importantly, the freedom to combat inflation using the conventional prescriptions makes the adoption of wage and price controls a moot question. This set of policy recommendations has a decidedly Keynesian ring. Although the title of the book mentions only monetary policy, Fellner incorporates fiscal policy into his program. His approach is clearly one that accepts some degree of fiscal fine-tuning, a position that he would reject in later years. One component of the recommendations contained in his *Monetary Policies and Full Employment* that did survive the years, and which he never relented in advocating was the rejection of unemployment rate targets which could be achieved only at the risk of inflation. It is surely fair, but hardly damning, to point out that in this book, compared with his later work in which a more consistent policy direction was pressed, Fellner's policy views do suffer from a split personality.

A more generous reading of the policies advocated in *Monetary Policies and Full Employment* can be made, if the matter of consistency is set aside. This is the view expressed by Irma Adelman who chooses to call Fellner a limited Keynesian, whose warnings about the dangers of overexpansion were prophetic. She seeks to stress the sense in which his fears came to pass in the post-1965 period, when serious inflationary pressures developed at the same time that policy was in pursuit of some very ambitious employment goals. Gottfried Haberler, a longtime Fellner friend and associate at the AEI, also sees much to be admired in *Monetary Policies and Full Employment*. In 1946 the economics profession was still swept up in the Keynesian Revolution. The experience of the Great Depression had led to widespread acceptance of the belief that monetary policy was ineffectual. While control of the growth rate of the money stock could prove useful in restraining an overheated economy and encouraging non-inflationary growth, attempts to revive an economy mired in a deep depression by manipulating the money stock will fail. The phrase often used to describe this policy asymmetry is that "you can pull on a string, but you cannot push on one." This is the infamous liquidity trap of early Keynesianism, wherein the demand for idle balances is perfectly elastic. A central bank may conduct open market purchases and inject reserves into the banking system. But fear and uncertainty may prevent that newly created liquidity from being used by its holders to purchase bonds, and if bond prices cannot be bid up, interest rates cannot be bid down. Interest rate sensitive spending categories will not respond. Experience during the 1930's did nothing to weaken this argument. The decade witnessed the failure of monetary policy to restore anything resembling a return to normal conditions. The monetary authorities pumped reserves into the system. But a banking system ravaged by a prolonged crisis lent out very timidly, providing little impetus for an economic revival. Whether the weakness exhibited by monetary policy in the 1930's can be specifically attributed to the existence of a liquidity trap was and continues to be debated. By the 1940's many economists, if not completely accepting of the liquidity trap, were at least suspicious of the effectiveness of monetary policy. Fellner never accepted this prevailing attitude, and was fully prepared to reinstate monetary policy to its rightful place beside fiscal policy. The world was quickly becoming one in which there was only one useful policy lever, fiscal policy. As Haberler points out, Fellner's resuscitation of the importance of money came long before Milton Friedman and the monetarists mounted their counterattack on Keynesianism in the early 1950's. In the contemporary debate on macroeconomic theory and policy, few economists are willing to dismiss the role of monetary policy in economic stabilization, and Fellner's contribution in the restoration of money deserves to be remembered.

Haberler has also noted that the treatment Fellner gave to the microeconomic foundations of macroeconomics came decades before other economists recognized their importance. In *Monetary Policies and Full Employment*, he examines the effects of wage-price rigidities and non-competitive market structures on the processes of inflation and deflation.

Fellner demonstrated his versatility in 1949 with the publication of *Competition Among the Few*. After many years devoted primarily, though not exclusively, to macroeconomic issues, he turned his attention to microeconomics in a book that examined oligopoly. Its coverage is thorough, and the exposition largely nonmathematical. Much attention is given to presenting the existing body of oligopoly theory. Some refinements and extensions of the standard treatments are offered. By this time, a Fellner book warranted reviews in all the prestigious journals, and this one received the full treatment. George Stigler, price theorist and future Nobel Laureate, reviewed *Competition Among the Few* in the *American Economic Review*. He voiced some misgivings, as did other reviewers, and this book did not get the uniformly warm reception accorded Fellner's earlier two. The most notable feature of this book is its replacement of the restrictive Cournot-Edgeworth assumptions with a mathematical reaction function, making possible a more precise modeling of the mutual interdependencies that exist between oligopolistic rivals. But time has been kind to this book. The muted praise with which it was initially greeted has not prevented it from remaining a standard reference in the bibliographic citations of works published in the fields of oligopoly and market structure since 1949. Some admirers of the book have credited Fellner for bringing attention to the importance of non-price competition in oligopoly settings. "Competition" in an imperfect market structure suggests behavior quite different from that of the perfectly competitive model. While the highly stylized sense in which "competition" is used in perfect competition does not apply in an oligopoly situation, the notions of contest, rivalry and struggle can be very helpful in analyzing the market outcome in oligopoly.

Fellner's book promoted the wider use of these notions. More recently, respected microeconomist, James W. Friedman, has praised *Competition Among the Few* for its critique of the Cournot reaction function, and stated his belief that it can still be fruitfully read, since so many of the unsolved problems it identified remain untouched. Friedman believes that it was Fellner who coined the term "reaction function," which is now part of the permanent lexicon of the economist.

While Fellner continued to build his reputation as a macroeconomist throughout his years at Berkeley, the late 1940's were a time in which his scholarly interests reached out to embrace externalities, bilateral monopoly and oligopoly, and by the early 1950's, technological progress and economic growth, areas to which he would devote much effort in the coming years.

The atmosphere pervading the system of higher education in the State of California in the late 1940's was not an entirely healthy one. McCarthyism was about to move to centerstage on the American political scene. At about this time, the California State Board of Regents was considering the institution of mandatory loyalty oaths for all faculty in the state university system. Despite his conservative political instincts, this move was an uncomfortable one for Fellner. Aside from the immediate controversy surrounding the merits of mandatory loyalty oaths, faculty collegiality and morale understandably suffered under the weight of accusation and recrimination. The Fellners were distressed to see colleagues checking the political views of other faculty before making up guest lists for social events. But this inhospitable environment was not the only reason for Fellner's increasing restlessness with West Coast life as the decade of the 1940's came to a close. He had concluded that the major eastern academic institutions were more influential in setting the direction of economic policy. A move to the East Coast would afford him an opportunity to participate more closely in the public policy debate, and place him in a location more geographically convenient to the nation's capital should his hopes for a role in policy consultation be fulfilled. By 1950 Fellner's interest in fuller participation in the public arena led him to consider more seriously offers of academic positions at universities in the East, with added urgency no doubt provided by the increasingly disagreeable climate at Berkeley.

NEARER TO THE CENTER: YALE AND BEYOND

Fellner's growing reputation had earned him a visiting professorship at Harvard University for the academic year 1950-51. During that year, Lloyd G. Reynolds, the chair of the economics department at Yale University, had been successful in recruiting several prominent European-born economists, including Henry C. Wallich, who was to become a member of the Council of Economic Advisers in the Eisenhower Administration and later a Governor of the Federal Reserve, and Robert Triffin, the noted specialist in international economics. Reynolds was in the process of seeking out still more recruits. He made contact with Fellner during his stay as a visitor at Harvard, and offered him a professorship at Yale. Fellner quickly accepted, and arrived in New Haven for the start of the academic year in 1952.

James Tobin, a member of the Kennedy CEA, 1981 Nobel Laureate in economics and apotheosis of neo-Keynesianism, was a junior member of the Yale economics faculty in 1952, eagerly awaiting Fellner's arrival. Tobin's first encounter with Fellner had been a long distance correspondence between New Haven and Berkeley, when as a graduate student he had challenged a point in *Monetary Policies and Full Employment*. What excited Tobin about Fellner's appointment was that it was an indication that the administration of the university had made a commitment to build a first-rate economics department at Yale. Tobin has also noted that Yale made another important, though at the time not very visible, economics appointment in 1952. Arthur Okun, who later served on the Johnson CEA, assumed a junior faculty position that year. He began a productive interchange with Fellner that was transplanted from New Haven to Washington, D.C., when he moved to the Brookings Institution and Fellner joined the AEI. In a remembrance of Fellner's arrival at Yale, Henry C. Wallich reported that he was impressed with his firm rejection of wage and price controls, which were in place at that time during the Korean War and enjoyed some popularity with the general public and within academic circles. Fellner never wavered in his opposition to controls. Years later, some observers, seeing this same rigid opposition to incomes policy of any sort, even in its mildest forms, thought it an odd break from Fellner's more customary pragmatism.

The move East made it possible for the Fellners to resume their valued and longstanding friendship with John von Neumann, who had moved to America in advance of the Fellners and settled at Princeton University. This renewed friendship made the path between Princeton and New Haven a much traveled one for the two families. Around this time, Anna went off to study French at Radcliffe College, where she joined her intermittent childhood friend, Marina von Neumann, one year her elder and daughter of family friend John von Neumann. It was in 1971 that Marina, by then married and known as Marina von Neumann Whitman, became the first woman to serve on the President's Council of Economic Advisers. Upon her resignation from the Council, it was William Fellner, father of her friend Anna, who was to succeed her.

In the early 1950's Fellner continued to distinguish himself both within and beyond the academic community. In 1952 he was given honorary membership in Phi Beta Kappa. He continued to serve as a consultant to the U.S. Treasury Department. In 1956 one of his most important books was published, *Trends and Cycles in Economic Activity*. Fellner had been focusing mainly on macro- and microeconomics in the 1940's. The next decade saw him devote more of his energies to the question of economic growth by authoring numerous journal articles and one book, *Trends and Cycles in Economic Activity*, on the subject. One reviewer rightly pointed out that this book returns to the issues bearing on stable, sustainable long-run growth, the questions that concerned the classical economists and gave birth to economic analysis. Long-run economic growth had continued to occupy the minds of some of the great economic thinkers, including Karl Marx and Joseph Schumpeter. The Great Depression and World War II had diverted the attention of the economics profession from the subject of growth, and Fellner's book was just one of many signs of a rekindling of interest in a time-honored field.

Trends and Cycles in Economic Activity is probably best understood if it is recognized as an excellent synthesis of the existing corpus of work on economic growth, rather than as a work of original insights. This should not in the least detract from Fellner's effort, but was, in addition to his well-established capacity to produce original works, yet another example of his genius. His ability to take a body of knowledge that was diffused and widely scattered throughout the literature, and recast it as a unified whole was one of his virtues as a scholar. The coverage of this book is quite broad. It includes the technical and analytical aspects of trends and cycles, as well as related topics such as cyclical disturbances and policy. One unique feature of this book is a thirty-page chapter that provides what Fellner calls condensed narratives of every major economic downturn since 1825. The heart of the book is contained in its third part which describes the requirements to be met for uninterrupted growth. Many admiring readers, including Charles Schultze of the Brookings Institution, believe there is no finer statement of those requirements than what Fellner has given us. The factors governing the ability of an economy to offset the underlying tendency towards diminishing returns through a sufficient flow of technological and organizational improvements are described. The significance of the character of such improvements in light of relative factor scarcities is deftly treated in a lengthy appendix to the book's third part.

Fellner was rewarded for the continued excellence of his work, and by the late 1950's he began to get some well-deserved international recognition. He was named the Alfred Marshall Lecturer at Cambridge University for 1957-58, and he was also able to lecture extensively at Oxford University during his stay in England. His Marshall lectures and those at Oxford were devoted to the question of the relevance of the neutrality of money proposition and Say's Law in an economy experiencing growth. Fellner found that these two notions must be substantially modified if they are to have any meaning for a growing economy. He believed that the prosperity of the Western economies owed little to the notions implied by Say's Law. It was instead a result of the stream of technological innovation that those economies proved capable of generating. The views he expressed in his lectures made in England are nicely captured in an article published in *Oxford Economic Papers*. In 1959 he became Sterling Professor of Economics, an honor reserved for the very best of the Yale faculty. In 1959 Fellner was appointed by the Secretary-General of the Paris-based Organization of European Economic Cooperation (OEEC), Sir Robert F. Hankey, as a member of the OEEC's Group of Independent Experts on Rising Prices. This group was formed to study the problem of inflation in the Western economies, and its work culminated in the publication of *The Problem of Rising Prices* in 1961, which Fellner co-authored with five other economists of international reputation.

The late 1950's and early 1960's were a time during which Fellner's pedagogical and administrative duties at Yale mounted. He was known for his effectiveness in the classroom. According to James Tobin, he had a reputation for patiently searching for the kernel of truth or substance in even the most wayward remarks of his students. Fellner had perceived what he believed to be a serious gap in the undergraduate economics curriculum. He thought it important to inform the student of economics on the relationship between contemporary theory and its historical antecedents, as well as the manner in which economic analysis has been influenced by the changing problems it confronts over time. The existing structure of the economics major left these questions untouched, and he volunteered to organize a new two-semester course to remedy the deficiency. The result was a course which blended the history of economic thought and the scientific methodology, as it pertains to economic analysis, with contemporary economic theory, or, as Lloyd G. Reynolds viewed it, to treat modern economic analysis in historical perspective. This enabled the student to modify the model learned at the undergraduate level to account for subsequent theoretical developments, which would continue to occur long after the end of formal education. One of Fellner's concerns was that those who received some degree of training in economics often became captive to whatever the conventional wisdom was at the time of their exposure to economics. On the title page of his *Trends and Cycles in Economic Activity*, Fellner quotes the British economist, Sir Alexander Gray, who had written: "No point of view, once expressed, ever seems wholly to die; and in periods of transition like the present, our ears are full of the whisperings of dead men." This sentiment is reminiscent of the closing passage of *The General Theory of Employment, Interest and Money*, in which Keynes notes that practical men "are usually the slaves of some defunct economist," and that those in authority often "are distilling their frenzy from some academic scribbler of a few years back." These two men, Keynes and Fellner, with largely opposing points of view, did share the common fear that, as expressed by Keynes in his *General Theory*, "there are not many who are influenced by new theories after they are twenty-five or thirty years of age, so that the ideas which civil servants and politicians and even agitators apply to current events are not likely to be the newest." Fellner was committed to the eradication of this intellectual myopia, and his course for undergraduates at Yale was but one way in which he sought to give life to that commitment.

Fellner's lecture notes for this undergraduate course became the inspiration for his book, *Emergence and Content of Modern Economic Analysis*, published in 1960. It is the kind of *tour de force* that has become extinct in an age in which economics has become fascinated with specialization and technique. It is eclectic in its mode of presentation, and is at once a treatise on economic methodology, history, thought, modern theory and policy. There was little of importance that had occurred in the discipline of economics that did not receive attention in this unique book, which, in the words of its preface, seeks to avoid the harm which "may result from equipping the student with contemporary economic theory if they are not made aware of the fact that much of this theory will become outmoded in their own lifetime." Lloyd G. Reynolds has described this book as filled with penetrating insights into classical economic thought. Yet it is surprising that this book received so little notice. Perhaps so didactic a work from a scholar known for grander things was regarded as unworthy of his abilities. Whatever the reason, it remains an undiscovered treasure for the serious reader in economics. Fellner is able to accomplish admirably the task set out for this book: to show the field of economics to be alive, in a state of constant evolution; and to make explicit the political judgments that influenced the development of economic thought in the past, and those which inform the contemporary debate.

John F. Kennedy's election to the presidency in 1960 led to the appointment of several Yale economists, most notably James Tobin, to important posts in the newly formed administration. Fellner's views were far more conservative than those of these departmental colleagues, soon to be on their way to Washington. He offered his encouragement to them, perhaps with a tinge of envy, and did what he could to ease the burden on the economics department caused by their absence. Scholarship was the activity held dearest by Fellner, and he generously relinquished a good portion of the time he had available to devote to it in order to accommodate his colleagues. To ease the staff shortage, Fellner willingly accepted an increased teaching load, and when his turn came, assumed the position of department chair from 1962 to 1964.

Fellner's was a supple mind always ready to strike out in new directions. His lifelong friendship with John von Neumann surely meant that he was well acquainted with the field of decision-making under conditions of uncertainty. Though he had an interest in the effect of uncertainty on certain forms of economic behavior, and had done some writing in the area, his interests never went specifically to decision theory. This changed in 1961 when his interest in the field became far more direct. IIc was invited to participate in a symposium on decision-making sponsored by the *Quarterly Journal of Economics*, the results of which were published in its November, 1961 issue under the heading "Symposium: Decisions under Uncertainty." Fellner's newfound interest eventually inspired the authorship of four journal articles and a book, and brought him into debate with those who had given their entire careers to the field.

A large literature had developed around the idea of portraying a decision-maker's risk preferences in the form of a mathematically specified utility function. When confronted with the necessity of making a decision in the face of uncertainty, that is, one in which several outcomes are possible, the decision-maker, armed with the knowledge of his or her utility function (determined by posing a series of gambles or lotteries to the decision-maker), need only make a simple calculation. The utility of each possible outcome is weighted by its probability of occurrence, yielding an expected utility. If the expected utility is positive, the course of action being evaluated should be pursued. If alternative courses of action are being assessed, the one with the highest positive expected utility should be chosen. Whether or not it is used for comparative purposes, this approach takes account of risk since the utility function employed in the decision calculus is constructed to reflect the decision-maker's risk preferences. Work in this field proceeded rapidly in the postwar era amidst optimism that it would prove to be of great practical value. An elaborate apparatus was constructed around this framework, including a set of axioms that stipulated the conditions that must be met in order to assure that the decision-maker was acting rationally. One important distinction made concerning processes giving rise to probabilistic outcomes is that between risk and uncertainty. A risky outcome ordinarily implies one in which the outcome is probabilistic, but the underlying probability distribution is known. The toss of a fair coin would fall into this category, as do the insurable risks faced by insurance companies taking advantage of historical experience and the law of large numbers. But what of the circumstance in which the underlying probability distribution is not known? This can be called a situation characterized by uncertainty as opposed to risk, and it requires that the decision-maker formulate his or her own subjective probabilities. In cases such as this, it would not be unusual for the decision-maker's subjective probability beliefs to be quite precarious. For example, a variety of economic decisions may be contingent upon the state of the energy market. Assume the following possible states of nature: (A) the price of crude oil remains low and its flow to the industrialized nations is unimpeded; (B) the flow is unimpeded but the world oil cartel is able to enforce very high prices; and (C) world oil supplies are near to exhaustion with little hope for the development of suitable substitutes. The economic policy of a government, the capital expenditures of a firm, and the portfolio held by an individual investor would differ depending on which of the three states of nature occurs. It is possible to design a strategy appropriate to each state, but the ultimate success hinges largely on one's ability to perform a nearly impossible task, to assign reasonably accurate probabilities to the three states of nature. It was on this particular aspect of decision-making under uncertainty that Fellner made his entry into the field.

In his contribution to the *Quarterly Journal of Economics* Symposium, Fellner asserted that the rational decision-maker, when faced with an uncertain situation in which subjective probability beliefs are precarious, may "slant" or "discount" (revise downward) the probabilities used in calculating the expected utility of a course of action. These "semiprobabilities" will not sum to unity, thus violating one of the most cherished axioms of decision theory. Furthermore, Fellner reported that he had conducted experiments in which Yale undergraduates were confronted with situations involving uncertainty, and their behavior was in his view both rational and supportive of his concept of "slanted" probabilities. Critics were quick to point out that, according to the standard conventions governing the use of the decision-theoretic framework, Fellner's suggested approach could not be reconciled with the postulate of rationality. For the interested layman, the ensuing debate followed an all too familiar pattern in economics: it descended into the arcane. For the specialist, it turned on the clarification of certain technical issues: standard processes, randomization, asymmetrical probabilities, and so on. The debate was finally closed when Fellner co-authored an article with one of his critics, K.R.W. Brewer, which clearly stated their common area of agreement concerning when "slanting" is, and when it is not, consistent with rational behavior. Again, the discussion takes a technical turn, hinging on whether the decision-maker's choice is limited, and how such limitations are regarded. Fellner's approach may not have as wide an applicability as he orginally claimed, but he was successful in pointing to the need for generalizing the Savage axioms, which had hitherto gone unchallenged in decision theory.

Aside from his contributions to the literature directed to this debate, Fellner's interest in decision theory begot an article in the *Review of Economics and Statistics* in 1963 with some fresh insight, and a book, *Probability and Profit*, published in 1965. In his article, he makes explicit the operational utility and subjective probability concepts that underpin the mean-variance two-parameter portfolio selection models popularized by the work of Markowitz and Tobin. An increasing number of works had appeared in the economics literature owing some kind of debt to these models. Yet some of the basic concepts that sustained these models and their offspring in the literature had not been fully examined. Fellner demonstrates how the Markowitz-Tobin approach can be connected back to its roots in the quadratic utility function of a risk-averse investor by defining investment return as the surplus accruing to the benefit of the risk-taker and making use of his "slanted" probabilities in the event that subjective probability beliefs are precarious. He also extends his "reconnection" to examine portfolio diversification and efficiency. His most ambitious contribution to decision theory is his book *Probability and Profit*, a review of his previous work and an attempt to extend its use to new economic problems. His "slanted" probability becomes the centerpiece of a theory of profit in which the risk-averse investor is rewarded for engaging in activities with outcomes that can only be described in terms of his "semiprobability." Fellner goes on to use his model to explain several observed forms of economic behavior, but with less than complete success. Reviewers generally found the arguments made in this book unconvincing, feeling that it offered little additional explanatory power to existing theory. The most enduring feature of the book is its splendid bibliographical commentaries, to use Fellner's term. He selected fifty-two classic articles bearing on decision theory, going back two centuries to the seminal work of Bayes and Bernoulli. He provides a detailed annotation for every citation and takes care to connect each one to what is presented in the main text of his book.

Fellner's incursion into the previously comfortable and settled realm of decision theory is instructive. His formal background in the field was limited. Yet once he decided to contest the ideas of the specialists, decision theory was left changed, made better, more fully informed of its own promise and limitations. Few men have been able to roam so far and wide with such effect. But a final footnote must unfortunately be a discouraging one. Fellner's own interest in decision theory had flagged by the late 1960's. Perhaps his waning interest was a portent of what was in store for the field of decision theory. The early promise of utility theory and its application to decision-making under uncertainty never bore fruit. Not long after Fellner had permanently turned his attention to other questions, the hopes for a practical, applications-oriented decision theory had faded.

By the mid-1960's Fellner had developed a serious interest in the international payments system, an area in which he had done no formal writing. His versatility was to come to the fore again through his participation with the Bellagio Group. The Bretton Woods Agreement established a system of fixed exchange-rates in 1946. Periodically this system came under pressure as a result of divergent economic conditions in the various countries that were party to the agreement. These conditions often arose because countries pursued different economic policies, and the lack of policy coordination would ultimately put the fixed rate structure under stress. The early 1960's was a time when the chronic problems associated with the payments system entered into another acute episode. As related by Haberler, the Kennedy Administration, under the direction of Treasury Secretary Douglas Dillon, decided to begin a major study of the international monetary system. Major trading nations and representatives of key international institutions would be invited to participate. However, the study would be conducted without the quarrelsome assistance of academic economists, who, it was felt, never sufficiently agreed on anything, and so had little to offer the policymaker in need of very specific advice. To counter this view, Fellner joined with Fritz Machlup of Princeton University and Robert Triffin, a Yale colleague, to organize a group of academic economists, eventually numbering thirty-two, to consider the problems of the international monetary system. Their first meeting was held in Bellagio, Italy, at a villa left to the Rockefeller Foundation. Thus, the group was thereafter called the Bellagio Group. The purpose of this and subsequent meetings was to convince government officials that, although differences among academic economists were inevitable, there did exist a consensus on how to proceed in solving international payments problems. Fellner was on the forefront of this effort. Lines of communication between the governmental study group and the committee of academics were forged. Beginning in 1964, joint conferences between the academic economists and the central bank and finance-treasury officials from the Western governments were held on a regular basis, and this larger gathering then became known as the Bellagio Group. Keen observers noted with irony the admission of government officials into this study group, given that officialdom was originally intent on completing its agenda without the assistance of academia. It is widely believed that these joint meetings were instrumental in convincing the governments of the West that there was no alternative to a shift from the system of fixed exchange-rates to one of flexible rates.

Fellner believed that the collaboration required among governments to manage a fixed rate system imposes intolerably high burdens on policymakers. He was an early supporter of flexible exchange-rates, but his advocacy was cautious. He feared the dangers posed by the transition period. If the move to complete flexibility were too rapid, economic disruptions could result that might sabotage the eventual return to fully flexible rates. He favored a gradual increase in exchange-rate flexibility. In policy terms, he urged that the fixed rate system be reformed to permit a wider band around which a currency could vary, and a shiftable-parity level that would enable currencies to respond to larger exchange-rate pressures. He did not view such reforms as permanent features of a new system of international payments. These were always temporary halfway measures, intended to smooth the path to the ultimate goal: market-determined exchange-rates. During the period leading up to the suspension of gold convertibility in 1971 and the introduction of controlled floating in 1973, Fellner continued to call for such changes as a system of band-and-crawl flexibility, and the initiation of limited flexibility beginning with the stronger currencies. Fellner did not favor the restoration of the gold standard. Believing the factors governing gold production highly uncertain, he could see no near-term alternative to a responsibly managed fiat money. Technical issues were not at the core of his faith in flexible rates. It was his belief that with floating rates the possibility of a declining exchange-rate provided less disciplined policymakers with an incentive to refrain from inflationary demand-management policies. For a competent government intent on assuring price stability, it would be easier to resist pressures against its policies with a system of flexible exchange-rates.

By the late 1960's Fellner had long been recognized for his work in economic theory, at both the macro- and micro- levels, and economic policy. He had in less than ten years built a reputation in two new specialities, decision theory and international monetary economics. The move to Yale had made possible greater collaboration with the very best in his profession, as well as increased consultative activities with government agencies. He was literally at the top of his profession, and fittingly, he was elected president of the American Economic Association in 1969. Bestowed by his peers, it was this achievement that gave him the greatest personal satisfaction in a long and distinguished career. The highlight of his term in office was his presidential address delivered at the eighty-second annual meeting of the association, held that year in New York on December 29, 1969. His topic concerned the activities that generate technological progress. While Fellner wished to use economics to solve problems, Herbert Stein has cited the opening sentences of his presidential address to show that economics meant more to him than just problem-solving. There were the joys of knowing, of understanding and of explanation as an end in itself. Fellner began his address: "Much of mankind's accumulated knowledge performs functions other than that of increasing our command over goods and services in the usual sense of these words." He continued by saying that the contributors to our knowledge have "been motivated largely by a desire to improve their understanding of the world into which they were born," and that harnessing that knowledge for solely materialistic purposes would provide "an unduly drab account of man's quest for knowledge."

By 1970 Fellner had established important contacts within the policymaking community, and his association with the AEI in Washington, D.C. had begun. His travel between New Haven and Washington became so frequent that he decided to maintain a residence in both cities, a practice which he was to continue even after his retirement from Yale. His more frequent contacts with top administration officials led to his inclusion in an AEI study group that met in the summer of 1970 with Paul McCracken, who was then chair of the Council of Economic Advisers in the Nixon Administration and also had a longstanding relationship with the AEI. The purpose of McCracken's consultations with this group of AEI economists was to assist in the identification of policy areas in which AEI study would be helpful. The result of this effort was a volume of essays, *Economic Policy and Inflation in the Sixties*, published by the AEI in 1972 and a forerunner to its annual *Contemporary Economic Problems* series. This volume reviewed the policy mistakes of the 1960's, and offered recommendations for the future conduct of policy. Fellner contributed the introduction and an essay. His essay revealed policy views that were to figure importantly in his CEA service, and which would undergo added refinement later during his tenure at the AEI. Fellner believed that the use of demand-side management, that is, expansionary monetary and fiscal policies, in the pursuit of unrealistically low unemployment rate targets inevitably results in chronic and accelerating inflation, and that this had been the key policy failure in the post-1965 period. As inflation worsens, he thought government would have to shift to a policy of restraint. But the rise in unemployment and the lost output would then lead to a return to a stimulative posture, and the cycle of stop-go would repeat itself. According to Fellner, wage and price controls would then be enacted to cure the inflation problem, giving policymakers free rein to use demand-side stimulation to restore full employment. However, as a firm advocate of a market-based economy, he was convinced that such controls do great damage to an economy that relies on market-determined prices to allocate its resources in a way consistent with the demands of its society; to intervene in this delicate communciations system between consumers and producers is to inhibit the ability of a market economy to bring prosperity and assure continued improvement in the material standards of life. Aside from the shortages and distortions they might introduce into the economic system, Fellner saw wage and price controls as a nightmare to administer. As legitimate appeals are heard from those unfairly affected, a program of controls with originally benign intent will edge towards chaos. Fellner warned that to restore some semblance of order to the control program it would become necessary to implement a more rigidly enforced system of controls. His political instincts told him that when bureaucrats, well-intentioned though they may be, make economic decisions heretofore reserved to the individual, then all has been lost. In his mind, economic controls never represented a viable policy option. Their vigorous application will ultimately lead to a regimented society in which our most basic freedoms have been abrogated. But Fellner's message was that this path need not be taken. He argued that there is no substitute for price stability in a market economy; it is the *sine qua non* for the proper functioning of a system in which prices convey useful information. Fellner further argued that the rejection of inflationary policies in favor of demand restraint need not mean that policymakers ignore the employment burdens imposed on certain disadvantaged segments of society by the restoration of price stability. His views can be safely called conservative, including the belief that inflation was the major menace threatening the continuation of American prosperity. But he was not doctrinaire in those views. His essay also revealed an appreciation for what it takes to make policy recommendations politically feasible. He had proposed what he called his "second-best" solution: a policy of monetary and fiscal restraint to assure non-inflationary growth combined with a government-subsidized jobs program to provide work for those whose employment prospects are harmed by a policy aimed at non-inflationary employment goals. These ideas were not new to Fellner; their genesis can be traced back to his *Monetary Policies and Full Employment*. They had been and would continue to be refined. But most importantly at that time, they were gaining attention within very influential circles. During this same period, he took the battle directly to the enemy with a 1971 article in the *Brookings Papers on Economic Activity*, a respected publication of the AEI's archrival Brookings Institution. He took aim at the theoretical superstructure which supported the notion that policymakers can in fact choose from a menu of inflation-unemployment combinations, the infamous Phillips Curve. In the main, this trade-off suggests that higher employment goals are achievable at the price of accepting a higher, though reasonably predictable, rate of inflation. Fellner rejected the existence of such a stable trade-off. He took a position that came to be known as the Accelerationist View, a view more widely associated with Milton Friedman and Edmund Phelps. According to this view, attempts to reduce the rate of unemployment below what is warranted by labor market conditions through the use of expansionary monetary and fiscal policies will provide a temporary stimulus, with output rising and employment increasing. However, wage and prices pressures will develop, especially if monopoly elements exist in the form of strong labor unions and firms with market power. An inflationary episode will ensue, which, through a new round of wage and price increases, will remove the profitability from the situation generated by the initial macroeconomic stimulus. Employment will return to its original level, but the new higher rate of inflation will persist. In the long-run, a demand-side stimulus has but one lasting effect, an acceleration of inflation, the result of the failure of policymakers to recognize the ultimate effect of a policy that creates excessively tight labor markets.

In 1971 the Fellners made their first visit to their native Hungary since their departure in 1938. Much had happened in Hungary in the intervening years: a world war, the Communist take-over, and the uprising of 1956. On the personal level, Fellner took satisfaction in knowing that he had been able to bring all four of his brothers to the safety of the United States in the aftermath of World War II. His return to Hungary in 1971 had been the outgrowth of his acquaintance with a Hungarian government ministry official who had spent six weeks in an exchange program at Harvard University. This official suggested that he would like to reciprocate by sponsoring a six week tour of Hungary for Fellner and his wife. Fellner had not been outwardly sentimental when it came to his homeland. He had made it a routine practice to refuse all invitations to attend public functions at the Hungarian Embassy in Washington. He had not been active with any Hungarian-American organizations, although in 1974, after his CEA appointment, the American Hungarian Foundation presented him with its first annual Abraham Lincoln Award. Unlike Valerie Fellner, he was not inclined to admit openly to a burning desire to return to his native soil. But when the offer for a visit came, he accepted, though viewing it as another exchange, not a pilgrimage.

For Valerie Fellner, their return to Hungary was a stirring experience, bringing with it a flood of memories of their early life there. On the exterior, Fellner allowed himself no such feelings, except, according to Valerie Fellner, for one brief moment of sentimental reflection as he watched the barges ply the Danube from the balcony of their hotel room in Budapest. However, his personal correspondence with friends in the United States during his visit leaves a very different impression. Those letters reveal a person genuinely engaged in the visit, and were filled with vivid descriptions of everything from the luncheon menu at the best restaurant in Budapest to such cultural attractions as the museum in the Buda section of the capital, the latest news on an archeological dig, and the best place to find good Gypsy music. The rural scenery and familiar cityscapes had to his eye kept their beauty.

Fellner had a penchant for secrecy. He later warned friends not to carry his letters from Hungary should they visit. He cautioned the tourist to be tactful in choosing a subject for conversation and careful in deciding with whom to speak. While no subjects had been off limits in closed sessions with other academics in Hungary, he had himself been circumspect in the selection of topics for public discussion, sticking mainly to American economic problems. His only difficult moments came in television and newspaper interviews, when he felt expected to respond in a way favorable to the state, but he was able to avoid graciously any such endorsements. To him, the Hungarian people had retained their dignity and seemed willing to speak openly about their problems. He believed that men and women of ability and courage were pressing for economic and political reforms. The standard of living, while low by Western standards, had improved, and the distribution of wage and salary income was surprisingly similar to that in the United States. There were shortages of prized commodities and foreign-exchange, as would be expected in an East-bloc country, and public services were in a sorry state. But conditions were measurably better than in the Soviet Union.

Fellner's return in June, 1971 had its triumphant side. Under the sponsorship of the Institute of Economics of the Hungarian Academy of Sciences, he had been scheduled to address an assemblage at the University of Budapest. His hosts were caught unawares by his unexpected popularity. A modest lecture hall was reserved for what would surely be a small gathering to hear this conspicuously conservative, and somewhat obscure, expatriate. Long before his lecture was to begin, the hall had filled to capacity, this to the great consternation of those enthusiastic arrivals who had the misfortune to show up shortly before the publicly announced starting time. A mad scramble to accommodate this overflow audience ensued. To their relief, embarassed officials were able to move the site of Fellner's address to the largest lecture hall at the University of Budapest.

Fellner had been pleasantly surprised at both the enthusiasm his fellow Hungarians had for the macroeconomic debate going on in the West, and the interest shown in his public appearance in Budapest. He did not disappoint his audience that June evening. His address touched on themes that had occupied much of his time recently. He explained his rejection of the Phillips Curve trade-off between unemployment and inflation. Attempts in the United States to push unemployment down to 4%, when full utilization was consistent with a higher rate, had led to a chronic and accelerating inflation. He expressed his preference for reaching more ambitious employment goals through a public sector jobs program, not inflationary demand-side management.

AT THE CENTER: SERVICE ON THE COUNCIL

The United States had proven reluctant to acknowledge the responsibility of government to work to assure the proper functioning of the macroeconomy. The long decade of the 1930's brought with it one of the defining experiences of American history: the Great Depression. Half-hearted and ineffectual attempts were made to end it, but it was the vast spending on armaments during World War II that finally provided relief. At the conclusion of the war, there were fears of a return to the stagnation of the 1930's. With the passage of the Employment Act of 1946, government recognized its obligation to prevent such a recurrence. In the language of the legislation, it is the declared policy of the Federal Government "to promote maximum employment, production, and purchasing power." Beyond its declaration of policy, the Act provided for the establishment of a Joint Economic Committee of the two Houses of Congress and the creation of a Council of Economic Advisers. The duties of the Council would include assisting in the satisfaction of another provision of the Act, the preparation of the annual Economic Report of the President to be submitted to the Congress.

The Council of Economic Advisers has evolved over time. Its original policy advisory role has become one of strong advocacy in some administrations. The peak of its influence on macroeconomic policy was probably during the Kennedy-Johnson Administrations, when Keynesianism reached its high tide with the tax cut of 1964. The three members of the Council have been drawn largely from the community of academic economists. There has always been a natural tension between these academics and the politicians who appoint them. Advisers accustomed to the openness and free flow of ideas characteristic of the college campus can find their suggestions less than appreciated by officials who must also weigh their political palatability. Lyndon Johnson's CEA chair, Walter Heller, was warned repeatedly to keep private his worries about the inflationary potential of a war on poverty conducted simultaneously with the war in Viet Nam without a tax increase. In time Heller resigned his position, but his misgivings were not publicly divulged. In the Reagan Administration, CEA chair Martin Feldstein was prone to making some very blunt and pessimistic disclosures about the course of the Federal budget deficit. His public warnings led to discomfort in the executive branch, and his hasty departure from office. Serious consideration was then given by the Reagan White House to the feasibility of abolishing the troublesome CEA. Sensing Congressional resistance, another plan to silence the Council permanently by subsuming it under either the Treasury or Commerce Department was proposed. But a more compliant Council was installed and the storm passed. The institutional structure of the CEA was left intact. The lesson is that from its very inception successive administrations have had to contend with defining the proper political role of the CEA.

This problem bedeviled the Nixon Administration in the aftermath of the 1972 presidential election. Their critics maintained that during the campaign the chair of the CEA, Herbert Stein, had made public pronouncements concerning economic developments that were designed more to curry favor with the electorate than to convey an honest sense of what was very often bad news. These complaints continued through 1973. With Marina von Neumann Whitman's announcement of her intention to resign, there was the opportunity to select a replacement to shore up the Council's tarnished credibility. Whitman was the first to suggest Fellner's name, and this was greeted with enthusiasm by Herbert Stein, though he did not know Fellner personally nor had he ever met him. It is to Fellner's great credit that the discussion turned to him in the effort to restore the standing of the CEA in the mind of the public.

Richard Nixon was not thought to have brought much interest in economics into office with him in 1969. Early in his first term he relied on the more immediate members of his administration for advice on economic matters, such as Arthur Burns and George Schultz. His neglect of his CEA in the policy formulation process continued with his New Economic Policy. The centerpiece of that policy was comprehensive wage and price controls and its authorship belonged primarily to Treasury Secretary John Connally. Nixon regarded foreign policy as his strong suit. Domestic issues, like the economy, were important more in the sense that they posed a risk to his reelection hopes, and were best handled by the politically adept in his administration. Thus, following the 1969-70 recession, care was taken to stimulate the economy by conventional monetary-fiscal means to improve the employment picture. The New Economic Policy announced on August 15, 1971 would suppress the symtoms of inflation, if not its underlying causes, by wage and price controls. These initiatives were placed in the hands of those with no formal background in economic policymaking. The views of John Connally and Melvin Laird, former Defense Secretary and later Domestic Affairs Adviser, were in the ascendancy, and the opinions of professional economists within the administration, including those on the CEA, were rarely sought.

By mid-1973 the Watergate ordeal was in its full fury. A beleagured President Nixon grasped at every opportunity to silence his critics. Among the flurry of accusations to be countered were those concerning the use of the CEA as a propaganda organ, whose mission was to gloss over some painful realities and put the best possible face on the latest economic results. The selection of a new member to the CEA with personal integrity beyond reproach could help to counter this perception. If the coming nomination needed to emphasize honesty, independence and bluntness, Fellner was the ideal candidate. Reports that Fellner was under serious consideration for the CEA opening surfaced well in advance of his formal nomination. On August 14, 1973, just one day before the effective date of Whitman's resignation, a long story by Hobart Rowen speculating on Fellner's likely nomination appeared in *The Washington Post*. Fellner's many virtues were extolled, and his stature within the profession discussed. Rowen quoted an unnamed economist who described Fellner as "an intellectual giant" and perhaps "the most distinguished name ever to be" suggested for service on the Council. While the story notes the surprise of some colleagues that Fellner would consider the offer given his age, other observers believed Fellner's grey eminence to be one of his important qualifications for the job given the circumstances. Rightly or wrongly, some claimed that Stein's very competent but youthful colleagues on the Council, Marina Whitman and Gary Seevers, were unable to help raise the status of the CEA in policy deliberations. This may be a distortion given Nixon's disinclination to make use of his Council from early in his first term. The Council's fall from grace, compared to its high standing a decade before, stemmed mainly from the neglect and disuse that accompanied Nixon's style of governing. The status of the Council by 1973 probably owed less to the youth of its membership than it did to the inevitable consequences of its eclipse and steady decline in the Nixon years. This advisory body, though playing a convenient propaganda role, had become moribund in a policy sense. The sudden revival of interest in it perhaps had more to do with Nixon's increasingly difficult Watergate predicament than it did with a passion for good government. Whether intentional or otherwise, the lot of the CEA was to improve beginning around the time of the first mention of Fellner's name as a nominee. The Nixon

Administration was intent on advancing its own credibility, and the image of the economic policy apparatus was in need of improvement. As time passed, Nixon and his circle of close advisers became almost entirely preoccupied with mounting his Watergate defense. White House officials who in better days would have gladly arrogated to themselves the formulation of economic policy had their attention focused elsewhere. No such usurpation was possible in the hysteria and obsession of Watergate. In the vacuum that followed in its wake, power and influence flowed back to its rightful place in the CEA. Morever, a deterioration in economic conditions gave added impetus to the Council's reversal of fortune. Economic circumstances were worsening, and the appearance was that no one was at the helm.

Fellner had retired from Yale in July, 1973 as Sterling Professor of Economics Emeritus. The academic year prior to his retirement was spent on leave. Gottfried Haberler had long been urging him to join the AEI on a full-time basis, and plans for Fellner to become a Resident Scholar at the Institute had been finalized. The Fellners were traveling in Europe in the summer of 1973. While vacationing in the Swiss Alps, Fellner was informed in a telephone conversation with CEA chair Herbert Stein that the administration had decided to offer him the vacancy on the CEA. Fellner's sense of duty admitted no course other than to accept. This was a very willing acceptance, the fulfillment of a long-held desire to take measure of himself at the highest policymaking level, to test himself at the center. The formal announcement of his nomination came on September 24, 1973, and was widely praised, both by the press and within the community of academic economists. Most press accounts appearing the next day reported that Fellner would likely succeed Stein as CEA chair.

Although his views were conservative, Fellner's nomination won the support of economists from all schools of thought. The overriding consideration was his independence of mind and scholarly achievement, and the hope that these qualities could help to rejuvenate the CEA. What then followed was a very curious episode for an unconfirmed nominee. Fellner was to engage in an act of public candor that gave him a celebrity unusual for a nominee to the CEA, or for that matter, to any post. Shortly before the announcement of his nomination, Fellner had completed a study on recent economic policy, and a press conference had been scheduled for September 27, 1973 at the AEI for him to make public his findings and take questions. Such sessions were routine at the AEI. But given the appearance of Fellner the nominee, interest far exceeded what was customary, and he did not disappoint.

Economic policy under Nixon had been the very model of inconsistency. The chief concern early in the administration was inflation. With encouragement from the White House, the Federal Reserve followed a restrictive monetary policy. The ensuing recession brought little relief from inflation, but caused some alarm as the administration set its sights on the next presidential campaign. Mandatory wage and price controls were imposed in 1971 to eliminate the symtoms of inflation. With the formulation of economic policy firmly in the hands of political tacticians, monetary and fiscal policy remained very expansionary throughout the election year of 1972 to forestall any rise in unemployment. To Fellner's way of thinking, these policy reversals, the lack of consistency, administrative controls and the failure to establish a credible program to restore price stability embodied all that had gone wrong with economic policy. Against this backdrop Fellner appeared before the press to discuss the AEI's upcoming publication, *A New Look at Inflation: Economic Policy in the Early 1970's*, to which he contributed the preface and "Employment Goals and Monetary-Fiscal Overexpansion," an essay critical of the Nixon Administration's economic policy.

In his essay Fellner reiterated many of the positions that had figured importantly in much of his recently published work. For many years a 4% unemployment rate had been accepted as the operational definition of full employment and the goal of policy. Fellner stated that changes in the demographics of the labor force made this an unrealistic goal. The entry of married women and teenagers into the labor force in vast numbers meant that job searches typically became more frequent and longer, giving an upward bias to the measured unemployment rate. He viewed attempts to force the unemployment rate down to 4% as inflationary, and thought a 5% goal to be more realistic, and achievable without risking added inflationary pressures. He characterized the progress toward the restoration of price stability as uneven. Balanced budgets and monetary restraint focusing on money growth rather than interest rates were needed. While admitting that his recommendations carried the risk of recession, Fellner believed that continuation of the current policy of excessive expansion would guarantee a much more severe downturn at a later date. For those unable to find work with a macroeconomic policy that aims for a 5% target rate of unemployment, Fellner urged that a government-subsidized jobs program be enacted. Having conveyed the essentials of his essay to the press, Fellner then entertained questions. As he elaborated on his positions, there seemed to be little in current policy with which he was in agreement: the administration had indulged in excessively stimulative policy during the previous presidential election campaign; wage and price controls were "bad economics", and would ultimately prove to be "bad politics," and should be brought to an early end; and to be workable, wage and price controls require a strict program of rationing and allocations, which would be at odds with American economic and political freedoms. Economists within the administration had quietly hinted at their own personal distaste for controls, while making clear their intention to implement them as best they could. In contrast, Fellner was uncompromising in calling for no delay in the abolition of all controls. His jobs proposal was a non-inflationary way to bring the unemployment rate down to 4.5% by creating work for 400,000 unemployed, costing between $2 and $3 billion and financed largely by the elimination of unsuccessful employment programs. Stating his reservations about the plan recommended by White House Domestic Adviser Melvin Laird for an immediate tax increase to be followed at a later date by a compensating refund, Fellner said that he feared the refund might come as the economy was showing strong improvement. He was able to muster some praise in his support for Nixon's veto of a proposed increase in the minimum wage. Fellner was not inclined to air his political views in public. Privately, he was in full support of the American effort in Viet Nam, and thought Watergate an exercise in political foolishness that could cost the nation a great leader. But at his press conference, he did reveal that though registered as an independent he had voted for Richard Nixon in both the 1968 and 1972 elections.

Fellner's virtuoso performance received coverage in newspapers across the country, with many carrying the same Associated Press photo showing him at the podium, one arm swung wide in grand gesticulation. Many wondered what the effect would be on his chances for confirmation. Just days before, favorable action on his nomination by the Senate was a virtual certainty. Having ingratiated himself with no one in his performance before the press, his confirmation hearings suddenly became an eagerly awaited event. On October 3, 1973, President Nixon held a press conference dominated by the emerging Watergate scandal. But in response to a question about the recommendation made by Fellner in his press conference the previous week that a 5% unemployment rate target be adopted, Nixon acknowledged the "outspoken comments" of his nominee, and admitted that he had found economists to be "the most independent breed of the human species except for members of the press." In fine form despite the mounting threats to his presidency, he remarked that his "economic advisers are not always right but they are always sure in everything that they recommend." He did succeed in deflecting attention from the disputed unemployment rate target without acceding to Fellner's position by saying that his goal was to see that every American who wanted to work could find a job, and that numerical goals were of lesser importance.

The fear was that others in the confirmation process would be less generous. On October 5, Herbert Stein faced the press, and was told that Fellner believed controls to be bad economics and bad politics. Stein replied testily that the nominee "was not selected for his mastery of politics." This was a comment from a presumed supporter, and Fellner was yet to face the wrath of Senator Proxmire at his confirmation hearings. Fellner's belief in a 5% jobless goal was viewed in some quarters as evidence of a lack of sympathy for the disadvantaged. Others pointed to his proposed jobs program as proof that he was a conservative with a conscience. The matter of a caring policy loomed large as his confirmation hearings approached.

The hearing was held on October 11 before the Senate Committee on Banking, Housing and Urban Affairs. William Proxmire, the Wisconsin Democrat, was expected to play his usual part as unrelenting inquisitor. Those hoping for verbal fireworks were to be badly disappointed. The proceedings were conducted in a very cordial atmosphere. Aside from the preliminary remarks of Committee chairman John Sparkman, Democrat of Alabama, and a friendly question from Republican Senator William Brock of Tennessee, Proxmire was allowed to dominate the session. He had been reading some of Fellner's recent writings, and as were many other members of Congress, was struck by Fellner's candor and outspokenness at his AEI press conference. While favoring openness concerning economic matters, Proxmire sensed that, given Fellner's views, his nomination signaled a marked departure from past policy. Proxmire's major misgiving was the possible abandonment of the 4% jobless target, and he cited the experience of the late 1960's when unemployment was below 4% without any serious inflation. Fellner responded by saying that on the contrary that period was one of accelerating inflation, and that economic growth was then interrupted by a recession brought on by efforts to control that inflation. Frequent repetition of this stop-go cycle would lead to unemployment averaging in excess of his 5% target. Proxmire said his impression was that the recent inflation resulted primarily from critical shortages of certain commodities, not from excessive demand stimulation or labor shortages. Fellner agreed given the current jobless rate of 4.8%, and added that his warning of accelerating inflation was made in connection with the pursuit of a 4% unemployment rate target by monetary and fiscal stimulus. Proxmire was heartened that Fellner called for subsidized employment to alleviate some of the hardship his policy of restraint would entail. But he remained unconvinced that a 4% jobless target meant inflation, since the many women eagerly entering the labor force at that time would ease any feared labor shortage. Fellner explained that the empirical evidence suggested that any labor category experiencing increased entry would have elevated rates of measured unemployment because new entrants typically engage in more frequent and longer job searches. After noting that the increased entry observed for women and teenagers followed this familiar pattern, he then described cross-country comparisons as unreliable due to variations in the way in which unemployment is measured. Stating that white collar workers were sharing the burden of unemployment more evenly with blue collar workers, Proxmire wondered whether this did not suggest that an unemployment rate lower than Fellner's 5% rate was then consistent with price stability. Fellner rejected this notion, saying that for a full appreciation of recent employment trends account must be taken of the increased proportion of secondary wage earners in the labor force. Surely the security of having someone else in a household employed makes a job seeker less reluctant to accept unemployment while conducting a job search, and measured unemployment rates must be interpreted with this in mind. Proxmire feared that government would abandon its traditional concern for the improvement of employment prospects. Fellner noted that the increase in the overall unemployment rate since the 1950's was explained by the short duration unemployment of new entrants, not by government indifference. Asked about job discrimination, Fellner thought that its effects would not show on employment *per se*, but might have a bearing on wage differentials, which have historically been explained by the longer and more frequent withdrawals of women from the labor force associated with marriage and child rearing. Although it may be difficult to substantiate discrimination in the aggregate employment statistics, he urged that prejudice be rooted out wherever found. Asked who would get priority for participation in his proposed jobs scheme, Fellner thought those suffering long duration unemployment should get first consideration. A recently approved negative income tax proposal, which unlike his jobs proposal had the advantage of working through the private sector, drew his sympathetic response. He hoped that the potential for political abuse in the form of demands for more generous benefits could be averted in his proposal through inclusion in the legislation of a provision for training. He regarded the current emergency employment program as unsuccessful since it operated in large part for the benefit of the short duration unemployed. Fellner then reiterated his opposition to wage and price controls, hoping for their elimination by year's end.

The hearing drew to a close with a few final questions from Proxmire, whereupon he proclaimed his respect for the nominee, whose competence he declared above reproach. While admitting to "very strong policy differences with him and reservations as to his position" on a variety of issues, he nonetheless moved that Fellner's nomination be favorably reported to the full Senate. In less than one hour, Fellner had emerged from the hearing unscathed, his confirmation assured, an outcome far from certain only a few days earlier. The oath of office was administered to Fellner on October 31, 1973, and he joined Chair Herbert Stein and Member Gary L. Seevers on the Council of Economic Advisers.

The responsibilities of the CEA are divided among the chair and the two council members. It is the chair who is in direct consultation with the president, and represents the CEA on a variety of executive branch policy bodies. The two council members directly supervise the Council's staff, represent the Council at a wide range of meetings in and out of government, and on an informal basis divide between them the responsibility for the various functional economic areas under Council purview. During all or a part of his tenure on the Council, Fellner had the responsibility for business conditions, short-term forecasting, monetary and fiscal policy, international finance, manpower training and employment, developments in the labor markets, financial markets, housing, the economic role of women, taxation, social security, health, education, and welfare. Seevers was in charge of areas such as energy and natural resources, environmental problems, and anti-trust questions. He also had Council responsibility for the Economic Stabilization Program while the major portions of the wage and price controls were in effect, and food and agriculture, his specialty as an economist.

The Employment Act of 1946 requires that the president submit an economic report to the Congress each year, and that the Council submit an annual report to the president. In reality, the Council's report is transmitted to the president, who, after appending a brief message, submits it to the Congress as the Economic Report of the President. Thus, the bulk of the report, consisting of several chapters and appendices, is in fact the work of the Council and its staff. The main chapters of the report cover key issues, which during Fellner's CEA tenure included current economic developments and policy, inflation, energy, agriculture, and the international outlook. Problems of special concern are ordinarily explored in appendices. Fellner was at the least a very active contributor to the reports published during his Council service, and Haberler has described him as the principal author of both the 1974 and 1975 Economic Reports. But since the annual report is presented as the product of the teamwork of the Council and its staff, no part of it is publicly attributed to the efforts of any particular individual.

It is safe to say that in the deliberations of the Council Fellner's views were most influential in the area of macroeconomic policy. In retrospect, the prominence that Fellner achieved while on the CEA is surprising, given that he was but a member, not the chair. In other administrations, it has been unusual for any member of the CEA, the chair included, to be known to the wider public. This was not so in the late Nixon Administration, in which Herbert Stein had already achieved some notoriety. The circumstances surrounding Fellner's nomination guaranteed him a degree of celebrity. His membership on the CEA did signal a dramatic policy shift in the struggle to curb inflation. Controls as employed had been thoroughly discredited, and had become increasingly unpopular with a public that had begun to appreciate more fully their inconvenience and unfairness. The new approach was in reality the old time medicine: demand restraint. In practical terms, given the political distaste for tax increases, this meant restrictive monetary policy and if possible, cuts in the Federal budget. What Fellner brought to policymaking was the idea that there were no substitutes for a policy of demand restraint. Inflation must be ended, or else the viability of the system of private enterprise would itself be threatened, the system to which he attributed America's prosperity. At the same time, he did not regard controls as an option. They had demonstrated their unworkability, and if carried further, would erode both economic and political freedoms. No alternative to demand restraint existed. Fellner arrived at the right time with the right message. Government officials were disenchanted with controls, knew something had to be done to restore price stability, and there was no presidential election campaign to assure the usual policy compromises. No doubt the neglect engendered by the preoccupation of White House operatives with Watergate also gave economic policymakers and advisers a freer rein. Fellner's views went beyond the simple advocacy of a policy of demand restraint. It was important how that policy was pursued. The belief had to be created in the mind of the public that price stability was the single overriding goal of government policy, and would be pursued regardless of the consequences. Government would not be deterred from its policy of restraint even if it threatened a recession. Once the public sensed the tenacity of government officials in their pursuit of price stability, economic behavior more consistent with price stability would emerge. For some time following his appointment to the CEA, Fellner's views were the centerpiece of macroeconomic policy, and he played a pivotal role in representing those views to the public. As a kind of administration point man, he was active in making public addresses to explain economic policy, and was very accessible to the press.

In February, 1974 the first Economic Report of the President since Fellner's appointment was published. There was some interest in whether his recommended unemployment rate target of 5% would figure in the report. In briefing reporters, Fellner said that the Council was reluctant at that time to press for the abandonment of the 4% goal. In a compromise of sorts, the report contained two full employment budgets. One was based on the conventional 4% unemployment rate, and the other assumed full employment to be a 4.6% jobless rate given an unchanged age-sex composition for the labor force. Fellner noted that though the 4% goal was "in abeyance" for the current year it had not yet been formally discarded. In his various public appearances, he showed no timidity in stating his positions. In late February of 1974, he spoke before The Conference Board at the Waldorf-Astoria in New York City, sounding a familiar warning: despite signs of economic weakening, government must resist the temptation to pump up the economy; the most important economic problem is inflation; and should policy fail again, political pressures may develop to reinstitute some form of controls, in all likelihood, entailing far more regimentation. A credible anti-inflation policy had to be established, and he sensed a desire on the part of the public for government to show some firmness in its policy; and a jobs program could assist those unintentionally harmed by such a policy. In an interview following the speech, Fellner took issue with a recent statement made by President Nixon in his State of the Union address. Nixon had said that there was no chance of a recession. Fellner thought such reassurances to be counterproductive, since they signal the unwillingness of government to risk a recession to bring inflation under control. Fellner insisted that inflationary behavior in wage and price decisions could not be discouraged if market participants are convinced that policymakers will reverse course and stimulate the economy at the first sign of weakness. If the government is to demonstrate conviction in the battle against inflation, it must be willing to risk an economic downturn. Those who persist in their inflationary wage and price behavior will presumably suffer should a recession occur. Excessive wage concessions will put products at an added disadvantage in a slowdown, and layoffs will result. Thus, the willingness to risk a recession can discipline labor in its demands. Similarly, fear of recession will discipline the suppliers of the firm's other inputs, such as raw materials, and will assure that the firm itself will be prudent in setting its output prices. When producers and input suppliers are convinced government will accept a recession to maintain price stability, policy is said to be credible. If policy is credible, inflationary behavior will be deterred, and as a result, there will be no need for government to make good on its threat to allow a recession to take place. With this gospel according to Fellner, no policymaking authority, not even a president, should ever "say that the probability of recession is precisely zero per cent."

Fellner's duties on the CEA required frequent travel, often overseas. For example, in April, 1974, he and several CEA staff economists traveled to Japan to visit that country's Economic Planning Agency to continue an exchange of views on economic matters initiated during the previous year, and to extend an invitation to a delegation from the Economic Planning Agency to come to Washington the following November.

At the time of Fellner's nomination, nearly every news account of it speculated that he would eventually move up to chair the Council. However, throughout the spring and summer of that year, Herbert Stein remained as CEA chair. As Watergate moved centerstage, interest in Stein's alleged political misadventures faded. The administration was also falling woefully behind in filling vacancies that had opened up in many important posts, and so Stein could help out by remaining longer. It is difficult to assess the speculation concerning Fellner as successor to Stein. Was it the invention of a press whose imagination got the better of it? Was it deliberate misinformation on the part of a desperate administration willing to try any expedient to improve its image? Or was it a genuine intention that simply got lost in the press of events? The truth may draw on each possibility. Stein was unpopular with a Washington press corps all too eager to announce his replacement. But such speculation, so long as it was not denied, could prove useful to an increasingly embattled administration. Whatever its true intent, the Nixon White House could deflect some criticism, attempt to strike a more respectable pose, and have its cause served by the continued mention of Fellner, a highly reputable economist, as likely successor to Stein. In the end, it was Stein who was able to decide when he would resign, and he eventually did so effective August 31, 1974, nearly a year after the announcement of Fellner's nomination to the CEA.

After Stein had made clear his intention to resign, President Nixon, in the waning days of his administration, made one of his last nominations. He announced that he would submit the name of Alan Greenspan for confirmation as the new CEA chair, an action at least in part attributable to Fellner's favorable mention of Greenspan as a possible nominee. Surely by this time, whatever hopes, if any, Fellner had to succeed Stein had vanished, and it is not likely that the position held any interest for him at that late date. Fellner thought Greenspan to hold views compatible with his own. Especially important was their shared belief that inflation was the most serious problem facing the nation. Greenspan also had an appealing style that might in some unknown way serve an administration struggling to survive. But by the time the new chair was sworn in, on September 4, 1974, Nixon had resigned.

For Fellner CEA service entailed long hours and late nights, carried out with devotion, and the details of which were, according to intimates, treated like military secrets. By the fall of 1974 he was sixty-nine years of age. He had retired from Yale the year before to pursue a labor of love, economic research with close colleagues at the AEI, which he then had to forgo to join the CEA. His circumstances were not unlike those of the many academics who have served on the CEA over the years. They held tenured positions on faculties at the most prestigious universities, from which they took leave of absence. These leaves were not open-ended, and many economists have left the Council of Economic Advisers to avoid the expiration of their tenure. In most such cases, CEA service is limited to one to two years. It is possible that Fellner may have considered this as the appropriate length of service. On September 24, 1974, nearly one year to the day of his nomination, he announced his intention to resign from the CEA effective the following February, after the Council's annual report to the president was complete. He made clear that his decision was in no way a result of policy differences or any disenchantment with government work. He had found the work "very interesting, quite exciting, and exceedingly educational." Having taken on the burden of Council service at a comparatively advanced age, Fellner was understandably intent on resuming his research at the AEI.

Although he announced his plans to resign five months in advance, Fellner nonetheless remained a very active member of the CEA. The arrival of Greenspan, another strong personality, on the Council in no way made Fellner a lame duck member, and his very visible role continued. The month of September, 1974 was a peculiar one for the American polity. A new man had assumed the presidency, without having faced the electorate either as a candidate for the vice presidency or the presidency. No sooner had President Ford taken office, when inflation returned with a vengeance. The effects of the quadrupling of crude oil prices by the OPEC cartel in November, 1973 combined with shortages in certain key sectors held out the prospect of substantial and continued price increases for the foreseeable future. In office barely a month, Gerald Ford decided to declare his own war on inflation, and part of his battle plan was to call a series of meetings, or inflation summits as they came to be known, to discuss possible courses of action. Participants included members of Congress, high government officials, of which Fellner was one, and several of the nation's most respected economists, mainly from the academic community. These meetings were conducted throughout the months of September and October, and one memorable result, though embarassing in the light of subsequent developments, was the WIN, or Whip Inflation Now, button. No one could dispute the severity of inflation; it was to reach double-digits for the first time since the removal of price controls following World War II. But unbeknownst to the administration at the time, the nation was on the verge of its worst economic downturn since the Great Depression years. WIN buttons disappeared as quickly as they had come on the scene, as policymakers tried to contend with the twin evils of high inflation and rising unemployment.

Fellner was very much a part of these high level meetings, and his views, as on previous occasions, gained him some public attention. Ford had planned twelve preliminary meetings to give a voice to various national constituencies, to be followed by a plenary session, the "summit conference" on inflation in Washington. Fellner participated in a preliminary session held at the Waldorf-Astoria in New York City on September 22. The agenda of this pre-summit meeting was to establish a policy consensus for an anti-inflation program. Cutting the Federal budget had emerged as a favored option in some of the earlier preliminary meetings. The consensus that began to develop at the Waldorf-Astoria meeting, which, unlike earlier meetings, was dominated by professional economists, viewed budget cuts as counterproductive given the signs of an economic slowdown. Econometric forecasts presented by Otto Eckstein and others indicated that reduced government spending would give little relief from inflation but would surely cause the unemployment rate to rise, not a worthy trade-off in the view of many conference participants. It had been argued in government circles that budget cuts could make it possible for the Federal Reserve to ease monetary policy further, and give a boost to sectors suffering from high interest rates. It was this view that the New York session was rejecting.

At this meeting, it was Fellner who came to the defense of the administration's position, which he been instrumental in formulating. Skeptics, while still in favor of an easing of monetary restraint, now thought budget cuts too risky given the delicate state of the economy. In a discussion paper presented at this pre-summit, Fellner argued that a cut in Federal outlays might have a neutral effect on employment, while slowing inflation. His own predisposition was to regard the achievement of price stability above all else, and this might necessitate risking a recession. Talk of budget cuts would show government resolve; abandonment of cuts would confirm the usual pattern of policy reversal at the first sign of distress. The theoretical rationale for Fellner's continued insistence on a policy of fiscal restraint was the crowd-out effect. With deficit spending, private borrowing is crowded-out by government credit demands. Savings is diverted from the private sector, where it would presumably be used to improve the productive capacity of the economy. Fellner asserted that budget cuts would reduce government borrowing, and release additional savings for use by private borrowers who will make productive investments beneficial to the economic well-being of society. Reduced borrowing by government should ease interest rates, providing the private sector with the needed incentive to expand its investment in new plant and equipment. Within the range that he was suggesting, Fellner did not believe that spending cuts would adversely affect the trend in real output, if the ensuing release of credit were to flow into those industries, such as housing, chemicals and steel, then operating at capacity utilization. Given the tightness being experienced in many industries, an expansion of industrial capacity would reduce inflationary pressures. The outcome of the economic summits was an official Ford Administration policy position calling for tax increases and budget cuts, both to fight inflation. The economic program unveiled on October 8, 1974 included a 5% income-tax surcharge for 1975 to be levied on corporations and the majority of those in the middle and upper income brackets, and nearly $5 billion in spending cuts. Tax increases and budget cuts were to be soon forgotten, as policymakers came to realize the full dimensions of the developing recession, a contraction far deeper than expected.

As the recession deepened in late 1974, press interest in Fellner's opinions brought him the occasional role of prognosticator. He claimed that current rates of production in the American automobile industry were not sufficient to maintain the existing automobile fleet. Since normal replacement needs were not being satisfied, this augured well for future sales, and Fellner predicted that a surge in car sales would lead to rapid recovery from the sharp recession. His role as economic forecaster for the popular press was a minor one, yet it had a touch of irony. His forecasts were always carefully hedged, and with good reason. He did not believe that forecasting was one of the strengths of the economics profession. He was often critical of econometric models that, despite their claims to precision, yielded inaccurate forecasts, serving only to tarnish further the reputation of the already beleaguered economics profession.

With economic conditions worsening, some in the Ford Administration began to think the proposed tax hike was inappropriate, and that a policy reversal might be needed. It was an awkward situation, and one to which Fellner's considerable skills were brought to bear. On December 3, in a speech before the National Economists Club in Washington, he very guardedly broached the subject of a possible tax cut. While urging patience and cautioning against economic stimulus until inflation eased, Fellner said policymakers should know what they "wish to do if and when additional support measures should become appropriate." Only if inflation subsides and significant economic weakness persists should consideration be given to expansionary measures. If those conditions were met, Fellner was quite specific about what form a stimulus should take. Tax cuts would be the preferred approach, not increased government spending, and the cuts should be aimed at reducing the effective income tax rates paid by individuals and corporations. This was to be accomplished by revising the tax structure to remove the distortions caused by inflation. Individuals were being pushed into higher income tax brackets because their nominal incomes were rising, even though their real incomes may have been declining. The same unlegislated tax increases also affected capital gains and corporate profits, since it was nominal rather real returns that were taxed. If tax relief was needed, Fellner believed it should be extended to capital gains and corporate profits, and not limited just to individuals. With his characteristic bluntness, he admitted that relief for individuals would prove politically popular. But the impact of inflation on the taxation of capital gains and corporate profits had been even more severe, and had to be redressed without regard to political considerations.

CEA chair Alan Greenspan had addressed the same group the previous day. He too fretted about expansionary moves taken in haste that might jeopardize the gains made against inflation. His remarks favoring tax cuts were aimed more at preempting increased Federal outlays, for which there was growing Congressional sentiment. Greenspan claimed that action on taxes would be more expeditious, and easier to reverse in the future if needed, than expanding Federal spending programs. Unlike Fellner's plan, he had made no reference to tax reduction as a means by which to undo inflationary distortions in the tax system. The trial balloon launched by Greenspan and Fellner met with the customary evasions, equivocations, denials and disclaimers from other Ford Administration officials. Their speeches were a convenient way to broach the subject of tax cuts, and give the White House greater room to maneuver. Fellner's reservations about returning too quickly to economic stimulation were shared by Greenspan and others within official circles. Treasury Secretary William Simon also feared that "a magnificent opportunity" to solve the problem of inflation would be lost if a move to expansionary policy were made too soon. Fellner believed that once a rebound began the economy would for a while be self-propelled, as inventories were replenished and stocks of durable and semidurable goods were built back up. Therefore, fiscal policy had to avoid too great a stimulus, or one continued too long.

Near the end of his tenure on the CEA, Fellner became optimistic that the nation had "turned a corner" in its effort to restore price stability. In mid-February he delivered a speech to a Civil Service Commission audience in Kings Point, New York, in which he presented his views on the need to reform the Federal tax system to remove the distortions wrought by inflation. According to Fellner's estimates, these distortions had raised the tax bill of individuals and businesses by $30 billion during 1974, a year in which economic conditions had progressively deteriorated, made worse by this increased tax burden, unintended though it may have been. Although a move to an indexed tax system did not appear immediately feasible, Fellner insisted that indexation be a part of any future tax considerations. Bracket creep and the effect of inflation on the personal exemption, standard deduction, inventory valuation and depreciation allowances had been briefly reviewed in the Economic Report of the President published just days earlier, but no formal commitment to an indexed tax system had been made. A study with similar findings was released around the same time by the Joint Economic Committee. It indicated that the increased tax burden induced by inflation had a greater impact on many families than did increased food and transportation costs. Revision of the tax codes to remove the adverse effects of inflation was an issue on which Fellner would expend much time and effort in the coming years. It seems fitting in retrospect that his last public address as a Council member was devoted to expressing his concerns on the need for a tax system indexed to take proper account of changes in the price level.

Fellner's last day of Council service was February 25, 1975. The arrival of Alan Greenspan at the CEA as its chair had apparently led to some strains within the CEA and its staff. He had come to government service from his very successful economic forecasting firm, Townsend-Greenspan and Co., which *Business Week* described as "a one-man band." His reputation was built upon his uncanny ability to make accurate economic forecasts. That reputation was not to remain unsullied for long. At one of the various economic pre-summits held during his first month on the Council, he predicted the economy would hold steady, and recommended to President Ford that a tax surcharge be implemented to fight inflation. In fact, the economy stood on the verge of its worst decline since 1937. Press accounts eventually began to surface that claimed Greenspan had brought his habit of running a one-man show to the Council, an institution which by its enabling legislation had been organized around the concept of teamwork. Fellner was an early supporter of Greenspan's nomination. But the new chair's alleged failure to consult with either the other members or the staff of the CEA in the revision of economic policy in late 1974 and early 1975 was blamed for strained relations between the two. It would be easy to overstate their differences. Fellner's departure had been announced within weeks of Greenspan's arrival, and so there could be no connection between the tensions that existed at the CEA and Fellner's resignation. Fellner had simply become accustomed to the teamwork and the open, consultative style of the CEA, one familiar to him from his academic experience. By February, both Gary Seevers and Fellner had made public their plans to leave the Council. Seevers was off to become a commissioner at the newly created Commodity Futures Trading Commission. Fellner was to return to the AEI. By the time of Fellner's resignation, the economic policy of the Ford Administration had undergone a radical change. A tax surcharge was still official policy in early December of 1974. But by the following February, it had been replaced by a proposal for a $16 billion tax cut. It was reported that Seevers and Fellner were resentful of Greenspan's failure to consult with them in this dramatic reversal of policy. The more serious disagreements at the Council were between the chair and the staff economists. Memories of the erroneously upbeat economic forecast delivered by Greenspan the previous fall were still fresh. While Greenspan had reluctantly accepted the need for tax cuts, he was inclined to favor a temporary tax break: a one-time tax rebate for households, and a one-year boost in the investment tax credit for business. The staff economists at the CEA felt that their views on the need for a proposal with much more expansive and permanent tax cuts were not being fully represented in White House policy deliberations. The departure of Seevers and Fellner came at an inopportune time, when the economy was deep in recession, policy was confused, and there was a palace revolt at the Council. Sympathetic though these two might have been, especially Seevers, who had begun his work at the Council as a staff economist, they were moving on. Two new members, Paul Macavoy and Burton Malkiel, and a change in approach on the part of the chair did eventually restore a harmonious atmosphere at the Council.

AT THE AEI: INFORMING THE PUBLIC DISCOURSE

In July, 1973, having spent the previous academic year on leave, Fellner formally retired from Yale University with the title of Sterling Professor of Economics Emeritus. His association with the AEI had begun in 1970 as an Adjunct Scholar. He had planned to join the AEI on a full-time basis as a Resident Scholar in the summer of 1973. Those plans were delayed by his CEA service, but in February, 1975 he finally arrived at the AEI, anxious to resume his scholarly research.

Founded in Washington in 1943, the AEI was originally known as the American Enterprise Association. It was little more than a propaganda organ for the interests of business until 1954. That year William Baroody arrived at the AEI, and began to mold it into a serious counterweight to the more liberal Brookings Institution. The oldest and most centrist of the conservative think tanks, the AEI is given much of the credit for infusing conservative ideas with intellectual respectability, especially in the 1970's, and making possible the political resurgence of conservatism. The right-of-center think tanks may have rejected Keynesian macroeconomics, but had at long last taken heed of Keynes' admonition that in the end "it is ideas, not vested interests, which are dangerous for good or evil." William Fellner fit nicely with the AEI, with its sober and scholarly approach, unlike the doctrinaire stance of the newer conservative research institutes.

With his return to the AEI, Fellner began in earnest his crusade for the indexation of the American tax system. In addition to the harm done to economic incentives through the interaction of inflation with the tax codes, Fellner also found that these unlegislated tax increases offended his democratic sensibilities. By June, 1975, his study, *Correcting Taxes for Inflation*, published under the auspices of the AEI and co-authored with Kenneth W. Clarkson and John H. Moore, had received wide press coverage, including prominent articles in *The Wall Street Journal* and *The Washington Post*. In July, Fellner was invited to write a lengthy article on tax indexation for the editorial page of *The Wall Street Journal*.

Fellner argued the case of both the individual and corporate taxpayer. For the individual taxpayer, inflation had eroded the real value of the personal exemption and standard deduction. Even more pernicious had been bracket creep. With the graduated income tax system and its many income tax brackets, each progressively higher, inflation had moved many taxpayers to a higher bracket. For some the problem was especially acute, since if inflation outpaced the rate of growth in nominal income, higher taxes could be paid on a declining real income. On the corporate side, inflation had biased operating income upward, creating a larger tax liability and reducing profitability. This had occurred primarily because of the way in which inventory valuation and depreciation were treated for tax purposes. Goods sold out of inventory were expensed for tax purposes at historical cost, that is, at the cost at which the firm had acquired them. In an inflationary environment, revenues had been better able to keep pace with inflation through price increases. Thus, inflation typically widened the gap between revenues and expenses, and led to greater tax payments. In effect, firms were paying taxes on phantom inventory profits. Yet firms must replace what they sell out of inventory. But the replenishment of inventory through purchases from suppliers was done at a new, higher cost, reflecting the effects of inflation. The way in which taxes were computed failed to take account of the new, higher cost at which inventory is replaced. The depreciation charge suffered from the same inadequacy. Depreciation expense reflected historical, not replacement, cost. Plant and equipment used up in the production process had eventually to be replaced, and typically at a higher cost given the inflation that had taken place over the life of the asset. But the tax laws allowed an expensing that presumed no price increases for plant and equipment. Again, since taxable income was larger than what was justified by replacement cost, the corporate tax burden had become exaggerated.

Fellner saw in this tax system unfairness and inequity. He also saw serious implications for savings and capital formation, and regarded some form of tax indexation as an absolute necessity. In concept, it is possible to fully index all dollar values used in tax computation, that is, to adjust upward dollar values to reflect the movement in some price index. Fellner's proposal in *Correcting Taxes for Inflation* was a more limited form of indexation, but one which undoes the major damage caused by inflation. Tax brackets, the personal exemption, and the standard deduction were to be indexed, and on the corporate side, inventory and depreciation expenses would be indexed to gauge replacement costs more accurately. While he was one of the initiators of the movement to index taxes, Fellner was not a fan of the general indexation plans proposed to cope with inflation, plans that would have indexed wages, debt repayments and other payments, in addition to taxes. He believed that such a comprehensive system would steepen price expectations and cause inflation to accelerate. His opposition was also rooted in the belief that an indexation scheme would divert attention from what was truly needed, a policy of monetary and fiscal restraint.

Fellner was not happy with the Tax Reduction Act of 1975. While admitting that it did provide relief to individual taxpayers as a group, he viewed it mainly as an unsatisfying mixture of inflation correction with redistribution of the tax burden. The tax benefits had been skewed towards lower income groups, and little had been done to redress the tax problems of business. Congress had granted a temporary increase in the investment tax credit, but there had been no consideration of the replacement cost issue and its use in the computation of business taxes. Since basic changes to the tax structure may affect economic incentives, Fellner urged that any future legislative action keep the removal of inflationary distortions separate from the matter of redistribution of the tax burden.

Throughout the recession year 1975 and into 1976, many economists continued to call for tax cuts to spur economic recovery. Fellner joined in those calls, but for a very different reason. His support was always based on the need to undo the harmful distortions wrought by many years of inflation. His study of the problem had revealed that the tax system had seriously eroded the power of the automatic stabilizers within the economy. When an economy recedes, tax payments based on the reduced level of economic activity decline, serving to ease the slowdown and foster conditions for a rebound. Fellner had found that the tax-raising effect of inflation had effectively neutralized this automatic stabilizer. His point was amply illustrated in an estimate that received widespread press attention: tax revenues in 1974 were $16 billion higher than what they would have been had his proposed tax law changes been in effect. He preferred the introduction of tax indexation in order to restore the power of this automatic stabilizer, rather than tax cuts aimed strictly at promoting expansion.

Tax indexation continued to absorb Fellner's attention in the years to come, and represents his greatest public policy legacy. Fellner had predicted on several occasions that serious interest in tax indexation would develop only if inflation worsened. It did worsen in the late 1970's and early 1980's, and he was eventually asked to consult with the Congressional Budget Office in framing legislation to index taxes. The provisions he suggested were passed as part of the major tax bill enacted in 1981, and became effective in 1985.

By the time of his departure from the CEA, Fellner had achieved a degree of celebrity. In the years following his Council service, such popular periodicals as *U.S. News & World Report, Forbes, and Newsweek,* as well as some of the nation's most respected newspapers, including *The New York Times, The Wall Street Journal,* and *The Washington Post* had sought out his opinions on economic matters. In the period immediately after his Council work, he had a brief fling as economic forecaster with *Dun's.* This was a reprise of the uncomfortable role he played within the Ford Administration: economic prognosticator for the press. But this time, it was as a private citizen offering non-official views. In June of 1975, *Dun's* trumpeted on its Washington Desk page that it could report the assessment of "one of the nation's most astute economic forecasters," a portrayal which surely made Fellner cringe, given his well-known wariness for the econometrician's trade. Whatever his misgivings, he volunteered his thoughts on the outlook for auto and housing sales, couched in his characteristically guarded terms. Since both the automobile and housing stocks had not been maintained during the recession, Fellner believed that restoring those stocks to their pre-recession levels would contribute much to the economic recovery. But in view of their high cost, he was more restrained on the role of automobile and housing sales in sustaining economic growth for the longer-run. At some point, continued recovery from the recession would come to depend on increased investment in new plant and equipment by business.

The previous two years had brought stagflation to its fullest fury, with double digit inflation and a jobless rate peaking near 9%. Despite the fact that the marketplace had come to expect very high rates of inflation, Fellner was by May, 1976 expressing the belief that policy had begun to recondition those expectations to a lower level. The year 1976 was for him one of renewed optimism concerning the economy, and also one of important personal achievement. In 1972 the AEI had published *Economic Policy and Inflation in the Sixties*, followed by *A New Look at Inflation: Economic Policy in the Early 1970's* in 1973. Both were significant and visible successes for the AEI. Fellner suggested that such an effort be mounted each year, and conceived of an annual AEI volume which would be devoted to a discussion of current economic issues. The AEI's annual *Contemporary Economic Problems* series was born, and Fellner was selected to be its editor, a title that was changed to Project Director with the 1978 edition. The preparation of each volume often required the contributors to meet in a seminar setting under Fellner's direction at various points throughout the year. A volume was published each year from 1976 to 1981, with the 1983-84 edition the seventh and final one completed under his supervision.

In 1976 Fellner's last book, *Towards a Reconstruction of Macroeconomics*, was published. Macroeconomic theory and policy had been slowly enveloped in crisis. The policy dilemma of stagflation as perceived by the authorities was one which required them to either accept higher unemployment or cause more inflation. The curse of stagflation also began to bring forth new theories to contend with the ruling Keynesian orthodoxy. Monetarism was enjoying a revival, and rational expectations and supply-side economics were receiving a more detailed elaboration. Fellner decided to enter the debate with his book, which is more accurately a recapitulation of the theoretical and policy views he had long espoused, and less a true and complete reconstruction of macroeconomics. The main thesis of the book is his credibilty effect, or hypothesis, which claims inflation can be halted only through the consistent application of a policy of demand restraint.

Fellner had long believed that inflation was the most serious threat faced by market capitalism. *A Reconstruction* was intended to return price stability to its place as the most important objective of macroeconomic policy. Fellner's view was that policymakers in the post-1965 era had caused inflation to steepen in an attempt to achieve unrealistic employment goals based on the misguided trade-offs suggested by Phillips Curve analysis. The resulting inflation was not welcomed, but fear of adverse employment consequences led to a willingness to accommodate it. Markets were no longer conditioned to the expectation of price stability. Fellner did grant that policymakers would occasionally become concerned with inflation when it surged in response to excessive nominal demand creation. However, such concern was ephemeral, and policy would ease at the first sign of increased unemployment. A cycle of stop and go would be perpetuated in which inflationary expectations steepen, and inflation worsens with each cycle. Left unattended, the eventual day of reckoning could be very painful since the restoration of non-inflationary growth might require a prolonged and deep recession.

A Reconstruction was meant to provide an alternative to this day of reckoning. In this book, Fellner reconsiders some of the macroeconomic debates that have raged in the aftermath of the publication of Keynes' *General Theory*. While dismissing Say's Law and deflation as useful ideas in moving an economy out of a deep depression, he also takes Keynes to task for encouraging the belief that inflation is the equilibrating mechanism by which a macroeconomy can be restored to full employment. While reiterating his criticism of the neo-Keynesian reliance on inflationary demand-side management, he also warns that the monetarist's insistence on a constant growth rate for money may not always be appropriate. Fellner proposes that the policy authorities attempt to achieve the highest level of real economic activity consistent with price stability, by which he means a zero rate of inflation, and provides a discussion of how the maximum level of economic activity consistent with price stability can be determined. The public cannot be fooled by a policy of overexpansion, which will provoke labor and producers to raise wages and prices in order to protect their real incomes. An incomes policy instituted to suppress these inflationary symptoms would prove to be but the first step down the road to centralized control of the economy. Government has no other option but to pursue a credible policy of non-inflationary growth which conditions the expectations of the public to price stability. Policy must offer guidance and discipline to labor and producers, and to be credible it must convey a willingness to risk a recession should the behavior of market participants be inconsistent with price stability.

Fellner hoped the ideas in *A Reconstruction* would leave a lasting mark on macroeconomics. However, its impact was modest at best. Fellner criticized Keynes' *General Theory* for its exclusive focus on the problem of unemployment. Fellner's critics made a similar charge, claiming the exclusive focus of *A Reconstruction* to be inflation, with the problems of assuring and maintaining full employment all too comfortably ignored. Fellner often repeated his fear for the continued viability of market capitalism in the face of chronic inflation. Those who disagreed with Fellner felt that he was blinded to the threat posed to market capitalism by his policy recommendations, which, if adopted, might entail a prolonged and difficult period of very high unemployment.

In 1977 Fellner returned again to Hungary, and was once more taken by surprise by the great interest there in Western economic controversies. In April he delivered a lecture to the Hungarian Economic Association in Budapest, and a version of his remarks was published in its journal, *Acta Oeconomica*. He examined what was to him a crucial distinction between the neo-Keynesian and monetarist schools of thought: the time frame adopted for policy purposes. In his view, monetarists tend to have a long-run orientation in which the short-run behavior of market participants must conform to the long-run goal of price stability. Neo-Keynesians have an employment objective as a long-run goal, and are willing to manipulate the short-run through monetary and fiscal fine-tuning to achieve that goal. Monetarists are cost conditioners. But neo-Keynesians are cost accommodators, and Fellner was very critical of this perceived aspect of their approach, since in his view it was the root cause of accelerating inflation.

Following a time-honored European scholarly tradition, a group of Fellner's past and present colleagues, some of them former students, organized the publication of a book of essays, a festschrift, to pay tribute to him on the occasion of his seventieth birthday. The editors of the volume were Bela Balassa and Richard Nelson. Balassa, a fellow Hungarian, had profited greatly under Fellner's mentorship as a Yale graduate student. Nelson was a former faculty colleague at Yale. Their lives had been enriched through their association with Fellner. In gratitude they assembled a collection of essays that touched on themes which had figured importantly in his work. The result was the 1977 publication of *Economic Progress, Private Values, and Public Policy: Essays in Honor of William Fellner*. Balassa, the original inspiration behind the project, recalled later that Fellner was far too modest to expect a festschrift, but overjoyed to receive it.

By the spring of 1978, with the Ford Administration replaced by a Democratic White House, Fellner became increasingly dissatisfied with the direction of economic policy. To foster continued growth, President Carter had recommended a $25 billion tax cut. Subsequent to this proposal, the employment picture improved dramatically and unexpectedly. The administration found itself in the uncomfortable position of appearing ungenerous and confused, as it publicly mulled over the advisability of withdrawing its tax plan. Much unwanted advice was provided from the sidelines, and Fellner was not reticent in sharing his views. He recommended a tax cut of no more than $7 billion. The rate of unemployment had fallen to 6%, making inflation the main threat and deficit reduction a policy priority. Fellner was fearful that monetary policy had become too easy, and in terms bordering on Calvinist, excoriated government for cheating the people through inflation bred by excessive money creation. He began to voice the opinion that, since policymakers had lost all credibility in the fight against inflation, the task of re-establishing credibility made recession unavoidable. Government had reacquired its bad habits, and was again using unwarranted money growth in an attempt to achieve unrealistic employment goals. Although the public had lost faith in policy, Fellner still believed a consistently applied policy of demand restraint could end inflation within three years at relatively low cost in terms of lost output and employment opportunity. But he believed that time was running out, and warned that continued delay might necessitate a recession to restore price stability. The disruption brought to world energy supplies in 1979 by the Iranian revolution assured that there was no respite from inflation, and the policy environment was again a very forbidding one. Carter Administration tax policy was once more a favorite target of its critics, Fellner included. By his estimate, should the extant 9% inflation rate persist, bracket creep would boost the tax bill for individuals by 15%, a delicious prognosis used by the growing legions of Carter's critics, including the editorial page of *The Wall Street Journal*.

Fellner had long been an admirer of Germany, a generous view for a man of Jewish ancestry all too familiar with the German nation's unhappy past. He saw the Third Reich as an aberration, a nation *in extremis*, brought to its knees and made vulnerable to totalitarianism by the economic ill of inflation, the dangers of which he had warned ceaselessly. But Fellner was a man of cultivation, a lover of the arts, fluent in many languages, including German, whose most important academic training took place in Berlin. His disgust for the Nazis could not shake his admiration for German culture or his faith in the German people. He had traveled widely in West Germany, and developed many close professional associations with economists and government officials, most notably Herbert Giersch, former member of the Federal Republic of Germany's version of the CEA, the Council of Economic Experts. The respect and admiration was mutual, and the West German Government chose to honor Fellner with the award of its Commander's Cross of the German Order of Merit. At the award ceremony held on January 8, 1979 at the West German Embassy in Washington, his remarks were characteristically gracious towards the German people. He, like most economists, was greatly impressed with the postwar West German economic miracle. But some Germans felt an unease, that in some unhealthy way their recovery had fostered material progress at the expense of cultural values. Fellner used the occasion of his award to offer re-assurance. Rather than supplanting future West German cultural achievements, he stated his belief that their strong economic performance would in time be seen to have nurtured a rebirth of German cultural accomplishment.

From the time of his departure from the CEA until the end of 1979, Fellner's technical writing was a blend of oft repeated themes and refinements and modifications to earlier positions. While acknowledging that there was no unique and immutable natural rate of unemployment, he argued that the unemployment rate to be targeted by policy at any point in time should be that consistent with a zero rate of inflation. Structural rigidities in the labor market would define the non-inflationary unemployment rate, and those rigidities and the zero inflation jobless rate they imply can, from time to time, change. Achieving a horizontal price trend in a post-recovery economy required growth in money GNP on the order of 5%, a balanced budget to encourage capital formation, and the renunciation of any preordained employment goal. Fellner came to believe that the M_2 definition of money bore a more dependable relationship to money GNP than did the narrower M_1, and urged that monetary policy be framed in terms of M_2. For 1977 he recommended that M_2 grow at 10%, which would reduce unemployment by 1%. After a complete recovery had been assured, M_2 growth would have to be gradually slowed. Fellner's views on monetary policy were not doctrinaire, and though he found much to agree with in the positions taken by the monetarists, he did not share their enthusiasm for a monetary rule.

Fellner believed price stability to be a necessary condition for sustainable growth, and continued to argue that a credible anti-inflation policy, if adopted, would achieve its objectives without a prolonged and damaging transition period. He began to study the broader ramifications of the inflation problem, finding that the decline in the rate of productivity growth was in part a consequence of high and uncertain inflation. Similarly, inflation was identified as the cause of the shift in household portfolios away from the financial assets that provide capital for the productive activities of business enterprises. Both the productivity slowdown and these asset shifts have serious implications for the continued improvement in material standards of living, and gave an added urgency to Fellner's calls for a firm policy to end the curse of inflation.

By the late 1970's, two new schools of thought were percolating through the field of macroeconomics: supply-side economics, and rational expectations. The supply-side view did not have the usual academic pedigree. It was to an important extent the brainchild of politicians and journalists, and served as the inspiration for Reaganomics. Fellner found little appeal in supply-side economics. As a man who always had great respect for empirical evidence, he was disturbed by its facile claim that cuts in marginal tax rates would lead to smaller budget deficits, and eventually a balanced Federal budget. The genesis and substance of rational expectations was more to Fellner's liking. It had undergone a long incubation period under the care of respected economists at some of the nation's finest universities. Haberler regards Fellner as an anticipator of rational expectations, noting that he had for decades discussed the influence of the expectations of market participants on the outcome of policy measures. But by no means did Fellner accept rational expectations in full. Rather he found within it some important truths, what he chose to call its "valid core." He believed that what was left after extracting this valid core was his credibility hypothesis. Rational expectations posits that market participants can learn to properly anticipate the effects of the systematic component of government policy. A policy stimulus under this reasoning would have no effect on real economic activity. Both producers and labor would use past experience to realize that such a stimulus is inflationary, bringing no lasting improvement in real terms. Without the prospect of an improvement in their real economic standing to serve as an incentive, they will not respond to a conventional policy stimulus. Fellner had for many years expressed his reservations about rational expectations theory, and his most detailed statement on the subject is found in "The Valid Core of Rationality Hypotheses in the Theory of Expectations," published in the November, 1980 issue of the *Journal of Money, Credit, and Banking*. He thought rational expectations needed to be qualified in several ways. For example, he was unwilling to accept the theory's presumption that policy is always systematic in the sense that it presents the marketplace with a mode of policy behavior which is detectable. Fellner claimed that in recent years policy unpredictably veered from expansionary to restrictive. With such repeated stop-go cycles, there was no systematic component of policy for market participants to anticipate. However, the valid core he found in rational expectations theory was that, when confronted with a credible and consistent policy line, the marketplace can properly anticipate its consequences and will adjust its behavior accordingly. A credible policy of demand restraint aimed at price stability can affect price expectations and lead to more favorable cost trends. For Fellner, the ultimate importance of rational expectations was to be found in the support it offered for his credibility hypothesis.

Fellner continued to preach his gospel of credibility as the 1970's wound to an end, but was worried about the policy then in effect, which he regarded as increasingly less credible. He believed that a credible and consistently applied policy of demand disinflation could gradually accomplish its objectives without causing any severe dislocations. He had favored a policy that would gradually restore price stability, but warned that if the pace were too slow, policy would no longer be credible. If policy credibility were completely lost, gradualism might fail, and policymakers would have to be prepared to implement a policy of abrupt disinflation.

In 1980 and 1981, Fellner, while still holding out hope for a policy of gradualism, felt an increasing sense of urgency concerning the inflation problem, and wrote about the shock absorbers that would be needed if an abrupt policy were instituted. Given their callability and refinancing provisions, many debt obligations might not require revision, but in the case of wage contracts revision would prove unavoidable. While giving consideration to the restoration of the gold standard as part of a system of shock absorbers, the unreliability of gold supplies continued to leave Fellner convinced that there was no feasible alternative to a responsibly managed fiat money.

In October, 1981, Fellner was able to express his views on the credibility effect in a unique forum. Seven former members of the Council of Economic Advisers, all of whom were either currently or formerly on the economics faculty at Yale University, met to discuss their Council experience. William Nordhaus, a Carter appointee, argued against demand restraint as means to end inflation, citing an estimate which showed that the inflation rate could be brought down to 3% only by accepting an 8% or higher unemployment rate for a period no shorter than five years. Fellner was quick to reply, saying that the assertion made by Nordhaus was "unprovable." He said if the Reagan Administration could demonstrate that it had a credible policy to curb inflation "the economy would fall in line," and the transition to non-inflationary growth would be brief and only slightly uncomfortable.

Those skeptical of the credibility effect have raised several objections, chief among them the belief that the transition period would be both prolonged and very painful, both in terms of unemployment and lost output. Fellner's position was particularly vulnerable to arguments about its employment effects. James Tobin was fond of noting that the opponents of the neo-Keynesian view were in favor of that rate of unemployment, however high it might be, which would result in a zero rate of inflation. Basil J. Moore had rebuked Fellner for a policy approach that would use unemployment and recession to punish unions and firms engaging in inflationary wage and pricing practices. But the victims would be the innocent, while those unions and producers that had market power would be able to escape relatively unscathed. Robert J. Gordon and others have advanced two additional criticisms. First, they have noted that maintaining a credible stance is complicated in a democratic society in which the turnover of policy advisers is high, and political leaders, subject to fairly frequent re-election cycles, are unable to bind successors to their policies. The second argument made against the credibility effect pointed to historical episodes during which demand restraint had been consistently applied for a prolonged period without provoking the desired response from wages and prices.

The debate over the credibility effect continued in the aftermath of the 1981-82 recession, the most serious in the postwar era. While critics pointed to the depth of the contraction, with the unemployment rate peaking at near 11% and real GNP declining by 2.5%, as evidence contradicting the credibility hypothesis, Fellner saw the recession as confirming its validity. He described the economic downturn as more rapid and less painful than predicted, because the authorities had established a credible disinflationary policy. Like many arguments in economics, this one could not be resolved unambiguously since it entails personal value judgments that must weigh the importance of price stability against employment. But Fellner found himself with little company on this issue even among conservatives. Lindley Clark of *The Wall Street Journal*, a longtime Fellner admirer, wrote that the disinflationary process in 1981-82 was not gradual as Fellner had predicted, but abrupt and severe. In the period following the recovery from the recession of 1981-82, during which the threat of double-digit inflation eased, the credibility hypothesis faded from the macroeconomic debate.

Fellner had become increasingly vocal in his opposition to Carter Administration policies, and was greatly relieved by Ronald Reagan's election in 1980. His hopes were high for a fresh start, and he happily served on the Inflation Policy and International Monetary Policy Task Forces during the transition. But the demand restraint Fellner looked for was not to be found in the large supply-side tax cuts passed in 1981. Fellner was never partisan enough to silence his own dis-enchantment. In 1982 he was very critical of the Reagan Administration, calling its program to end inflation too timid, and its budget policy both based on unrealistic assumptions and bereft of any genuine attempt at deficit reduction. While chiding the nominally conservative White House for its fiscal heresy, Fellner also continued to attack what he regarded to be the true nemesis of democratic capitalism: neo-Keynesian economics. Under the influence of the neo-Keynesian view, policy prescriptions had come to be based on the concepts of the high-employment budget and potential output, about which Fellner had some major reservations. He believed the approach very unreliable since, in his view, estimates of potential output were made without the inclusion of key supply-side variables. Additionally, those variables are extremely difficult to predict, and their inclusion by no means guarantees that the high-employment budget will be based on accurate estimates of potential output. By Fellner's reckoning, fiscal policy predicated on these elusive concepts would be inflationary, lead to larger budget deficits, and divert savings from productive private investment in order to finance these increasingly larger deficits.

The year 1982 brought Fellner his last major award. His work was greatly admired in Western Europe, especially in West Germany. He had close ties with the Federal Republic's diplomatic corps, which played no small part in his receipt of the Commander's Cross in 1979. In West Germany itself, a nation historically obsessed with the maintenance of price stability, his work, particularly that on the inflation problem, was followed with care by economists in and out of government. Herbert Giersch, a former member of the West German Council of Economic Experts and longtime Fellner friend, as well as many other Fellner admirers in the Federal Republic decided that he should be recognized for his contributions to the field of economics. The outcome of their efforts was that Fellner was awarded the Bernhard-Harms Prize, the most prestigious honor that can be afforded to an economist in West Germany and one that some regard as second only to the Nobel Memorial Prize in Economic Sciences. Previous recipients included Harvard economist Wassily W. Leontief in 1970, a Nobel Laureate, originator of input-output analysis, and like Fellner, holder of the Ph.D. in economics from the University of Berlin. The Bernhard-Harms Prize is given by the University of Kiel's Institute of World Economics, to which Fellner traveled for the award ceremony held on June 26, 1982. That day Fellner presented his last major public lecture. Entitled "Economic Theory Amidst Political Currents: The Spreading Interest in Monetarism and in the Theory of Market Expectations," and later published in slightly abridged form in *Weltwirtschaftliches Archiv*, his lecture drew on many of the themes that had figured importantly in his work.

Fellner began his address with a reference to the late German-born Harvard economist, Joseph Schumpeter, and his famous speech, "The March into Socialism," delivered at the annual meeting of the American Economic Association in 1949. Fellner admired Schumpeter's work, and was sympathetic with his belief that the market economies of the West were headed for socialism, not due to Marxian internal contradictions within the capitalist system, but as victims of their own success. Schumpeter's thesis held that market capitalism could not survive the hostility of intellectuals who would spread contempt for private property and bourgeois values, pillars of the capitalist system. The public sector would grow until economic decisions had effectively been removed from private hands and given over to a bureaucracy under the control of the political authorities. Fellner agreed with Schumpeter's view that bureaucratic power and direction was at best a secondary factor in the trend toward socialism. Fellner believed that in the twentieth-century it had been the short-run orientation of voters which had hastened the advance of socialism. In his view, many voters came to expect an ever-increasing bounty from the welfare state, and sought to achieve those gains through the ballot box, rather than through economic activity. In 1981, Fellner had contributed an essay to a volume celebrating the fortieth anniversary of the publication of Schumpeter's *Capitalism, Socialism and Democracy*. In that essay, Fellner remarked that market economies have shown a surprising resilience to government intrusion, but that the post-1965 economic performance betrays a systemic weakening. However, before his audience in Kiel in June, 1982, the chord he struck, though cautious and tentative, was one of renewed optimism.

The more sanguine view expressed by Fellner had been prompted by what he perceived to be a greater interest on the part of policymakers in alternatives to conventional neo-Keynesian demand-management policy. These were seen as countercurrents to the increasing intrusiveness on the part of government into the operation of market economies. The two alternatives to orthodox policy discussed by Fellner were monetarism, and rational expectations. Fellner freely admitted that a stable income velocity of money is the key to the successful use of the monetarist approach, but that the requisite stability is never guaranteed. Despite the risks posed by this stability problem, he still believed the virtues of monetarism to be sufficient compensation. Monetarism provided a policy variable, the money stock, which the authorities were capable of controlling, and the intervention in the functioning of the economy to control it was relatively limited. Fellner believed that the full structural econometric models which formed the basis of neo-Keynesian policy prescriptions were undependable, since they required assumptions about variables beyond the control of the policymaking authorities. Fellner was fearful that attempts to circumvent the unreliability of these models might include bringing certain economic variables directly under the control of government through centralized and comprehensive economic planning. But he was heartened by the renewed interest in monetarism, taking it as a sign that policymakers preferred its simplified short-cut policy approach to those which risked more profound infringement on the operation of the marketplace. The interest in rational expectations was similarly characterized, though Fellner made it clear that he accepted only its "valid core." The interest of policymakers in the role of market expectations was taken as a good omen. According to Fellner, the post-1965 inflation was in part a result of the reliance on the full structural neo-Keynesian models which had failed to recognize that the marketplace takes the policy stance of government into account in forming its price expectations. Fellner was again fearful that the inflationary consequences of a policy that failed to take account of expectations would not lead to those flawed models being discarded or modified, but would result in an even more intrusive policy, the imposition of wage and price controls. He ended his address on a hopeful note, taking the recent interest in monetarism and rational expectations as evidence that past mistakes would not be repeated. The economic and political freedoms that had been fostered by unfettered markets could be preserved; "The March into Socialism" was not inevitable. The adoption of a credible policy aimed at disinflation was the best way to insure against that dreaded "March."

Entering the last year of his life, Fellner stressed issues and ideas that had long occupied a prominent place in his work. In an essay written for a volume published in 1983 for the centennary observation of Keynes' birth, he granted that the Keynesian savings-investment equality as an equilibrium condition was a seminal breakthrough in economic thought. But he rejected again the Keynesian belief in the tendency of market economies towards mass stagnation due to insufficent private investment spending, and castigated the neo-Keynesian views which he felt had bred inflationary demand-side management. He was unhappy with the unprecedented Federal budget deficits that had emerged in the Reagan years, which had encouraged consumption spending at the expense of the private investment spending needed to restore productivity growth. Fellner was generally approving of the actions of the Federal Reserve, including its move to widen the band of acceptable money growth due to the instability that had beset the velocity of money. He did fault the central bank for what he believed to be its failure to make clear to the public its commitment to price stability. In his view, a clearer commitment would have given policy added credibility. Since its inception in 1970, Fellner had been a regular participant on the Brookings Panel on Economic Activity. At the Brookings Panel meeting scheduled for September 15, 1983, he and Phillip Cagan were to present a paper on their study which claimed to show a curtailment of wage inflation as a result of the authorities having finally established a credible disinflationary policy. It is indeed fitting that Fellner's last moments were devoted to mounting yet another defense of his cherished credibility hypothesis. But on the morning of September 15, 1983, while preparing to attend the Brookings Panel meeting scheduled for later that day, he died suddenly of a heart attack in his Washington, D.C. home at the age of seventy-eight.

Fellner's passing was a reminder that those European economists, like Gottfried Haberler, Henry Wallich, Fritz Machlup and many others from that same tradition, who came to the United States in the 1930's to enrich and energize the economics discipline, have become a vanishing breed. Though it is safe to call Fellner a classical liberal in the nineteenth-century tradition, beyond that, his views defy easy categorization. He was more comfortable with the ideas of Joseph Schumpeter than with mainstream neo-Keynesianism. He believed an economy under market capitalism to be inherently stable, that it was government policy that often became a destabilizing force. Thus, he sought to keep within well-defined bounds the ability of government to intervene in the economic system.   Macroeconomic thought throughout most of the postwar period had accepted the idea that modern industrial economies, far from being intrinsically stable, were susceptible to shocks at unpredictable intervals and required the stabilizing hand of government. While the cleavage between Fellner's views and the mainstream set him at odds with the most prominent Keynesian economists of his era, it did not place him easily within one of the other competing schools of thought.   He personally rejected the label of monetarist, noting that he lacked the unalterable confidence in the predictability of the velocity of money generally associated with monetarism. At times he did appear to advocate the use of a monetary rule, that is, a constant rate of growth in the money stock. Yet on other occasions he supported adjustable money growth targets, and was willing to allow the monetary authorities to exercise judgment in certain special circumstances. This led to the accusation from uncompromising monetarists that he was promoting the ultimate apostasy, policy discretion. In the policy debate over rules versus discretion, Fellner often found rules to be helpful. Yet he was convinced that at times rules need to be adjusted, and sometimes, though perhaps rarely, to be completely discarded. But even this small concession to discretion was regarded as heresy by some monetarists. One of Fellner's main complaints against the neo-Keynesians had been that their elaborate econometric models fostered the illusion that they incorporated all the policymaker needed to know in order to conduct efficacious policy. Monetarism did not represent eternal truth to him. But he did feel that it offered policymakers the opportunity to take advantage of a simple economic regularity that had proved to be reliable under ordinary circumstances: the near constancy in the rate at which the money stock is turned over, the velocity of money. Fellner did not regard this constancy to be guaranteed at all times. Yet he thought it a sufficiently close approximation to reality most of the time, enough to make monetary policy a useful tool in helping to end the scourge of inflation.

Fellner's views on the role of fiscal policy also make the monetarist label a forced one. Monetarism asserts that the crowd-out effect associated with fiscal policy is complete, that is, an increase in government spending will result in an equal reduction in private investment spending. Thus, discretionary fiscal policy is dismissed as a determinant of the overall level of real economic activity. If the Keynesian notion of speculative demand is rejected, as the monetarists do, money demand is not influenced by the interest rate, and there is reason to believe the fiscal policy crowd-out to be complete. Fellner had always been dubious of the concept of speculative demand, and so was sympathetically disposed towards the monetarist view of fiscal policy. Yet rather than dismiss it completely, he chose to stress the importance of the built-in stabilizers of fiscal policy. Though hardly admiring of the big government that had given rise to them, he believed these stabilizers created an environment in which the simple monetary regularities could become established. Fellner's interpretation makes it possible to concede some sort of stabilizing role to fiscal policy, a kindness not granted by those subscribing to a more rigid brand of monetarism.

The theoretical and policy positions that Fellner held were clearly eclectic. He was a pragmatist in the best sense of the word. Where others might claim the evidence had revealed some rigorous theorem, he was more circumspect. His viewpoints were informed by a careful study of history. While many conservatives had embraced a balanced budget amendment as the answer to Federal deficits, Fellner was skeptical. Experience had taught him that democratic societies can invent endless evasions to subvert their own constitutional constraints. The strength of his historical orientation is disclosed no more forcefully than in his belief that inflation left untamed would prove the final undoing of market capitalism. He had witnessed the great hyperinflations that ravaged the economies on the European continent in the interwar period. Haberler states that he was deeply affected by the "claims inflation" of that era, the process by which group rivalries and social conflicts were resolved. Fellner was alarmed by the relaxed view of "claims inflation" held by so many of his contemporaries in the post-1965 period. James Tobin had commented that there were far more dangerous means through which to resolve the inconsistent income claims of competing groups within society. Such acquiescence was troubling to Fellner, and his distaste for the market power exerted by labor unions can be traced to the adjustment difficulties he thought they caused by their ability to perpetuate the process of "claims inflation."

Fellner always made clear that he was not a proponent of unqualified laissez-faire capitalism. He believed that society has a responsibility to assure the subsistence of all of its members. But the accomplishment of this task should never be allowed to compromise other important objectives, price stability being a primary one. It is in this sense that Fellner was a partisan of conservatism, urging that we do all that is necessary to nurture and preserve those institutional arrangements that have accounted for the continued growth in the prosperity of the Western nations, and to foster the spread of democratic capitalism to the rest of the world.

On October 1, 1983, Fellner was eulogized at a memorial service held at American University in Washington, D.C. Tributes were paid by Gottfried Haberler, Herbert Stein, James Tobin, Henry Wallich, and Bela Balassa. It was not just Fellner the economist who was remembered, but "Willy," the man and friend who had commanded their respect and attention for so many years. A litany of praise was recited: the impeccable manners and Old-World courtliness; the courtesy and conciliatory tone always shown to others; the sophistication without pretension; the epitome of the civilized and cultured man, fluent in several languages and well-versed in English, German and Hungarian literature; a scholar of the first rank whose work was informed by a sense of history. Fellner had a strong appreciation for the tentative nature of our understanding of economic behavior. Stein mentioned Fellner's respect for the truth and respect for others, that he never confused his own ideas with the "unassailable verities," and that the positions he took were undogmatic, carefully qualified and tempered with humanity. Since the reflections of colleagues of like mind are expected to be generous, the most telling remarks often times come from an adversary. It was James Tobin, a former colleague at Yale and the embodiment of neo-Keynesianism, who perhaps best expressed Fellner's enduring legacy to the economics profession by voicing his admiration for Fellner's "focus on essential issues, respect for evidence, and intellectual integrity."

CHAPTER II
Works by Fellner

1. BOOKS BY FELLNER

Fellner, William J. *A Treatise on War Inflation: Present Policies and Future Tendencies in the United States.* Berkeley: University of California Press, 1942.

> This book was the first publication of the University of California's newly formed Bureau of Business and Economic Research. Fellner claims that the chaos and inflation usually accompanying wars financed primarily by borrowing can be avoided. He recommends a sound fiscal policy combined with monetary restraint. War inflation is discussed, and its prevention through the removal of redundant income is explained. A non-inflationary approach to the American war effort would include the use of progressive income taxation, borrowing household and corporate savings, price ceilings and rationing. Political agreement on an equitable sharing of burdens is needed, and the income tax provides the mechanism by which to allocate those burdens. The corporate income tax could harm incentives and efficiency, especially in the postwar period, and is not recommended.

Monetary Policies and Full Employment. Berkeley: University of California Press, 1946.

> This book, originally published under the auspices of the University of California's Bureau of Business and Economic Research, was reprinted in 1983 as part of the Garland Publishing Series on *Gold, Money, Inflation and Deflation.* Secular stagnation and its chronic mass unemployment are discounted. The problem confronting American economic well-being is cyclical unemployment. It would be a mistake for government to guarantee full employ-

ment. Inflation would follow such a guarantee, and lead to direct government controls, which would be as destructive to the social fabric of a democracy as mass stagnation. Fellner recommends using expansionary fiscal and
monetary policy at first sign of recession, to be halted if either business investment revives or inflationary pressures appear. His proposals resemble
Keynesian fine-tuning, which he so adamantly opposed later. Policy should
aim for an acceptable level of employment, not guarantee full employment.
Fellner emphasized the dangers of overly ambitious employment goals
throughout his career.

Competition Among the Few: Oligopoly and Similar Market Structures. New York:
Knopf, 1949.

This work provides a thorough exposition of the various oligopoly theories
and bilateral monopoly, including the Stackelberg solution, institutional considerations, and social welfare effects. Collective bargaining, labor-manage-
ment relations, and anti-trust are some of the public policy issues addressed.
Given imperfect coordination among firms in oligopoly, Fellner develops a
model of qualified joint profit maximization. This book's most lasting contribution is the replacement of the restrictive Cournot-Edgeworth assumptions
with a mathematical reaction function to make explicit the mutual interdependencies among oligopolistic rivals. Fellner argues that the case against
monopoly is a stronger one than that against oligopoly, because the latter can
encourage technological advance and may also improve the distribution of
income. This book was not universally well-received when published, but
remains an important reference in the oligopoly literature. The second edition (1960), published by Augustus M. Kelley, has a new and interesting introduction.

*Trends and Cycles in Economic Activity: An Introduction to Problems of Economic
Growth.* New York: Holt, 1956.

This is probably Fellner's most important book. It is perhaps best viewed as
a lucid synthesis of existing work rather than a work of original insights. Yet
it is still regarded as one of the finest statements of the conditions that must
be satisfied for an economy to enjoy sustained growth. The technical aspects
involved in identifying trends and cycles are presented. An entire chapter is
devoted to narratives of every major world economic downturn since 1825.
Fellner's main thesis is that sustained economic growth depends on three fac-

tors: (1) the capacity to offset diminishing returns through technological and organizational improvements; (2) sufficiently mobile resources; and (3) a flexible monetary mechanism to assure price stability. Cyclical disturbances and policies to foster growth in early and later stages of development are also considered.

Emergence and Content of Modern Economic Analysis. New York: McGraw-Hill, 1960.

Fellner based this book on the lecture notes he had prepared for an undergraduate economics course at Yale. Its didactic focus may explain why this excellent book did not receive the attention it deserved. ˙Fellner was convinced that students of contemporary economic theory must come to appreciate its historical antecedents, the extent to which economic thought is influenced by the problems confronted in each era, and the tentative, evolutionary nature of economic understanding. These purposes are accomplished admirably in this book, which opens with a discussion of deductive and inductive reasoning, and normative and positive economics. It then covers the Ancients, Mercantilism, Physiocracy, the Classical School, Marxian views, and Neoclassical economics. The key features of modern microeconomics and macroeconomics are developed. The book concludes by applying economic analysis to a variety of policy questions, including monopoly, full employment, and international problems. Few books have captured the vast sweep of economic thought as this one does.

The Problem of Rising Prices. Paris: Organization for European Economic Cooperation, 1961, co-authored with Milton Gilbert et al.

In 1959 Fellner was appointed by the Council of the Organization for European Economic Cooperation to be a member of a Group of Independent Experts to study the problem of rising prices. The study endorses stable prices as desirable and feasible, and maintains that inflation is the by-product of policies instituted to maintain high employment and growth. The causes of inflation and the effectiveness of the measures taken to assure price stability are examined. The study covers 1953-60 in the U.S. and other, mainly Western European, countries. The record of price inflation for the study period is reviewed. Excess aggregate demand and excessive negotiated wage increases are the main causes of inflation, while temporary factors and monopolistic pricing are of minor importance. Fellner and Lutz state their own reservations concerning the Group's endorsement of wage guidelines. Balance of payment issues are also given consideration. Appendices with supporting charts and tables comprise the bulk of this book.

Probability and Profit: A Study of Economic Behavior along Bayesian Lines. Home-wood, Ill.: Irwin, 1965.

This book is an outgrowth of Fellner's participation in a symposium on decision-making under uncertainty in 1961. Observed behavior held to be irrational by the standard axioms of decision theory is rationalized by the concept of semiprobability. When subjective probabilities are precarious, they can be slanted, or revised downward, to form semiprobabilities. These then enter as decision weights into the calculation of the expected change in utility from a given course of action. Fellner uses his semiprobabilistic concepts to construct a theory of profit, making the controversial claim that his approach provides a better explanation of some economic behavior than does existing decision theory. Applications are presented and conclusions drawn, including the belief that average cost pricing may be a rational tendency in the face of uncertainty. An excellent bibliography of fifty-two major works in decision theory with detailed commentaries is provided.

Towards a Reconstruction of Macroeconomics: Problems of Theory and Policy. Washington, D.C.: American Enterprise Institute, 1976.

Whether this book truly reconstructs macroeconomics is debatable. However, its main thesis, the credibility hypothesis, is argued with force and eloquence. Policy aimed at price stability can succeed only if market participants are convinced that a policy reversal will not occur if adverse, transitional employment effects appear. This is Fellner's idea of credible policy. A less credible policy will eventually require a greater decline in output to restore non-inflationary growth. Phillips Curve trade-offs do not exist. Demand-side management predicated on such beliefs will only lead to accelerating inflation. The private enterprise system cannot endure without a reasonably stable price level. Continued inflation will result in comprehensive wage and price controls, which are inconsistent with Western democratic values. Actual inflation should roughly equal expected inflation, or else public expectations become conditioned to steepening inflation. Demand-management should aim for a predictable and horizontal price trend. The deflationary propositions implied by Say's Law, as well as the inflationary ones seen in the Keynesian system, are rejected. Deficiencies on both sides of the neo-Keynesian-monetarist debate are cited. Fellner opposes incomes policy, and favors a gradualist approach to the restoration of price stability.

2. ARTICLES AND ESSAYS BY FELLNER

Fellner, William J. "Savings, Investment, and the Problem of Neutral Money," *Review of Economic Statistics,* November, 1938, pp. 185-92.

> This article, translated from the German, was Fellner's first publication in a major American journal. He asserts that it is impossible for economic policy to prevent monetary disturbances from affecting the real economy, that is, there is no way to maintain neutral money. Attempts by policymakers to counteract the a-neutral effects of such disturbances may lead to even greater economic instability.

"Hicks and the Time-period Controversy," *Journal of Political Economy*, August, 1940, pp. 563-78, co-authored with Howard S. Ellis.

> In his *Value and Capital*, Hicks presents a theory of interest which he claims to be a synthesis of those theories that incorporate a time-period element and those that do not. Time-period theories were built around the idea that the value embodied in capital goods is ultimately transformed into value in the form of consumption output, and that the average time period within which this transformation occurs is inversely related to the interest rate. Opponents of this view reject the notion of a meaningful time period. Hicks develops a concept similar to that of bond duration which purports to show the average time deferment of a future stream of "surpluses" to be inversely related to the interest rate. Fellner and Ellis view Hicks' time-period as an appendage which is not integrated into his theory of interest, and dismiss his claimed synthesis.

"Alternative Monetary Approaches to Interest Theory," *Review of Economic Statistics*, February, 1941, pp. 43-48, co-authored with Harold M. Somers.

> An attempt is made to reconcile the loanable-funds theory of the interest rate with the approach taken by Keynes in his *General Theory*, the liquidity preference theory of the interest rate. A graphical analysis is presented which purports to show that both approaches yield identical results. Keynes claimed the demand for idle money balances to be an important determinant of the interest rate. However, the authors view the introduction of the notion

of idle balances as an unnecessary complication which provides no additional insight into the determination of the interest rate.

"The Technological Argument of the Stagnation Thesis," *Quarterly Journal of Economics*, August, 1941, pp. 638-51.

In the United States, the early followers of Keynes developed a stagnation thesis, which held in part that technological improvement provides little economic stimulus for mature economies because the innovations they tend to experience are not ones which lead to an increase in capital employed per unit of output (a "deepening" of capital). Fellner rejects this view, believing there to be no reliable evidence showing that innovations had become less capital deepening as capitalism matured. He also claims that technological improvement that deepens capital implies nothing about the strength of the economic stimulus it provides.

"Uncertainty and Idle Balances," *Proceedings of the Twentieth Annual Conference of the Pacific Coast Economic Association*, December, 1941, pp. 40-45.

The empirical evidence suggests that the level of idle balances rose substantially in the post-1929 period. Fellner agrees, but rejects the explanation of the speculative theory of hoarding. That theory asserts that idle money will be preferred to interest-bearing securities if an interest rate increase is expected that would cause a decline in security values more than sufficient to wipe out the yield on securities. He finds this theory implausible since it requires the widespread public expectation of an increase in the interest rate and declining bond prices, when in fact the time period was characterized by an uptrend in bond prices. Fellner gives his own theory, in which idle balances are held by business if it is believed that producer losses have become more likely while at the same time access to credit has become more difficult. Such a combination of events could force a liquidation. Holding idle balances offers protection against this possibility. Comments by Robert E. Rapp follow.

"Monetary Policies and Hoarding in Periods of Stagnation," *Journal of Political Economy*, June, 1943, pp. 191-205.

Uncertainty leads firms to invest less than that level consistent with profit maximization, that is, firms maintain safety margins. In a period of stagnation, profit expectations decline and these safety margins may be viewed as inadequate. The restoration of these margins will necessitate a reduction in investment even if the trend in interest rates is downward. In regard to idle balances, a rise in the rate of interest will diminish safety margins and increase the firm's demand for such balances. Yet a higher interest rate reduces such hoarding by making it more expensive. On balance, the interest elasticity of idle balances is small. If both private investment and idle balances are interest inelastic, then the only kind of policy with any hope of success is government spending financed by borrowing from the central bank.

"External Economies and Diseconomies," *American Economic Review*, September, 1943, pp. 493-511, co-authored with Howard S. Ellis.

In the presence of external diseconomies, Pigou argued that the level of ouput in a competitive market would be in excess of what is socially ideal since rent is not properly included as part of social cost. A tax on output would assure a market outcome consistent with the social optimum. Pigou was subsequently found to be in error when it became widely agreed that rent is not a social cost. The authors contend that it does not necessarily follow that the competitively-determined and socially-ideal levels of output coincide in the case of external economies, which do represent a true offset to social cost. The market will produce less than the social ideal. A permanent subsidy would be appropriate if the external economies are of the sort that vanish if output contracts. Irreversible external economies would require only a temporary subsidy.

"Period Analysis and Timeless Equilibrium," *Quarterly Journal of Economics*, February, 1944, pp. 315-22.

The income-expenditure model is used to compare the multiplier and equilibrium in the Robertsonian and Swedish models with that for the Keynesian system. The period analysis of the Robertsonian and Swedish models produce roughly equivalent outcomes in terms of the cumulative increase in income from a temporary increase in expenditures. Under certain conditions, the results of the Keynesian approach are also similar. However, one very important qualification is made. Fellner says that if the expenditure increase is assumed permanent the time dimension can no longer be ignored, that is, timeless equilibrium must be abandoned. The multiplier must be defined in terms of dollars over time, and the dynamic aspects connected with the time required to restore equilibrium become important considerations.

"Postscript on War Inflation: A Lesson from World War II," *American Economic Review*, March, 1947, pp. 76-91.

Fellner examines the tax policies that would have been needed to eliminate inflationary pressures in the American economy during World War II. His analysis is framed in terms of the cost of living, and uses the concepts of ex ante and ex post inflation potential in the determination of the required tax policy. He finds that a proportionate tax of 10% applied to all income without exemption, and superimposed upon the existing tax structure, would have eliminated all inflationary potential from the economy. The government would not have had to resort to war bond drives. Out of concern for the possibility of adverse effects on savings and incentives, the use of a proportionate tax increase is preferred to one that incorporates some progressivity in it. The application of the approach suggested by Fellner to the problems of peacetime inflation is briefly discussed.

"Hansen on Full-Employment Policies," *Journal of Political Economy*, June, 1947, pp. 254-56.

Fellner reviews Alvin Hansen's *Economic Policy and Full Employment*, in which compensatory fiscal policies are suggested as a remedy for cyclical instability. Though some merit is seen in such policies, Fellner does not feel that Hansen fully appreciates their limitations. He would reserve serious government intervention to situations of mass unemployment. The full employment guarantee contemplated by Hansen will create chronic upward pressure on wages and prices, a possibility that Hansen does not give adequate consideration. Inflation of this kind will lead to administrative controls that are incompatible with democratic values. Fellner feels Hansen has not confronted the question of how political freedom is to be balanced against economic objectives.

"Prices and Wages under Bilateral Monopoly," *Quarterly Journal of Economics*, August, 1947, pp. 503-32.

The theory of bilateral monopoly is applied to the labor market to examine wages and employment under collective bargaining. Using indifference analysis, it is shown that a labor union will find it advantageous to contract for a combination of wages and employment on an all-or-none basis rather than simply for wages if its wage-employment preferences involve a trade-off between the wage rate and the amount of employment. The effect of a wage increase on general equilibrium is considered. Employment will rise if the investment displaced by the wage increase is more than offset by the reduction in uncertainty faced by producers. In a reconsideration of bilateral monopoly theory, the cases in which either the seller or the buyer is assumed to dominate are found invalid since alternative outcomes exist in which both parties benefit. The indeterminacy characteristic of bilateral monopoly is discussed.

"Monetary Policy and the Elasticity of Liquidity Functions," *Review of Economics and Statistics*, February, 1948, pp. 42-44.

Fellner responds to criticism from James Tobin relating to the shape of the liquidity preference function. He agrees that the function will become horizontal at a sufficiently low rate of interest, but argues that an economy usually operates along the inelastic range of the liquidity preference function. This being the case, alteration of his policy prescriptions is not warranted. In a deep depression, expansion cannot be produced by either open market purchases or government spending financed by borrowing from the public or the commercial banks. With inelastic liquidity preference, only government spending financed by borrowing from the central bank will bring expansion. Fellner contests Tobin's empirical estimate of the liquidity preference function, claiming its methodology flawed.

"Average-Cost Pricing and the Theory of Uncertainty," *Journal of Political Economy*, June, 1948, pp. 249-52.

Firms often operate in circumstances in which their demand functions and cost functions are not known with certainty. This being the case, Fellner argues that it is not optimal for firms to simply produce at that level of output for which expected marginal revenue is equal to expected marginal cost. Firms are treated as risk averters, and the best guess rule does not afford maximum safety from losses that result should the best guess turn out to be wrong. In a world of uncertainty, firms may choose to maximize safety margins. Fellner shows that such behavior closely approximates average full-cost pricing. Discrepencies between theory and observation are resolved in light of the way rational firms alter their behavior in the face of uncertainty.

"Employment Theory and Business Cycles," Chapter Two in *A Survey of Contemporary Economics, Volume I*, edited by Howard S. Ellis, Homewood, Ill.: Irwin, 1948, pp. 49-98.

> The state of employment and business cycle theory is examined. Contemporary theories of employment are cast largely in terms of the savings-investment framework, rather than the quantity theory approach, because the propensities to consume and save are generally regarded as more predictable than the habits governing money demand. Employment theory needs to be integrated with the theory of economic fluctuations, and some recent savings-investment models may make this possible. The stagnationist hypotheses are found unconvincing since there is no evidence unambiguously supporting the view that mature economies face chronic underemployment. Overinvestment and underconsumption theories of the business cycle are critiqued. Uncertainty and market rigidities as potential barriers to full employment are assessed. Compensatory fiscal policies can be useful to relieve mass unemployment, but will be inflationary when used as part of a full employment guarantee.

"Note on 'Stocks' and 'Flows' in Monetary Interest Theory," *Review of Economics and Statistics*, May, 1949, pp. 145-46, co-authored with Harold M. Somers.

> A mathematical model is presented which indicates that a theory of the interest rate can be formulated either in terms of flows or of stocks. An approach employing the flow concept will produce results identical with those for the stock approach. This paper is intended to add additional force to an argument made by the authors in a previous work, namely, that Keynes' concept of liquidity preference does not constitute a major departure from the loanable funds theory.

"Collusion and Its Limits Under Oligopoly," *American Economic Review*, May, 1950, pp. 54-62.

> The term "collusion" typically means the spontaneous coordination of business policies, rather than direct contact or explicit agreement. This tendency towards coordination results from the fact that oligopolists, being few in

number, recognize their mutual interdependence, and can react to their rivals. The relative bargaining positions of firms in an oligopolized market are subject to unpredictable changes, and this effectively limits the degree of their collusion. Permissible competition is usually confined to cost-saving innovations, new advertising, and product variations. Constraints on behavior are observed, and violators face retaliation. Anti-trust policy should focus on the elimination of artificial barriers to entry.

"Stock and Flow Analysis: Comment," *Econometrica*, July, 1950, pp. 242-45, co-authored with Harold M. Somers.

Lawrence R. Klein took issue with the claim made by the authors in their previous publications that the choice between a stock and a flow approach in a theory of the interest rate is irrelevant. Klein also wrote that the liquidity preference theory of the interest rate is not identical with the loanable funds theory. He believes that their error is rooted in a confusion of the stock and flow concepts. Fellner and Somers state that Klein's criticism derives mainly from his peculiar definition of stock analysis, and that their definition is one that is in widespread use by others. They hold to their original positions concerning stock and flow analysis and Keynes' liquidity perference.

"Stock and Flow Analysis: Note on the Discussion," *Econometrica*, July, 1950, p. 252, co-authored with Harold M. Somers.

In a continuation of their debate with Klein, Fellner and Somers express the view that certain differences of opinion have been bridged. They agree that liquidity preference theory is distinct from loanable funds theory, but only if the interest rate can move even though the supply of and demand for claims is in equality. However, they do not believe this to be what Keynes intended by his liquidity preference. While they feel that Klein has unfairly termed their approach "static", it is conceded that his type of dynamic approach may prove more useful in economic analysis.

"'Competitive' Output in Bilateral Monopoly," *Quarterly Journal of Economics*, November, 1950, pp. 648-50.

In this brief note Fellner responds to criticism of a proposition in his article "Prices and Wages under Bilateral Monopoly," *Quarterly Journal of Economics*, August, 1947, made by James N. Morgan in the August, 1949 issue of the same journal. Morgan claims that bilateral monopoly cannot result in an output level that is "competitive." Fellner rejects Morgan's assertion that the seller-monopolist in his analysis must be assumed to act as a unilaterally monopsonistic buyer, thus vitiating his results. His use of the term competitive in quotes is said to be consistent with its use in describing non-competitive conditions, and was not intended to imply a perfectly competitive outcome. A short reply by Morgan follows Fellner's note.

"The Influence of Market Structure on Technological Progress," *Quarterly Journal of Economics*, November, 1951, pp. 556-77.

What effect does market structure have on the adoption of inventions? In perfect competition, a single cost-reducing unexpected innovation will be adopted, causing new entry, price reductions and output growth. With no barriers to entry and either monopolistic competition or monopoly, the outcome depends on special factors. With blocked entry, existing firms adopt an innovation only if marginal revenue intersects long-run marginal cost at an output level greater than (Fellner specifies greater than or equal to, but later issued a correction prompted by the criticism of Alvin Marty) that at which total cost with plant adjustment equals total variable cost without plant adjustment. This test assures that the fixed costs of the existing plant are taken into account. A correctly anticipated flow of innovations given blocked entry will be adopted if this test is passed and further superior innovations are unlikely. The case of free entry is qualified by special factors. Welfare effects and the patent problem are considered.

"The Capital-Output Ratio in Dynamic Economics," in *Money, Trade, and Economic Growth*, by David M. Wright et al., New York: Macmillan, 1951, pp. 105-34.

This article is Fellner's contribution to a volume of essays in honor of John Henry Williams of Harvard. The Keynesian framework, business cycle and innovation theories are all inadequate explanations of investment spending and its role in achieving full employment. Building on the work of Harrod, Domar, and others, including his own, Fellner constructs a model which shows the level of investment needed to sustain full employment equilibrium, taking as given the capital-output ratio, the rate of growth in full employment output, and the full employment level for savings. His theory must be substantially qualified should a discrepancy between savings and investment lead to adjustments in the capital-output ratio and the growth rate in output.

Such adjustments require that resource scarcities and uncertainty be incorporated into the analysis. The model is compared to the acceleration principle and underconsumption theories, and is applied in a quantitative appendix.

"The Robertsonian Evolution," *American Economic Review*, June, 1952, pp. 265-82.

Fellner was a fond admirer of the work of British economist D. H. Robertson. The admiration he showed for Keynes and his *General Theory* was considerably less generous. In this article, Fellner claims that much of the economics included in what is called the Keynesian Revolution has in fact evolved from the previous work of Robertson. The relationship between savings and investment, and its implications for the direction of macroeconomic activity are ideas which Fellner chooses to attribute to Robertson. The analytical apparatus developed by Keynes is compared to Robertson's. There are similarities, such as Robertson's recognition of the need for compensatory monetary-fiscal policy in the face of a deep depression. Keynes is portrayed as focusing so exclusively on the problem of unemployment that he failed to appreciate the inflationary dangers inherent in pursuing a program of full employment. Robertson's approach is viewed as superior because it can also address the question of price stability.

"Elasticities, Cross-Elasticities, and Market Relationships: Comment," *American Economic Review*, December, 1953, pp. 898-910.

Robert Bishop claims in his paper that difficulties arise in the classification of market relations based solely on the cross-elasticity of demand. He suggests a classification scheme which uses the ratio of price elasticity to cross-elasticity. Fellner's comment critiques Bishop's proposed scheme. Fellner believes that the idealized market structures of economic theory can be fully described based on cross-elasticities alone, thus making Bishop's more elaborate approach unnecessary. While granting that the difficulties pointed out by Bishop do arise in determining whether a real world market fits some idealized market structure, Fellner again rejects Bishop's approach. He recommends classification based on the use of a simple adjustment to cross-elasticity, which has the added virtue of avoiding the logical difficulties of Bishop's scheme.

"Long-Term Tendencies in Private Capital Formation: The Rate of Growth and Capital Coefficients," in *Long-Range Economic Projection: Studies in Income and Wealth, Volume XVI*, by The Conference on Research in Income and Wealth of the National Bureau of Economic Research, Princeton, N.J.: Princeton University Press, 1954, pp. 275-331.

> This paper is Fellner's contribution to a volume that studies long-range economic projection. He examines ways to generate long-run projections of investment for the U.S. economy, focusing on methodology rather than specific forecasts. He suggests that such projections be based on estimates of the long-run growth in output combined with estimates for the long-term relationship between capital and output. This method is compared to other variants of the acceleration principle, those proposed by Samuelson, Harrod-Domar, and Hicks. Using the Kuznets' data estimates that extend back to 1869, Fellner assesses the stability of the relationships critical to his approach. He compares his results with the conclusions of a study by the Council of Economic Advisers in the January, 1950 *Annual Economic Review*.

"Individual Investment Projects in Growing Economies: General Characteristics of the Problem and Comments on the Conference Papers," in *Investment Criteria and Economic Growth*, by Jan Tinbergen et al., Cambridge, Mass.: Center for International Studies, M.I.T., 1955, pp. 119-47.

> Fellner presented this paper at a conference sponsored jointly by the Center for International Studies and the Social Science Research Council. The issue addressed in this paper is the appropriate criterion by which to judge investment projects in growing economies. In the absence of government interference in the economy, projects which maximize the present value of future net income should be accepted. This simple rule must be qualified when government intrudes either by outright ownership or by a policy of subsidization, taxation or regulation. The infant industry problem is used as an illustration of that qualification. The impact on project acceptability of government concern with income distribution, monopoly power and external economies is discussed. A brief comparison with decision-making under the Soviet model is made. Comments on the papers of other conference participants are offered.

"Post-war Economic Tendencies in the United States," in *The Business Cycle in the Post-war World*, edited by Erik Lundberg, London: Macmillan, 1955, pp. 11-36.

This paper is the product of Fellner's participation in an international conference on the business cycle in the postwar era. Economic experience in the
United States from 1945-52 is detailed. Possible explanations for the general
prosperity of the period are presented, including defense spending, the
postwar restoration of the capital stock (behavior of the capital-output ratio
is important in this assessment), the contribution of construction activity, and
the high degree of postwar liquidity. The main features of the 1948-49
recession are reviewed. The American economy is viewed as less depression-
prone in the postwar era due to the added significance of automatic
stabilizers and a greater willingness to make use of compensatory government policy. Additional topics such as foreign aid, armaments, the capital-
output ratio, and monetization of the public debt are covered in appendices.
The volume in which this paper appears includes a summary record of the
discussion of all conference papers.

"Relative Emphasis in Tax Policy on Encouragement of Consumption or Investment," in *Federal Tax Policy for Economic Growth and Stability*, Papers Submitted by Panelists Appearing Before the Subcommittee on Tax Policy, Joint Committee on the Economic Report, 84th Congress, November 9, 1955, Washington, D.C.:
United States Government Printing Office, 1955, pp. 210-17.

This paper was one of many submitted to Congress on the question of tax
policy. With economic growth causing tax revenues to rise relative to fiscal
expenditures, Fellner agrees that the resultant fiscal drag might slow economic growth. Sounding like a fine-tuning Keynesian, he recommends a tax
reduction. Although the magnitude of its effect is less predictable, a cut in
corporate income tax rates is favored over a cut in individual income tax
rates. The rationale is that a cut in corporate taxes will encourage capital
formation and foster a more rapid rate of economic growth. The improvements in labor productivity that result will eventually raise real wage rates.
Thus, wage earners can also expect to benefit.

"The Balancing of Objectives Under the Employment Act of 1946," in *The Employment Act Past and Future*, Special Report No. 41, edited by Gerhard Colm,
Washington, D.C.: National Planning Association, 1956, pp. 87-91.

This essay was included in a volume commemorating the tenth anniversary of
the passage of the Employment Act of 1946. Fellner sees its main importance to be the formal recognition on the part of government of its responsi-

bility to put in place discretionary policies to assure full employment. The failure of the Act to make explicit mention of price stability and growth as desirable objectives is noted with regret. While accepting the idea behind the Act, the avoidance of a repetition of the deep depression of the 1930's, he remains true to character by sounding his concern that the pursuit of a full employment policy carries with it the danger of chronic inflation.

Discussion Paper for Session "Economic Growth I: Statement of the Problem of Keeping the U.S. Economy Moving Forward, But Steadily," *American Economic Review*, May, 1956, pp. 35-37.

> Fellner comments on an aspect of the problem addressed by the main papers of this session. Technological-organizational progress fosters economic growth only if it distributes its labor and capital savings impacts in accord with relative resource scarcities. With this in mind, Fellner is concerned that the trend toward a more service-oriented economy noted in Homan's paper may put a drag on growth unless the improvements in that sector are labor-saving. He disputes the claim in Abramowitz's paper attributing continued growth in output to growth in resource use. Output has grown in rough proportion to the capital stock and in higher proportion to other resource inputs, facts more plausibly explained by the more rapid technological-organizational progress.

"Quantitative Sufficiency of Innovations and Proper Distribution of Their Factor-Saving Effects," *Economie Appliquee*, Summer, 1956, pp. 283-313.

> This article was published in French. In reprint form, a brief abstract in English is provided. Fellner argues that technological improvements in the Western industrialized economies have been sufficiently plentiful and properly distributed in terms of their input savings effects to offset the tendency toward diminishing returns. Long-term trends along these lines in the United States are studied. According to Fellner, technological innovation has led to a clear uptrend in real wages, and a mild yet not very uniform downtrend in the returns to the capital input.

"Patinkin's Integration of Monetary and Value Theory," *American Economic Review*, December, 1956, pp. 947-55.

This article reviews Don Patinkin's *Money, Interest and Prices*, which attempts to formulate a unified theory of microeconomics and macroeconomics with the demand for real money balances serving as the connecting variable. Fellner regards Patinkin's model as firmly rooted in the neoclassical tradition, since it describes a system in which perfectly flexible wages and prices assure full employment. The static, non-dynamic nature of the model is seen as its chief weakness, one which tends to undermine Patinkin's claim to have removed the false dichotomy between monetary theory and value theory.

"Marxian Hypotheses and Observable Trends under Capitalism: A 'Modernized' Interpretation," *Economic Journal*, March, 1957, pp. 16-25.

The analytical apparatus of classical microeconomic theory is used by Fellner to assess the Marxian claim that technological progress is part of a process that inevitably leads to unfavorable downtrends in both wage rates and profit rates, culminating in the eventual collapse of capitalism. On a purely theoretical level, Fellner finds little to support the Marxian view. Assuming a Cobb-Douglas production function, his analysis indicates that innovating activity ordinarily increases the absolute returns to all inputs, although the relative share of some inputs may decline. It is also noted that historical experience has thus far contradicted the predictions made by Marx.

"Automatic Market Clearance and Innovations in the Theory of Employment and Growth," *Oxford Economic Papers*, June, 1958, pp. 184-204.

The manner in which Say's Law and the neutrality of money would hold in an economy in a stationary equilibrium of zero net investment is described. Along a path of dynamic equilibrium, in a growing economy with increasing resource supplies and technological-organizational knowledge, the neutrality of money is generally not valid and Say's Law must be modified to allow for the possibility that capacity utilization may be the norm but only at a substantially reduced rate of growth. The relative prosperity of the Western economies is attributed to the high level of technical innovation, not seen as the inevitable outcome of a system governed by Say's Law. The capital stock has risen relative to the supply of labor, but the level of innovation has maintained the productivity of capital. The character of that innovating activity (its balance between capital- and labor-saving) has prevented any appreciable decline in the rate of return on capital, while allowing for an uptrend in real wages rates.

"Politics, Economics, and Recession," *The Yale Review*, September, 1958, pp. 1-16.

Fellner sounds some themes that recur throughout much of his writing. He agrees that a deep depression requires substantial government intervention. However, relatively minor departures from full employment, such as the 1957-58 recession in the U.S., should be treated with benign neglect. Insistence upon the maintenance of a rigidly adopted level of employment will provoke inflation, and lead to comprehensive administrative controls, harming the performance of a market economy and diminishing personal freedoms.

"Relative Permanent Income: Elaboration and Synthesis," *Journal of Political Economy*, October, 1959, pp. 508-11.

Fellner discusses the study by Eisner in which it was concluded that consumption is more sensitive to income for between-group comparisons than for within-group comparisons. A group can be defined, for example, by occupation, or by age. Eisner believed his findings supported the permanent income hypothesis, since the transitory components of income within a given group tend to cancel, and income measurement then introduces much smaller distortions. Fellner says that the data in Eisner's study is also consistent with the relative income hypothesis. If a household moves between groups, rather within a given group, it will have to change its consumption more in order to establish its standing relative to the new group it has joined.

"Possibilities of Broadening the Tax Base, Reducing Tax Rates, and Promoting Economic Growth," in *Tax Revision Compendium*, Vol. 1, Compendium of Papers on Broadening the Tax Base, Submitted to the Committee on Ways and Means, 86th Congress, November 16, 1959, Washington, D.C.: United States Government Printing Office, 1959, pp. 193-99.

This paper was one of many submitted to the Committee on Ways and Means on the question of tax reform. In the 1950's, the tax base in the United States was small. Consequently, marginal tax rates were high. Fellner states that a tax system structured in this way is harmful to economic incentives, and is in need of reform. He proposes a 15% cut in individual marginal tax rates with increased personal exemptions. This would be coupled with a 7% retail sales tax on about 40% of all consumption expenditures. While some groups at low income levels may be slightly burdened, the combined effect would be revenue neutral. But the tax base would be broadened, tax rates reduced, savings encouraged, and incentives for behavior that promotes economic growth improved.

"Demand Inflation, Cost Inflation, and Collective Bargaining," Chapter Eleven in *The Public Stake in Union Power*, edited by Philip D. Bradley, Charlottesville, Va.: University of Virginia Press, 1959, pp. 225-54.

A distinction between demand inflation and cost inflation is drawn in which the former can be suppressed without reducing the level of resource utilization, whereas the latter can be controlled only by temporarily elevating the unemployment rate. If recent experience has been non-inflationary, cost inflation of the wage-push type can be ended with little additional unemployment. Left unattended, wage-push inflation tends to accelerate. Fellner regards the 1951-57 experience in the United States to be one of wage-push inflation, while Great Britain faced a demand inflation. With most unemployment in the United States of relatively short duration, he would accept more unemployment on a temporary basis to achieve price stability. Alternatives to restrictive monetary-fiscal policies as a means to control inflation are discussed. Price controls are rejected, while the extension of the anti-trust laws to labor unions, though not politically feasible, is given a sympathetic treatment.

"Professor Baumol's New Approach to the Theory of the Firm," *Kyklos*, Vol. 13, No. 1, 1960, pp. 110-12.

Fellner critiques the theory of the firm presented by William J. Baumol in his book, *Business Behavior, Value and Growth*. Baumol states that as a result of the separation of management from ownership the objective of the modern corporation is to maximize sales revenue subject to the constraint that some minimum level of profitability be achieved. Fellner sees this as simply another way of saying that competition tends to eliminate abnormally high profits. He also feels that there are inconsistencies between the macroeconomics and microeconomics that Baumol derives from his model.

"Rapid Growth as an Objective of Economic Policy," *American Economic Review*, May, 1960, pp. 93-105.

Addressing dissatisfaction with the rate of economic growth in the 1950's, Fellner recommends policies that will promote the kind of capital formation that incorporates technological advance. He warns that higher growth may aggravate cost-push inflation given the wage-setting power of labor unions. As various groups compete to maintain their shares of real income, accelerating inflation becomes a possibility. If conventional monetary-fiscal measures fail to assure price stability, other means may be necessary. He rejects wage and price controls in favor of broader anti-trust action against collusive behavior. Fellner notes that faster growth by way of more rapid capital formation will require a higher rate of savings, which can be fostered by tax reform. The corporate tax burden should be reduced, and tax relief afforded to individuals in exchange for a new tax on consumption. The merits of luxury taxes as a means to reduce income inequalities are considered.

"Two Propositions in the Theory of Induced Innovations," *Economic Journal*, June, 1961, pp. 305-08.

Fellner derives two propositions based on the existence of an adjustment mechanism which in market economies directs the choice of firms between a new labor-saving technology and a new capital-saving one. The choice depends on the relative input scarcities observed at the macroeconomic level. In classical microeconomic analysis, no such macroeconomic adjustment mechanism exists since atomistic firms respond only to given factor prices. Fellner's first proposition states that firms may be induced by a learning process to notice that factors of production are not in infinitely elastic supply at the macroeconomic level. If the supply of capital is rising relative to that of labor, a firm may choose a presently inferior labor-saving invention over a superior capital-saving one in anticipation of the unfavorable trend in wages rates. The second proposition states that firms facing a monopsonistic imperfection in the labor market will experience a relative increase in the wage rate as the labor input is increased. This would also lead to a preference for the relatively labor-saving invention.

"How to Accelerate Increases in Production," *Mercurio*, August 15, 1961, pp. 1-6.

Increases in output are fostered by the expansion of investment spending, especially that which embodies technological progress. Government can facilitate the needed increment to savings with fiscal policies that ease the corporate tax burden, and at the personal level, combine a cut in personal income tax rates with an equivalent increase in taxes on the consumption of luxury goods. Scientific research, education, and public health deserve priority on the spending side. Credit controls can be useful to curb inflation, and compensatory government spending should begin promptly at the first sign of recession. Western Europe has enjoyed a higher rate of growth than the United States, and Fellner attributes this to their adoption of tax policies similar to what he recommends.

"Distortion of Subjective Probabilities as a Reaction to Uncertainty," *Quarterly Journal of Economics*, November, 1961, pp. 670-89.

When a gamble or lottery is posed to a risk-averse decision-maker, the subject will assess the outcomes associated with the different possible bets by formulating subjective probabilities. These estimates are made through comparisons with the objective probabilities connected with well-understood stochastic processes, such as the flip of a fair coin. In the estimation procedure, the subjective probabilities become slanted, that is, they sum to less than one. Fellner claims that this nonadditivity property is consistent with the assumption of a rational subject. If a subject is observed slanting probabilities, it does not imply irrationality, but simply reflects the conditions of uncertainty under which the decision is made. Fellner conducted experiments to test his concept of slanted probabilities, and reports that his subjects exhibited behavior supportive of that concept.

"Appraisal of the Labour-saving and Capital-saving Character of Innovations," Chapter Four in *The Theory of Capital*, Proceedings of a Conference held by the International Economic Association, edited by D.C. Hague, London: Macmillan, 1961, pp. 58-72.

Fellner contributed this paper to an international conference on the theory of capital. Conceptual problems associated with characterizing innovations as either labor-saving or capital-saving are examined. The capital-output and capital-labor ratios are said to reflect the quantity rather than the character of innovations. An innovation is defined as relatively capital-saving if it lowers capital's share in national income, while raising labor's share, with the reverse holding in the labor-saving case. The potential effect of innovations of both characters on wage and profit rates is explored, and Fellner's framework is related to the Harrod-Domar growth model. Trends in capital-output ratios are reviewed, along with Solow's finding that innovations in the American economy from 1909-49 were neutral in character. Problems in the measurement of capital are presented. The volume in which this paper appears also contains a summary record of the discussion of all conference papers.

"Does the Market Direct the Relative Factor-Saving Effects of Technological Progress?," in *The Rate and Direction of Inventive Activity: Economic and Social Factors*, National Bureau of Economic Research, Princeton, N.J.: Princeton University Press, 1962, pp. 171-88.

This paper was one of many presented at a conference on inventive activity in 1960, all of which were published in one volume with substantial comments. Fellner is interested in whether market incentives exist which will guide inventive activity to be factor-saving in accord with relative input scarcities. Do high wages, which suggest relatively abundant capital and scarce labor, cause inventive activity to be directed toward the search for labor-saving inventions? Would high interest rates direct the search toward capital-saving inventions? For the perfectly competitive economy, Fellner answers these questions in the negative. If, reflecting macroeconomic scarcities, inputs are not in infinitely elastic supply, incentives directing the adoption of the appropriate inventions do exist. This volume begins with a helpful introduction by Richard Nelson. Edwin Mansfield's comments on the Fellner paper are particularly useful.

"Profit as the Risk-Taker's Surplus: A Probabilistic Theory," *Review of Economics and Statistics*, May, 1963, pp. 173-84.

The principles of operational utility and numerical subjective probability which underlie the two-parameter mean-variance portfolio selection model attributed to Markowitz and Tobin are made explicit. Fellner models an investor's decision concerning a single bet assuming quadratic utility with his concept of the risk-taker's surplus. Modification of the analysis for the case of highly uncertain subjective probability beliefs using slanted probabilities is discussed. The analytical apparatus is extended to cover a portfolio, a large number of "bets". Benefits from diversification are measured in terms of the increment to the risk-taker's surplus. The optimal degree of diversification and the exclusion of inefficient portfolios are considered.

"Slanted Subjective Probabilities and Randomization: Reply to Howard Raiffa and K.R.W. Brewer," *Quarterly Journal of Economics*, November, 1963, pp. 676-90.

Fellner responds to the criticism of Raiffa and Brewer, who assert that his method of slanting probabilities for decision-making under conditions of uncertainty cannot be reconciled with the postulate of rationality. His critics believe that the rational assessment of an uncertain bet can be made, not by slanting, but b randomization, a process by which probability beliefs for a nonstandard process can be made equivalent to those for a standard, stable process, such as the toss of a fair coin. Fellner shows this argument does not hold for events governed by asymmetrical probabilities. He also claims to show that randomization fails even in the symmetrical case in the event of a small number of trials, a situation that much of modern utility theory was designed to handle.

Introduction to *The Principles of Political Economy and Taxation*, by David Ricardo, Homewood, Ill.: Irwin, 1963, pp. v-xii.

The work of Ricardo is put into perspective. His long discredited labor theory of value is now of interest only to Marxists. His analysis of rent is illustrative of his use of abstraction as a means by which to remove unnecessary detail while still capturing the essence of a problem. The theory of comparative costs, though originally based on the labor-value framework, has survived as one of the great insights of economic analysis. Misjudging the pace of technical progress led to an unsuccessful analysis of technological unemployment and his mistaken stationary state. Yet Ricardo's conception of the race between technical progress and diminishing returns still informs modern growth theory. His concern for capital formation and distaste for government interference (the Poor Laws and Corn Laws) remain a part of contemporary discourse.

"Problems of Public Finance During the Sixties," in *Fiscal and Debt Management Policies*, by William Fellner et al., Englewood Cliffs, N.J.: Prentice-Hall, 1963, pp. 1-44.

This paper was contributed to a volume prepared for the Commission on Money and Credit. Fiscal policy issues are reviewed. With continued economic growth, what use should be made of increased Federal revenues? Three possibilities and their effects are examined: deficit reduction, tax cuts, or increased government spending. The implications of changes in the composition of Federal expenditures for changes in the tax structure are reviewed. The impact of various modes of taxation on economic behavior is assessed. His view is that the concern for equity has led to tax laws which discourage savings and work effort. He recommends a sales tax on non-necessities, elimination of the corporate income tax, and reduced reliance on the graduated income tax.

"The Slanting of Subjective Probabilities: Agreement on Some Essentials," *Quarterly Journal of Economics*, November, 1965, pp. 657-63, co-authored with K.R.W. Brewer.

In previous work, Fellner characterized as rational a procedure known as the slanting of subjective probabilities. In making decisions under conditions of uncertainty, this involves the use of subjective probabilities which do not sum to one. Critics of slanting claimed it to be irrational in certain situations. Brewer, one of those critics, and Fellner collaborate in this article to state more clearly those areas of agreement concerning the question of slanting. Slanting behavior is rational when the experimenter limits the subject in the choice of the event on which to place a bet, or when the subject is not indifferent towards the various possible events. If there are no limits or if the subject is indifferent, the slanting of subjective probabilities is irrational. The possibility of rational slanting points to the need for generalizing the Savage axioms to take account of the ability of the subject or the experimenter to exert an influence over a bet.

"Profit Maximization, Utility Maximization, and the Rate and Direction of Innovation," *American Economic Review*, May, 1966, pp. 24-32.

The rapid rise in research and development expenditures and the increasingly systematic approach to which it has given rise in the exploration of technological and organizational innovation has increased the number of innovation projects under consideration. This has enabled the risk-averse decision-maker to become a more willing innovator since a larger number of projects permits greater diversification to be achieved in the innovation process. Although fears have been expressed that a high rate of innovation can cause unemployment, Fellner cites the experience of the Western economies as evidence that innovation improves economic well-being. Theoretical support is discussed for the belief that innovation will be biased in a labor-saving direction in economies with rising capital-labor ratios and will suppress any rise in labor's share of output. While noting some of the limitations of this body of theory, Fellner is impressed with its ability to explain both the tendency for diminishing returns to be offset and the stability of distributive shares.

"Introduction," Chapter One in *Maintaining and Restoring Balance in International Payments*, by William Fellner et al., Princeton, N.J.: Princeton University Press, 1966, pp. 3-8, co-authored with Fritz Machlup and Robert Triffin.

Fellner and his co-authors explain the structure of the book. Part I is devoted to three comprehensive papers, and Part II to fourteen papers on special issues. The three papers in Part I are intended to assist officials in the formulation of policy. Written independently, they give broad treatment to the international payments question. Substantial overlap in both coverage and views in these three papers does not mean that they are identical. For example, Fellner fears that different policy pressures in the various countries may disrupt effective coordination, while Machlup and Triffin are less concerned. Fellner and Machlup put more stress on achieving greater exchange-rate flexibility than does Triffin. The special issues covered in Part II include: indicators of impending payments imbalance, external balance and employment policy, monetary-fiscal policy mix under fixed exchange-rates, use of selective controls as a policy alternative, and the policy responsibility of the surplus vs. the deficit country.

"Rules of the Game, Vintage 1966," Chapter Two in *Maintaining and Restoring Balance in International Payments*, by William Fellner et al., Princeton, N.J.: Princeton University Press, 1966, pp. 11-31.

An analysis of international adjustment problems is presented in the context of the Bretton Woods system. That framework requires continuous consultation among the Western monetary authorities to avoid crises that can result when countries adopt international economic policies that are at cross purposes. However, Fellner warns that this kind of collaboration, if incomplete, can pose risks to other policy goals such as price stability. Failure to achieve systematic collaboration in international economic matters can provoke a crisis that ultimately leads to the collapse of the fixed rate system. Although his remarks are intended to address problems within the existing fixed rate system, Fellner suggests that policymakers consider the ways in which the burdens imposed by close collaboration might be eased through greater exchange-rate flexibility.

"On Limited Exchange-rate Flexibility," Chapter Five in *Maintaining and Restoring Balance in International Payments*, by William Fellner et al., Princeton, N.J.: Princeton University Press, 1966, pp. 111-22.

> Fellner reproduces a statement signed by twenty-seven prominent economists calling for a widening of the band around which the value of a currency can vary, and more flexibility in changing the parity level of a currency. Wage rigidity makes it difficult to restore external balance under a fixed rate system without risking inflation in surplus countries or exchange controls in deficit countries. Greater exchange-rate flexibility provides more leeway in restoring payments balance without these undesirable side-effects as well as more responsible policy behavior. Fearing that speculation could be destabilizing in the initial stages, Fellner does not favor an immediate move to completely market-determined exchange-rates, but rather a more gradual move in that direction. Within the widened band, no official intervention would be allowed. The shiftable-parity provides for larger exchange rate movements.

"Measures of Technological Progress in the Light of Recent Growth Theories," *American Economic Review*, December, 1967, pp. 1073-98.

> Fellner examines Joan Robinson's Golden Age growth concept, which among other things suggests that the relative income shares of labor and capital will be constant. Two models are used: the Cobb-Douglas production function with Hicks-neutral innovation, and the CES production function innovation-frontier model. Two alternative measures of technological progress are used: a total factor-productivity index, and the rate of increase of output per labor hour times the labor elasticity of output. Both models with either measure indicate a tendency in the U.S. economy toward the satisfaction of the Golden Age conditions. The CES approach is preferred, since it explains the mild increase in labor's share observed for the American economy in the study period.

"Operational Utility: The Theoretical Background and a Measurement," Chapter Three in *Ten Economic Studies in the Tradition of Irving Fisher*, by William J. Fellner et al., New York: Wiley, 1967, pp. 39-74.

> The main purpose of this paper is to ascertain whether it is possible to endow cardinal utility with any operational content, that is, to use it to formulate

propositions that are testable by observing the choices made by individuals. Tests of the Hicksian ordinalist approach are discussed. Two operational versions of cardinal utility are presented: a certainty case based on an approach developed independently by Fisher and Frisch, and an uncertainty case based on the work of von Neumann and Morgenstern. The comparability of the measurements based on the two approaches is considered. The Fisher-Frisch methodology is used with Bureau of Labor Statistics family budget data to obtain an indirect estimate of the elasticity of the marginal utility of income, and the implications of the estimate are assessed. Though measurement problems lead him to qualify his results, Fellner claims his approach has a wider applicability than the ordinal framework.

"The Adaptability and Lasting Significance of the Chamberlinian Contribution," Chapter One in *Monopolistic Competition Theory: Studies in Impact, Essays in Honor of Edward H. Chamberlin*, edited by Robert E. Kuenne, New York: Wiley, 1967, pp. 3-30.

Given that very few markets fit the polar extremes of perfect competition and pure monopoly, Chamberlin's theory of monopolistic competition is a more realistic portrayal of the functioning of markets. His model suggests that competitive conditions are determined by the number of rival producers and the substitutability of their outputs. To assess the extent of competition in specific markets, reliance on these simple concepts may be preferable to the use of such measures as the concentration ratio, the Lerner index, and cross-elasticities. Diminished professional interest in market competitiveness along with a renewed interest in welfare economics causes Fellner to fret about greater governmental intervention in the marketplace. A review of Chamberlin's oligopoly theory reveals an antiquated mode of exposition, but a remarkably modern conclusion. Oligopoly situations characterized by relatively little uncertainty tend to produce market outcomes similar to those for the monopoly case.

"Specific Interpretations of Learning by Doing," *Journal of Economic Theory*, Vol. I, No. 2, 1969, pp. 119-140.

In the standard approach to learning by doing theory, reductions in input per unit of output are a function of cumulated output. Fellner specifies an alternative version, in which reductions are related to time. The competing versions offer the choice between "doing more" and "doing it longer" as the explanatory factor. The nature of the statistical errors generated by a "time" process improperly modeled as a "cumulative" one is described, and a procedure for identifying a "time" process through the analysis of these errors is given. Fellner applies his "time" version to athletic events, and finds it to be a satisfactory explanation of the improvement in performance in events that offer only a limited number of ways in which performance can be improved. Events which provide many such dimensions more closely resemble the process governing technical progress at the macroeconomic level.

"Specific Proposal for Limited Exchange-Rate Flexibility," *Weltwirtschaftliches Archiv*, March, 1970, pp. 20-35.

The Bretton Woods Agreement provided for fixed exchange rates with a system of adjustable pegs. Difficulties with attempts to maintain disequilibrium rates have led to serious consideration of more flexible alternatives. The side-effects of policy measures to restore balance of payments equilibrium with fixed rates are compared with those for flexible rates. Under fixed rates, policy authorities in countries with payments deficits (surpluses) are unwilling to impose the unemployment (inflation) needed to restore equilibrium. Fellner advocates a gradual move to more flexible rates through the institution of a system of band-and-crawl flexibility. Undervalued currencies and those that have maintained a stable relationship to the dollar would be the first candidates for the greater flexibility. Countries with overvalued currencies should establish a record of greater discipline in their monetary policy prior to the introduction of a crawl.

"Trends in the Activities Generating Technological Progress," *American Economic Review*, March, 1970, pp. 1-29.

This is Fellner's presidential address delivered to the American Economic Association in December, 1969 in New York. He considers the return from activities in the profit and non-profit sectors which contribute to technological progress, mainly education, and research and development. Two measures of the average social rate of return from these activities are estimated. One includes the progress-generating expense incurred in the non-profit sector, the other excludes it. The estimated rate is in excess of 13% for the former, and in excess of 18% for the latter. While both rates show a mild downward trend, each exceeds the rate of return on physical investment, thus implying that a shift of resources could be socially beneficial.

"Land in Fellner's Model of Economic Growth: Reply and Further Observations,"
American Economic Review, June, 1970, pp. 500-01.

> Fellner responds to Roger McCain's comments concerning his December,
> 1967 *American Economic Review* article on technological progress and
> growth theory. According to McCain, land can be explicitly introduced into
> the Fellner two-input model in a way that validates his results. Furthermore,
> the predictive power of the model improves, and Frey's criticism that neo-
> classical growth theory fails to explain differences in growth patterns between
> countries is resolved. The main focus of Fellner's rejoinder is on the re-
> quired modification to his two-input results if a third input is added. In the
> two-input model, the two measures of technological progress used both
> yielded the same results. This will not obtain in McCain's three-input case.

"A 'Realistic' Note on Threefold Limited Flexibility of Exchange Rates," in *Approaches to Greater Flexibility of Exchange Rates: The Burgenstock Papers*, edited by
George N. Halm, Princeton, N.J.: Princeton University Press, 1970, pp. 237-44.

> While favoring completely flexible exchange rates, Fellner views the institu-
> tion of such a system as unlikely in the near term. As an alternative, he rec-
> ommends a plan of threefold but limited flexibility which would be: (1) lim-
> ited in extent; (2) limited to those currencies tending upward in relation to
> the dollar; and (3) limited to a very small number of currencies, with the
> German mark being the strongest candidate for his proposal. Those coun-
> tries running chronic balance of payments surpluses with the United States
> experience the accumulation of large dollar balances. Given the gold incon-
> vertibility of the dollar, central banks committed to the repurchase of these
> balances may find their other policy objectives impaired. Fellner believes
> this dilemma can be avoided if surplus countries adopted a policy of gradual
> upward revaluation of their currencies in relation to the dollar. The revalua-
> tion of gold represents another alternative, but would make the control of in-
> flation more difficult, and would introduce other policy complications.

"Empirical Support for the Theory of Induced Innovations," *Quarterly Journal of
Economics*, February, 1971, pp. 580-604.

> Fellner examines the joint influence of rising capital-labor ratios and labor-
> saving technological innovation on labor's share of national income. His
> hypothesis is that rising capital-labor ratios tend to raise labor's share, but

this increase is offset by greater emphasis on labor-saving inventions in the innovational process, except when the growth in the capital-labor ratio is unusually steep. Time-series and cross-sectional data are used to test this hypothesis. The period 1920-57 is broken into four subperiods. The subperiod 1948-57 is the only one in which labor's share of income shows appreciable growth, and is also the only time period during which growth in the capital-labor ratio proved exceptionally steep. A regression analysis using cross-sectional data for the period 1948-57 indicates a statistically significant relationship between the rate of increase in labor's share and the rate of increase in the capital-labor ratio. Tests of the other three subperiods yield statistically insignificant results.

"Phillips-type Approach or Acceleration?," *Brookings Papers on Economic Activity*, No. 2, 1971, pp. 469-83.

Can American policymakers peg the unemployment rate at 4% and maintain a steady rate of inflation? Fellner says no, and states that his analysis shows 5% to be the lowest unemployment rate target consistent with non-accelerating inflation. A study by Gordon and another by Perry, both claiming that the empirical evidence supports the existence of a stable Phillips Curve, are assessed. Fellner believes the stability that these studies observe results from the way in which they "correct" the conventional measure of unemployment. Gordon was able to confirm a stable Phillips relationship only by correcting for what he called disguised unemployment, and Perry resorted to a measure of unemployment which adjusted for the age-sex composition of the labor force. Fellner suspects that these "corrections" mask whatever acceleration may be in the data, and fail to reflect policy-induced changes in price expectations. The process of accelerating inflation is described, and a program of public sector jobs is suggested as a means to avoid it.

Case for Moderation in the Economic Recovery of 1971: An Analysis Based on Observed Wage-Price-Productivity Relations, Special Analysis No. 4, Washington, D.C.: American Enterprise Institute, 1971, pp. 1-31.

Fellner is fearful that the officially announced policy targets for the recovery from the 1969-70 recession are too ambitious. More moderate targets for 1971, in terms of both the unemployment rate and GNP growth, offer a better chance of sustainable, non-inflationary growth. Policy must be carefully considered given that inflation did not ease during the 1969-70 recession. If monetary and fiscal restraint are not exercised during the recovery year of 1971, a recession will have been endured without any progress toward greater price stability, and the eventual task of reducing inflation will be even more painful. Fellner rejects the concept of potential output and the need to close the gap between it and actual output. He believes estimates of potential output to be very unreliable, and policies aimed at the achievement of such output levels carry a high risk of inflation.

"Tensions at Full Utilization: A Comparative-Economic View Rejecting the Phillips-Curve Approach," *Acta Oeconomica*, Vol. 8, No. 1, 1972, pp. 3-23.

The American experience of the mid-to-late 1960's is the basis for the rejection of the Phillips Curve trade-off which assumes that policymakers can target a low unemployment rate and still maintain a steady rate of inflation. Fellner's claim is that the adoption of a 4% unemployment rate target eventually led to the acceleration of inflation. The measured rate of unemployment can be a misleading guide to policy since it accounts for neither the intensity of the job search nor the duration of unemployment. Furthermore, a 4% overall target fails to recognize that serious labor shortages develop in the heavily demanded categories, while unemployment still exceeds 4% in those with much weaker demand. Using regression analysis, Fellner concludes that any attempt to push unemployment below 5% will accelerate inflation. Studies purporting to show that a stable Phillips Curve trade-off exists are criticized for using data corrections which mask accelerating inflation. The intensification of wage-push pressures and the acceleration of inflation can be avoided by the adoption of a public sector jobs program to employ those in labor categories with permanently excess supply.

"The Dollar's Place in the International System: Suggested Criteria for the Appraisal of Emerging Views," *Journal of Economic Literature*, June, 1972, pp. 735-56.

Fellner presents criteria for the appraisal of the variety of views on the international role of the dollar expressed in the aftermath of the suspension of the gold convertibility of the dollar in 1971. Many observers tend to underrate the technical difficulty of restoring the convertibility of foreign official dollar-holdings into an international reserve asset. A more promising approach is the establishment of a system of smooth exchange-rate adjustability combined with insuring the real value of foreign official dollar-reserves. While a case can be made for dollar convertibility under a genuine fixed rate system, its restoration would not be compatible with the newly instituted system of limited exchange-rate flexibility. A return to convertibility would carry the risk of both restrictive trade and payments practices and crisis in the event of renewed suspension.

"Aiming for a Sustainable Second Best During The Recovery from the 1970 Recession," Chapter Five in *Economic Policy and Inflation in the Sixties*, Domestic Affairs Study 4, by Charles McLure et al., Washington, D.C.: American Enterprise Institute, 1972, pp. 241-67.

> Fellner also wrote the introduction to this volume, the forerunner to the *Contemporary Economic Problems* series. This essay is a slightly modified version of AEI Special Analysis Number 20 published in December, 1971. Labor market rigidities make a 4% unemployment rate target unreasonable. Conventional monetary-fiscal policy could achieve it only by creating inflationary shortages in certain scarce labor categories. Fellner recommends a public sector jobs program in order to bring unemployment down to 4% in labor categories of chronically high joblessness. Though this is a second best policy, he claims it both politically feasible and less damaging than demand-side manipulation. It has a better chance of restoring economic stability than a policy of stop-go, wage-price controls or increased payments to the jobless.

Employment Policy at the Crossroads: An Interim Look at Pressures to be Resisted, Domestic Affairs Study 9, Washington, D.C.: American Enterprise Institute, 1972, pp. 1-28.

> In the 1950's, full employment could be safely defined as an unemployment rate of 4%. Fellner argues that by the early 1970's changes in the age-sex composition of the labor force require that the definition be revised upward to 5%. Attempts to push unemployment below 5% through expansionary monetary and fiscal policies will cause inflation to accelerate. Such policies would create extreme tightness in key segments of the labor market, leading to unfavorable wage trends. At the same time, little improvement would be experienced in segments with higher than average unemployment rates. Fellner suggests that public sector employment programs be refocused to target groups within the labor market with above average unemployment rates. This would allow an overall unemployment rate of 4% to be achieved without risking the acceleration of inflation.

"Controlled Floating and the Confused Issue of Money Illusion," *Banca Nazionale del Lavoro Quarterly Review*, No. 106, 1973, pp. 206-34.

> The move to controlled floating in March of 1973 is welcomed. Support-interventions to offset currency speculation should be used sparingly in order to avoid any possible rebureaucratization of the international payments system. An appraisal of the role of the International Monetary Fund is made in light of the new arrangements. In the absence of money illusion, the elimination of a trade deficit by a policy of deflation at fixed exchange-rates in an economy with rigid money wages will cause output and employment to contract. The same undesirable side-effect accompanies a policy of exchange-rate flexibility if the money wage rate rises. The role of labor unions in wage determination is thought to be a more important consideration than money illusion, and between the two policies, Fellner prefers the policy of exchange-rate flexibility. An assessment of the 1971 rate-adjustments concludes that they did not contribute to the continued deterioration of the American trade balance from 1971 to 1972.

"Employment Goals and Monetary-Fiscal Overexpansion," Chapter Five in *A New Look at Inflation: Economic Policy in the Early 1970's*, by Phillip Cagan et al., Washington, D.C.: American Enterprise Institute, 1973, pp. 135-72.

> Fellner also wrote the preface to this work. Changes in the demographics of the labor force make a 4% target unemployment rate inconsistent with non-inflationary growth. Inflation began to accelerate in 1965, and a deceleration started in the early 1970's. This recent progress toward restoration of price stability is being endangered by ill-advised and overly ambitious policies based on illusory Phillips Curve trade-offs. Economic circumstances are said to favor reliance on monetary rather than fiscal policy, with the monetary policy focus on tighter control of money supply growth, not interest rates. While this policy does carry the risk of recession, continuation of the current policy of overexpansion guarantees a far more severe downturn in the future. A jobs program is recommended to offset employment hardships from his more disciplined policy.

"The Chances of a Reasonably *Soft* Landing After a Period of Overheating," *Business Economics*, January, 1974, pp. 16-20.

Expansionary monetary and fiscal policies aimed at an unemployment rate target of 4% are regarded as both inflationary and unsustainable, given the tightness in the labor market at the time. A 5% target is suggested as more reasonable. Any unemployment hardship that results can be mitigated by a government-subsidized jobs program. The conditions under which the pressures from the overheated economy could be reduced without risking a serious recession are discussed.

"A Strange Expansion," *American Economic Review*, May, 1974, pp. 71-74.

According to Fellner, the economic expansion underway in the spring of 1974 was characterized by several peculiarities. Policies pursued during the early stages of the expansion had made estimates of the economy's long-run growth path unreliable, while significantly reduced exchange-rates for the dollar contributed to domestic price pressures. A substantial rise in food prices necessitated large wage increases in the private nonfarm sector, which employers regarded as steep but seemed inadequate to wage earners.

"The Controversial Issue of Comprehensive Indexation," in *Essays on Inflation and Indexation*, Domestic Affairs Study 24, Washington, D.C.: American Enterprise Institute, 1974, pp. 63-69.

Fellner has misgivings about the use of the indexation of money wages and other costs to control inflation. When actual inflation consistently exceeds what is expected, decision-makers are repeatedly disappointed by their real incomes. This causes inflationary expectations to steepen. Comprehensive indexation would make this tendency for inflation to accelerate more pronounced. Monetary-fiscal restraints imposed to control inflation would result in a more difficult adjustment period in terms of duration, lost output and unemployment. Indexation may prove more useful in promoting disinflation once inflation has stabilized. But the need for a cyclical setback to initiate price deceleration and the fact that a recession does not guarantee price deceleration show that indexation gives no easy answers, not even in the disinflationary case. Though skeptical about wage indexation, Fellner regards the indexation of taxes as a useful way to offset the distortions of inflation.

"Budget Deficit: The Relevant Dilemma," *The New York Times*, March 8, 1975, Letters to the Editor, p. 24.

A letter to the editor of *The New York Times* written by a group of economists suggested that a recent policy debate on the budget deficit was irrelevant. Fears of an inflationary increase in the money supply to finance additional debt were unfounded since, by accounting identity, private savings would increase by the amount of the additional debt. Fellner's response to this letter points out that the accounting identity, when properly stated, also allows for a decrease in gross private investment as a result of an increased budget deficit, the crowd-out effect. Reliance on increased deficits will cause interest rates to decline less during the recession, and will unfavorably affect the subsequent course of investment spending.

Discussion Paper on "The Payments Adjustment Process and the Exchange Rate Regime: What Have We Learned?," by Marina v. N. Whitman, *American Economic Review*, May, 1975, pp. 148-51.

Fellner discusses the problems that accompany the elimination of a trade deficit given fixed exchange-rates. A comparision is made with the case in which flexible rates govern. He notes that governments intent on pursuing inflationary policies can abuse either a system of fixed rates or one of flexible rates. However, a competent government wishing to assure price stability will be better able to resist pressures against their policies with flexible rates.

"Inflation and Overtaxation," *Wall Street Journal*, July 3, 1975, p. 21.

Inflation can interact with the tax system to create serious distortions. Tax revenues can increase more rapidly than money incomes. This results from a tax system in which inflation pushes individuals into higher tax brackets, while businesses are taxed on phantom inventory profits and take depreciation charges that do not properly reflect current replacement cost. Fellner is critical of the Tax Reduction Act of 1975, which merged a correction for inflation with a redistribution of income. These two matters should receive separate legislative treatment to avoid harm to economic incentives. The tax relief for businesses provided by the Act is called inadequate. Indexation of the tax code is the most important reform needed.

Correcting Taxes for Inflation, Domestic Affairs Study 34, Washington, D.C.: American Enterprise Institute, 1975, pp. 1-47, co-authored with Kenneth W. Clarkson and John H. Moore.

The distorting effects of inflation on taxation are examined. Rather than propose a general indexation scheme, the authors recommend the introduction of several specific forms of tax indexation. The individual income tax code should be revised to allow for the indexation of tax brackets, exemptions and the standard deduction. On the corporate side, inventory and depreciation expenses will more accurately reflect current replacement costs if indexed to the general price level. The Tax Reduction Act of 1975 is reviewed with the conclusion that it is a confusing mixture of inflation correction and basic change to the tax structure. While the tax reduction does much to remove the overtaxation imposed by inflation, the distribution of the cuts is very different from what it would be if the Act was aimed exclusively at the removal of inflationary distortions. It is suggested that inflation correction and structural change be kept separate in any future tax legislation.

"Lessons from the Failure of Demand-Management Policies: A Look at the Theoretical Foundations, *Journal of Economic Literature*, March, 1976, pp. 34-53.

Keynesian macroeconomics focuses on the elimination of involuntary unemployment by the use of inflationary demand-management policies that moderate real wages by raising the price level. Fellner does not believe such an inflation-unemployment trade-off to exist. Policies which continually target unrealistic employment levels will produce only accelerating inflation. American experience from 1965-74 gives no indication of a moderation of real wages in response to inflation. Policy should target price level stability. Whatever output and employment levels result must be accepted. This view does not constitute acceptance of a unique "natural" rate of unemployment, since that rate depends on the structural rigidities in the commodities and labor markets. The macroeconomic foundations of demand-management policy need to be reconstructed. A credible policy of price stability is one in which unemployment is not lowered below what is consistent with the price level target. Policymakers must distinguish between unemployment which can and that which cannot be reduced by expansionary demand policy.

"Interpretation of a Regularity in the Behavior of M$_2$," *Brookings Papers on Economic Activity*, No. 3, 1976, pp. 741-61, co-authored with Dan Larkins.

In the conduct of monetary policy, a monetary aggregate which has a stable relationship with GNP should be targeted. This criterion would be met if an aggregate has a constant velocity, or measured by its reciprocal, is a constant percentage of GNP. The M_2 definition of money is the subject of this study covering the period 1952-75. Over the subperiod 1962-75, its velocity appears to be nearly trendless, with small variations around that flat trend. The authors discuss in detail the factors that explain this "constant" velocity, including the effect of changes and innovations in the financial markets. Since interest rates had an upward trend from 1962-75, an attempt is made to identify the factor that offset this influence on velocity. Several regression analyses are performed, but none produce satisfactory results. Although M_2 seems to be a strong candidate as a monetary policy target, the authors warn that mechanical projection of its past behavior into the future is no substitute for careful judgment.

"Criteria for Demand Management Policy in View of Past Failures," in *Contemporary Economic Problems 1976*, edited by William Fellner, Washington, D.C.: American Enterprise Institute, 1976, pp. 85-108.

The objective of monetary and fiscal policy must be the achievement of maximum money GNP compatible with price stability. To be credible, such a policy must be aimed consistently at a zero rate of inflation. Once full recovery is made, non-inflationary growth will require that annual growth in money GNP be no more than 5 to 6 per cent. The persistent and growing Federal budget deficits must be eliminated to avoid any adverse effect on capital formation. The trend in expenditures must be brought under control to accommodate this need. In recent years, the Federal Reserve alone has been able to resist political pressures and fight inflation. Its policy independence must be maintained. The age-sex composition of the labor force makes the formulation of policy in terms of a numerically specified unemployment rate target unrealistic. Wage and price controls should be rejected due to administrative difficulties and the potential for abuse.

"Schools of Thought in the Mainstream of American Economics," *Acta Oeconomica*, Vol. 18, Nos. 3-4, 1977, pp. 247-61.

Fellner believes the essential distinction between the monetarists and the neo-Keynesians to be the time frame adopted for policy purposes. Monetarists tend to have a long-run policy orientation in which short-run market behavior adjusts itself to long-run policy goals. Neo-Keynesians favor fiscal and monetary policy fine-tuning in the short-run so as to ensure the desired long-run outcome. Fellner strongly criticizes neo-Keynesians, for both their short-run orientation and the use of unrealistic unemployment rate targets, which will lead to accelerating inflation. Comprehensive wage and price controls will inevitably follow. Neo-Keynesians are said to have failed to consider the impact of their policies on our economic and political institutions.

"Money Supply and the Budget: Current and Future Problems of Demand Management," in *Contemporary Economic Problems 1977*, edited by William Fellner, Washington, D.C.: American Enterprise Institute, 1977, pp. 83-116.

Fellner argues that the M_2 definition of money bears a more dependable relationship to money GNP than any other monetary aggregate. While fully recognizing that this economic "regularity" should not be mechanically projected into the future and that it can be affected by changes in other factors such as policy variables, he recommends a 10 per cent increase in M_2 for 1977 which should reduce the unemployment rate by 1 per cent. This rate of increase should be gradually slowed as the recovery becomes complete. Wage and price controls in any form should be avoided. The Carter Administration is said to have acted correctly when it reneged on a campaign promise by withdrawing its tax-rebate proposal. That proposal is said to typify the short-run policy orientation that makes it impossible to achieve long-run objectives such as price stability. Various measures are proposed to eliminate the unfair burden placed on individuals and corporations by the tax code during inflationary periods.

Problems to Keep in Mind When It Comes to Tax Reform, AEI Studies 167, Washington, D.C.: American Enterprise Institute, 1977, pp. 1-26.

Fellner examines an argument made by proponents of tax reform, namely, that broadening the individual income tax base through the elimination or reduction of exclusions and deductions would make possible the reduction of income tax rates. He finds that many proposals tend to exaggerate their broadening effect, but feels that certain reforms should be enacted regardless of their effects on revenue. He favors the indexation of the tax structure at both the personal and corporate levels in order to eliminate the added tax burden imposed by inflation. Fellner also advocates the elimination of the double taxation of dividends. To minimize the tax revenue loss, he recommends that this be accomplished by allowing corporations to deduct dividends for tax purposes.

"The Core of the Controversy about Reducing Inflation: An Introductory Analysis," in *Contemporary Economic Problems 1978*, William Fellner, Project Director, Washington, D.C.: American Enterprise Institute, 1978, pp. 1-12.

> A study by Cagan shows that in order to substantially reduce the rate of inflation policy must maintain slack in the economy for an extended period of time. This supports those economists who recommend a more direct attack on inflation through an incomes policy. Fellner rejects this viewpoint by noting that Cagan's estimates of the length of the transition period were made using data from past episodes when the public geared its behavior to the belief that government was not serious in its efforts to stop inflation. As Cagan himself suggests and Fellner reiterates, the length of a transition period can be significantly shortened if policymakers apply a consistent and credible policy aimed at gradually reducing the growth of money GNP. A firm policy of monetary-fiscal disinflation would have an expectations effect, restoring price stability without the need for a prolonged slack in the economy.

"Structural Problems behind Our Measured Unemployment Rates," in *Contemporary Economic Problems 1978*, William Fellner, Project Director, Washington, D.C.: American Enterprise Institute, 1978, pp. 83-112.

> Fellner repeats some favorite themes. The conventional approach used by policymakers to estimate potential output is based on a seriously flawed methodology which fails to account adequately for the institutional and structural rigidities characterizing the labor market. Minimum wage legislation and collective bargaining agreements are arrangements that make labor more costly and disemploy some workers. Unemployment compensation and transfer payments have become more generous, making unemployment a more attractive alternative. Shifts in the age-sex composition of the labor force are also an important consideration. The increased participation of women and teenagers has biased measured unemployment upward since re-entrants and new entrants take longer and more frequent job searches. The employment goals implicit in the macroeconomic policies based on the concept of potential output are not attainable given these rigidities. The continued pursuit of those goals will only accelerate inflation.

"A Critique of Fiscal Policies Based on the Conventional Concept of Potential Output," in *Tax Policies in the 1979 Budget: Highlights of a Conference*, edited by

Rudolph G. Penner, Washington, D.C.: American Enterprise Institute, 1978, pp. 11-16.

> In Fellner's view, a macroeconomic policy dedicated to closing the gap between actual output and potential output is bound to fail, and the 1979 Federal budget is predicated upon this notion. Potential output is too imprecise a concept to guide policy. Its inaccurate estimation procedures lead to excessively ambitious growth and unemployment targets, which imparts an inflationary bias to policy. The changing supply conditions in various input markets make extrapolation of growth in potential output from the pre-1973 period to the current period both unrealistic and dangerous. Policymakers who promise too much will be inclined to accommodate the inflationary pressures their policies produce, resulting in steepening cost trends. A summary of the discussion of this paper by conference participants is provided.

"The Credibility Effect and Rational Expectations: Implications of the Gramlich Study," *Brookings Papers on Economic Activity*, No. 1, 1979, pp. 167-78.

> Finding rational expectations too broad, Fellner advocates a similar, but more limited, viewpoint, the credibility effect, which assumes that the public can learn the behavior of policymakers only if policy is conducted in a consistent and understandable way. The American public is characterized as resigned to the need for a disinflationary demand policy, a course entailing a recessionary transition period. Fellner examines the wage equation used in a study by Edward M. Gramlich and suggests that the pattern of errors it generates are supportive of the credibility effect. The equation underpredicts wage inflation for 1971-77, when policy was accommodative to inflation, and overpredicts it for 1954-70, when policy was aimed at price stability.

"How Three Economists Size Up Inflation," *U.S. News & World Report*, November 26, 1979, p. 38.

> The key to bringing inflation under control is resolute behavior on the part of the Federal Reserve. It must convince the public that a policy of restraint will be maintained even if output and employment are adversely affected. The public must be dissuaded from believing that the Federal Reserve will not repeat its customary practice of restraint, followed by easing at the first sign of distress even though the inflation rate remains high. Public suspicions of a reversal of course make it more difficult to control inflation, and must be

dispelled in order for progress against inflation to be made. Disinflation should be gradual if a severe shock to the economy is to be avoided. However, if progress is too slow, policy will lose its credibility. Two other economists offer their views on the same issue.

"The Declining Growth of American Productivity: An Introductory Note," in *Contemporary Economic Problems 1979*, William Fellner, Project Director, Washington, D.C.: American Enterprise Institute, 1979, pp. 3-12.

The essays in Part One of this volume are devoted to American productivity growth. Fellner provides an overview of these essays and the issues they address. Possible causes of the pronounced reduction in the rate of productivity growth in the United States in recent years are reviewed. The work of Denison and Kendrick, including their contributions to the present volume, is discussed. The productivity problem has been widely studied, yet a substantial component of the decline in its growth remains unexplained. Fellner suspects that perverse policy may provide some part of the remaining explanation. It is his hope that future research will focus more closely on the possible role of such policy-related factors as inflationary policies, discentives created by the tax structure, and the added regulatory burden imposed on business.

"American Household Wealth in an Inflationary Period," in *Contemporary Economic Problems 1979*, William Fellner, Project Director, Washington, D.C.: American Enterprise Institute, 1979, pp. 153-89.

This study examines the trends in the composition of wealth for American households for the inflationary period 1965-78. The asset mix of the typical household portfolio changed due to the penalty exacted by high inflation. There was a shift away from those financial assets with returns unable to keep pace with inflation, such as common stocks, money, and claims on money payments fixed in nominal terms. During the study period, household wealth shifted away from financial assets to tangible assets, such as owner-occupied residential dwellings and durable consumer goods, which have prices that both rise with inflation and depend on their untaxed use value. There was a decided trend away from assets providing capital for the productive activities of enterprises, and toward those which yield use value directly to households.

"Neo-Keynesianism, Monetarism, and the Short and the Long Run," Chapter Three in *Theory for Economic Efficiency: Essays in Honor of Abba P. Lerner*, edited by Harry I. Greenfield, Albert M. Levenson, William Hamovitch and Eugene Rotwein, Cambridge, Mass.: The MIT Press, 1979, pp. 24-45.

> The recent macroeconomic debate is first framed in terms of opposing views on demand-management policy. The cost-accommodating view holds that policy should target low unemployment even if this means higher inflation. The cost-conditioning view calls for a policy aimed at price stability with unemployment adjusting to a level consistent with non-inflationary growth. The debate is then described in more familiar terms, the relative strength of monetary and fiscal policy. Monetarists give central importance to the monetary aggregates in the determination of nominal GNP, while neo-Keynesians emphasize fiscal policy. Although the overlap is not perfect, neo-Keynesians, with a short-run policy orientation, subscribe to the cost-accommodating view; monetarists, with a longer-run policy focus, accept the cost-conditioning view. In stating his own views, Fellner finds the overlap to be incomplete, since he favors the cost-conditioning view yet believes in the stabilizing power of fiscal policy.

Remarks reprinted as part of *In Memoriam, Arthur M. Okun, November 28, 1928-March 23, 1980*, Washington, D.C.: The Brookings Institution, 1980, pp. 24-25.

> Fellner eulogizes Arthur Okun, remembering him as a man of warmth, humor, and great professional achievement. Though often on the opposite sides of an issue, Okun is praised for both the fairness he showed to those who held opposing views, as well as the importance he set on seeing all points of view fully articulated. He was generous when proved correct, and gracious in admitting error. By promoting healthy intellectual exchange, he assured that out of debate would come greater wisdom.

Comments on "Inflation in Theory and Practice," by George L. Perry, *Brookings Papers on Economic Activity*, No. 1, 1980, pp. 243-48.

> Perry claims to have an explanation of recent inflation based on the introduction of a shift in the norm rate of wage increase into his model of the wage-setting process. This is accomplished within a neo-Keynesian framework that specifically rejects the natural rate of unemployment and the Accelerationist View of inflation. Fellner agrees that norm shifts have taken place, but

attributes them to a shift by the policy authorities to an inflationary posture. Perry's norm shifts are not the cause of the steepening price trend, but rather the inevitable result of demand-side policies geared to unrealistic employment targets. The restoration of price stability requires a credible policy based on a demonstrated record of consistent demand restraint, not on declarations of intention.

"The Valid Core of Rationality Hypotheses in the Theory of Expectations," *Journal of Money, Credit, and Banking*, November, 1980, Part 2, pp. 763-87.

Rational expectations models the formation of price level expectations by portraying market participants as using all relevant information, including the current policy regime. Fellner contrasts this with what he calls the standard "neo-Keynesian" macro models, which, in his opinion, rely too heavily on past trends to explain current price expectations. The strongest form of the rational expectations hypothesis asserts that the systematic component of demand-management policy affects only the price level, and that the policy authorities have no ability to influence any real economic variables. These claims are thought to be too ambitious, and several qualifications are suggested. What survives is the valid core, or what Fellner calls the credibility hypothesis, which retains the notion that the public will take current policy into account in forming its price expectations. Expectations can be conditioned to price stability by the consistent and credible use of non-inflationary demand-side policies.

"The Bearing of Risk Aversion on Movements of Spot and Forward Exchange Relative to the Dollar," in *Flexible Exchange Rates and the Balance of Payments: Essays in Memory of Egon Sohmen,* edited by John S. Chipman and Charles P. Kindleberger, Amsterdam: North-Holland, 1980, pp. 113-26.

An explanation is sought for the appreciation of many currencies against the dollar during 1977-78 that seems unwarranted given either interest or inflation rate differentials. Fellner believes the risk aversion of American households keeps interest rate differentials small. With their payment obligations denominated mainly in dollars, the acquisition of large foreign currency positions would be speculative. It is dollar holders with payment commitments in foreign currencies who can hedge with positions in those currencies. The market is dominated by households, not those making international business transactions. The behavior of households causes prompt exchange-rate movements in the spot market, reflecting economic processes that will work out over an extended period. The dollar's poor performance will continue until the demand restraint needed to reduce inflation is applied. This essay was also published as AEI Reprint No. 120 in January, 1981.

"Introductory Remarks on Demand Disinflation: What If Gradualism Should Fail Despite Its Merits?," in *Contemporary Economic Problems 1980*, William Fellner, Project Director, Washington, D.C.: American Enterprise Institute, 1980, pp. 1-8.

Fellner sees no alternative to a gradual return to the price level stability of the 1951-65 period through the adoption of a consistent, credible policy which allows money GNP to increase at an annual rate of 5%. It is estimated that in roughly four years price stability will be restored. Adjustments to the tax structure that remove inflationary distortions harming savers and investors can ease the transition. Should gradualism fail, thus requiring sudden stabilization, measures to soften the shock of such a major policy shift would be needed. Financial stress would result from nominal debts and wage bargains that were based on the belief that high inflation would continue. Legislation to revise such contractual obligations downward could be part of a wider program which includes a new currency backed by a promise of gold convertibility. The mere contemplation of such extreme measures should build the resolve needed to make the gradualist approach succeed.

"Corporate Asset-Liability Decisions in View of the Low Market Valuation of Equity," in *Contemporary Economic Problems 1980*, William Fellner, Project Director, Washington, D.C.: American Enterprise Institute, 1980, pp. 77-102.

Shifts in the composition of assets held by American nonfinancial corporations resemble those made by the household sector. Liquid assets performed poorly in an environment of high and uncertain inflation. Liquidity being more costly, corporations decided to economize on their holdings of liquid assets. But this less liquid position is also a riskier one. Common stock did not prove to be a very effective inflation hedge, and as a consequence, the market value of equity fell to almost one-half its equivalent replacement cost by 1979. The high cost of raising new equity led corporations to greater reliance on debt financing, higher debt-equity ratios, and riskier capital structures. By 1979 interest payments equalled dividends. Some have argued that depressed stock prices eliminate the danger posed by a market collapse. But a recovery of share values would be beneficial. Suggested changes in the tax code include elimination of the double taxation of profits.

"March into Socialism, or Viable Postwar Stage of Capitalism?," Chapter Three in *Schumpeter's Vision: Capitalism, Socialism and Democracy After Forty Years*, edited by Arnold Heertje, New York: Praeger, 1981, pp. 45-68.

The views of Marx and Schumpeter are compared and contrasted. Both foresee the eventual demise of market capitalism and the rise of socialism, but for very different reasons. Marx believes that the failures of capitalism will bring about its collapse; Schumpeter rejects the notion of class struggle and sees capitalism as falling victim to its own success. Although Schumpeter's prediction concerning the fate of capitalism has not yet come to pass, his analysis can be useful in understanding the various stages through which market capitalism has evolved.

"On the Merits of Gradualism and on a Fall-back Position If It Should Nevertheless Fail: Introductory Remarks," in *Contemporary Economic Problems: Demand, Productivity, and Population*, William Fellner, Project Director, Washington, D.C.: American Enterprise Institute, 1981, pp. 3-18.

Fellner reiterates his conviction that non-inflationary growth can be restored with a policy of consistent gradualism. Yet without admitting to a defeatist attitude, he does concede that there exists enough uncertainty about the authorities' ability to acquire the credibility needed for a successful gradualist program to justify interest in alternatives. Given that gradualism fails, a policy of abrupt disinflation should be adopted and shock reducers introduced. The terms of long-run payment commitments would have to be revised to avoid placing an undue burden on debtors and employers. All long-term debts would be made callable by the borrower, and multi-year wage agreements would be renegotiated. Conditions in the gold market make it unlikely that restoration of a gold-based currency can play a role in the achievement of price stability.

"Gold and the Uneasy Case for Responsibly Managed Fiat Money," in *Contemporary Economic Problems: Demand, Productivity, and Population*, William Fellner, Project Director, Washington, D.C.: American Enterprise Institute, 1981, pp. 97-121.

This essay is a slightly adjusted version of the one contributed to the festschrift in honor of Herbert Giersch, *Reflections on a Troubled World Economy*, and summarized in an entry below. The version in the present volume contains a very brief critique of two suggested modifications to the gold standard. The first was originally proposed by Irving Fisher, and calls for maintaining a constant real price for gold by adjusting its nominal price whenever the general price level changes. The other would substitute for the obligation of the authorities to buy and sell gold at a given nominal price the requirement that they buy and sell a comprehensive bundle of commodities at a fixed price, which would presumably approximate the general price level. Both proposed modifications are regarded as unpromising by Fellner.

"Shock Therapy or Gradualism?," in *Shock Therapy or Gradualism? A Comparative Approach to Anti-Inflation Policies,* Occasional Papers No. 8, New York: Group of Thirty, 1981, pp. 9-32.

Fellner returns to a familiar question: what should be done in the event that policymakers fail in an attempt at a gradual restoration of price stability? Previous efforts to cure inflation ended in policy reversals, suggesting that a policy of gradualism with perceptible speed could fail due to a lack of credibility. This would necessitate a policy of abrupt disinflation with the use of indexation to serve as a shock reducer. Since debt obligations are typically callable or subject to refinancing, they need not be indexed. Fellner's main shock absorber is a wage indexation scheme covering only those labor agreements that cannot be renegotiated by mutual consent, and which are in force while the disinflation is taking place.

"The Budget and the Economy: A Preliminary View," *The AEI Economist*, February, 1982, pp. 1-5, co-authored with Herbert Stein.

To assess the economic effects of the Federal budget, it is best to assume a path for the economy that is both satisfactory and feasible. The 1983 budget describes a path which is neither. It calls for a reduction in the inflation rate that is too timid, while projecting growth in real GNP that is overly optimistic. Furthermore, the budget projects a decline in inflation that is not consistent with its robust forecast for real GNP growth. The budget is criticized for its failure to make any serious effort at deficit reduction, diverting savings away from much needed increases in private investment spending.

"In Defense of the Credibility Hypothesis," *American Economic Review*, May, 1982, pp. 90-91.

> This paper is the text of Fellner's remarks delivered in a panel discussion on the problem of establishing credible anti-inflation policies. Though skeptical of many of the propositions associated with the rational expectations school, he does find their credibility hypothesis convincing. It maintains that a consistent policy stance can exert an influence on expectations, and ultimately affect cost trends in the economy. He regards this explanation of inflationary cost trends as superior to rival hypotheses that have been proposed.

"Economic Theory Amidst Political Currents: The Spreading Interest in Monetarism and in the Theory of Market Expectations," *Weltwirtschaftliches Archiv*, September, 1982, pp. 409-29.

> This is a slightly abridged version of the lecture that Fellner delivered on June 26, 1982, on the occasion of his receipt of the Bernhard-Harms Prize. He speculates on the likelihood that the Western economies will take Schumpeter's "March into Socialism." He is optimistic that such a course will be avoided. Neo-Keynesian fine-tuning has been responsible for the protracted inflation. Disenchanted policymakers are seeking less intrusive alternatives, causing monetarism and rational expectations to receive greater attention. Although he has some reservations about both of these schools of thought, he does see them as countercurrents to the increasing intrusiveness of government in the economy. Neo-Keynesian interventionism and the flawed models on which it is based must be abandoned. Non-inflationary growth can only be re-established through a credible policy that takes account of the public's ability to anticipate the effects of government policy.

"Criteria for Useful Targeting: Money versus the Base and Other Variables," *Journal of Money, Credit and Banking*, November, 1982, Part 2, pp. 641-60.

> A non-inflationary monetary policy requires adoption of a rule which commits policymakers to the targeting of some economic variable. A suitable target variable would be one related to some important objective as well as controllable in the short-run. On this basis, gold, the unemployment rate, aggregate real output, nominal GNP, and interest rates are rejected as possible target variables. Fellner views the monetary base, reserves, and M_1, narrowly defined money, to be strong candidates as the target variable. The

base and reserves are seen as inferior to M_1 because their instability might tempt policymakers to substitute their discretion for the policy rule. The regularity displayed by M_1 velocity should effectively limit the opportunity for the use of discretion. The effect of the increased availability of money substitutes on the suitability of M_1 as a target is discussed. A gradual restoration of price stability is preferred, but should it fail a policy of abrupt disinflation may be needed.

"The High-Employment Budget and Potential Output: A Critique," *Survey of Current Business*, November, 1982, pp. 26-33.

This article, a slightly different version of the one noted in the next citation, is immediately followed by a response from Frank de Leeuw and Thomas Holloway, who have used the high-employment budget and potential output concepts in work criticized by Fellner. They note Fellner's objection to the use of potential output for policy purposes, though it and the high-employment budget are no longer used for such purposes, but rather as indicators. Thus, no harm is posed by the present methods of measurement. While the crowd-out of private investment may deserve more attention, this can have no bearing on concepts proven useful as trend indicators.

The High-Employment Budget and the Potential Output: A Critique Focusing on Two Recent Contributions, AEI Studies 372, Washington, D.C.: American Enterprise Institute, 1982, pp. 1-18.

Fellner believes the concepts of the high-employment budget and potential output to be vague, and estimates of them very unreliable. The level of potential output in an economy depends on a large number of variables, including supply-side variables. However, models which make very specific estimates of potential output do so without the inclusion of these variables. Setting a high-employment budget to achieve a level of output estimated in this way leads to inflationary demand-side management. Proponents of these concepts emphasize the expansionary effect of budget deficits (and restraining effect of surpluses), but give no attention to their effect on the consumption-investment mix. After the consideration of some possible qualifications, Fellner concludes that budget deficits divert savings from private investment, and encourage consumption.

"Keynes in the History of Economic Thought," *The AEI Economist*, June, 1983, pp. 3-6.

> Fellner grants that Keynes' use of the relationship between savings and investment to show whether an economy is expanding or contracting is a significant achievement in economic thought. He faults Keynes' *General Theory* for promoting the erroneous belief that mature capitalist economies will stagnate due to a deficiency of private investment spending. Fellner's most serious criticism of the legacy of Keynes is that inflationary demand-side policies have become accepted as a means to reach a more favorable growth path.

"Tentative Lessons from the Recent Disinflationary Effort," *Brookings Papers on Economic Activity*, No. 2, 1983, pp. 603-08, co-authored with Phillip Cagan.

> This paper was Fellner's last, and was to be presented at a panel meeting held the day of his death. A widely employed wage model is slightly modified for use in the prediction of U.S. wage trends in the aftermath of the 1981-82 recession. The regression results indicate that the model overpredicts wage increases by a margin that becomes progressively larger from late 1981 to mid-1983. The authors attribute this curtailment of wage inflation to the ability of the authorities to establish a credible disinflationary policy, and see it as confirmation of the validity of the credibility hypothesis.

Comment on "Reducing Government Expenditure Growth: A British View," by Alan Peacock, in *Reassessing the Role of Government in the Mixed Economy: Symposium 1982*, edited by Herbert Giersch, Tubingen: Mohr, 1983, pp. 25-30.

> Fellner critiques Peacock's hypothesis which asserts that in a democracy growth in government expenditures is explained by the political power of voters at and below the median income to force the needed income redistributions. The critique centers on Peacock's use of the median income as the criterion by which to partition voters. Economically ambitious voters with below median incomes may be unwilling to vote for redistributions to protect their future economic positions. Furthermore, the observed increase in government expenditures in the United States during the 1970's stemmed mainly from increases in Social Security benefits, which redistribute income across time from youth to middle age to old age, rather than across income groups, and may reflect the unwillingness of democratic societies to allow their older

citizens to live in poverty. Given the ability of democracies to evade their own controls, Fellner feels that Peacock's enthusiasm for constitutional constraints as a means to control government spending will prove unfounded if the needed political conviction fails to materialize.

"Entrepreneurship in Economic Theory: The 'Scientific Method' and Vicarious Introspection," Chapter 2 in *Entrepreneurship and the Outlook for America*, edited by Jules Backman, New York: The Free Press, 1983, pp. 25-53.

> Conventional economic theory has found it difficult to incorporate explicitly entrepreneurial activity into its equilibrium models. Entrepreneurs by their very nature react to new market opportunities created in disequilibrum situations. Entrepreneurs make decisions in the face uncertainty, and society benefits most when government does not add to that uncertainty. This can be accomplished by the adoption of credible policies that have a long-run orientation. Fellner introduces the notion of vicarious introspection, an intuitive understanding of human behavior, and describes it as a useful tool in the investigation of human activity generally, and entrepreneurial activity in particular. Fellner believes that the research on entrepreneurship has focused on a mistaken conception of profit, and the essay concludes with a discussion and clarification of profit that should prove helpful in future research.

"Gold and the Uneasy Case for Responsibly Managed Fiat Money," Chapter Five in *Reflections on a Troubled World Economy: Essays in Honor of Herbert Giersch*, edited by Fritz Machlup, Gerhard Fels and Hubertus Muller-Groeling, New York: St. Martin's Press, 1983, pp. 91-116.

> Fellner does not favor a return to the gold standard as means to enforce noninflationary monetary discipline. The role of gold in the international payments system and movements in the real price of gold are put into historical perspective. Recent inflationary experience substantially increased the demand for gold at a time when gold production was expected to slow. With gold sales by the monetary authorities deemed inappropriate, increased demand for gold in an environment of limited supply suggests a continued rise in the real price of gold. Therefore, a policy seeking to establish a fixed nominal price for gold will result in a variable and unpredictable general price level deflation. In the absence of any improvement in the outlook for

gold production, no viable alternative to a responsibly managed fiat money exists.

"The Cost of Disinflation, Credibility, and the Deceleration of Wages 1982-1983," in *Contemporary Economic Problems: Disinflation*, William Fellner, Project Director, Washington, D.C.: American Enterprise Institute, 1984, pp. 7-19, co-authored with Phillip Cagan.

Various estimates implying the costs of a policy of disinflation to be substantial in terms of lost output and unemployment are contested. It is noted that the deceleration of wage increases during 1981-83 was much steeper than what standard models forecasted. The move to a restoration of price stability, while not without some cost, was more rapid and less painful than many analysts suggested. Regression analysis performed on several versions of a wage change equation indicates that the function has shifted, meaning deceleration of wage increases due to the 1981-82 recession exceeded that implied by previous experience. These favorable developments are attributed to the adoption of a more consistent, credible policy of non-inflationary growth. Such a policy can yield far more disinflation for a given level of economic slack than its critics grant.

"Monetary and Fiscal Policy in a Disinflationary Process: Justified and Unjustified Misgivings about Budget Deficits," in *Contemporary Economic Problems: Disinflation*, William Fellner, Project Director, Washington, D.C.: American Enterprise Institute, 1984, pp. 55-86.

Fellner criticizes policies which target employment and growth directly, noting that the inevitable outcome is stop-go sequences as policymakers periodically become concerned with rising inflation. He faults the Federal Reserve for its failure to make clear to the public its commitment to price stability, but approves of its use of target ranges for money growth given the erratic behavior of velocity in 1982. After reviewing the expansionary effect that increased budget deficits and more rapid money growth have on nominal demand, the large Federal budget deficits of the early 1980's are discussed. Higher real rates of interest brought on by larger deficits will alter the mix of final output away from investment goods towards consumption goods. It is undesirable to finance government expenditures using a method that will channel savings away from productive investment, thereby endangering productivity growth and continued improvement in living standards.

"Currents and Countercurrents in Political and Economic Thought," in *Essays on Macroeconomic Implications of Financial and Labor Markets and Political Processes*, Carnegie-Rochester Conference Series on Public Policy, Volume 21, Autumn 1984, edited by Karl Brunner and Allan H. Meltzer, Amsterdam: North-Holland, 1984, pp. 231-52.

This was Fellner's last published work. He reviews Schumpeter's ideas on the movement of democratic societies toward socialism, and agrees with Schumpeter that the onset of socialism is due to the short-run orientation of voters, not bureaucratic direction. Inflationary policies reflect voter choice, and hasten the march into socialism. While understanding of the Federal Reserve's widening of its money growth targets in 1982 due to unstable velocity, Fellner is critical of the monetary authorities' failure to make clearer to the public its commitment to price stability. He is encouraged by what appears to be greater acceptance by the public and policymakers of the necessity for a sustained policy of disinflation. Continued support might counter the tendency toward socialism. Comments by Anna Schwartz follow in which she is skeptical of the change in public attitude perceived by Fellner, and criticizes his acceptance of the exercise of discretion in some instances in the conduct of monetary policy.

3. BOOKS EDITED BY FELLNER

Fellner, William J., Editor. *Readings in the Theory of Income Distribution.* Philadelphia: The Blakiston Company, 1946, co-edited with Bernard F. Haley.

> The editors lament the unsatisfactory state of the theory of income distribution in their introduction to this volume. Articles on the concepts of income and distribution are presented. Articles on production theory and marginal productivity theory are included, since these topics have figured importantly in the development of the theory of income distribution. Several articles on wages, interest, profit and rent, the various distributive shares, are included. Many of the selections are classics in the literature. The list of contributors includes many of the most noted economists of this century, such as Kuznets, Stigler, Chamberlin, Machlup, Robinson, Lange, Kalecki, Robbins, Robertson, Lerner, Hayek, Knight, Keynes, and Hicks.

Contemporary Economic Problems 1976. Washington, D.C.: American Enterprise Institute, 1976.

> This edition was the first in the annual *Contemporary Economic Problems* series. This 1976 edition of essays begins with Fellner's lengthy guide to the volume in which he relates the individual works to the overall theme of the book. Some essays address structural, or microeconomic issues, and others focus on aggregative, or macroeconomic questions. But all deal with problems that arose out of the acceleration of inflation in the post-1965 period. Fellner dismisses bad weather and oil prices as the cause of the recent inflation, and rejects the belief that restraint in demand-management will cause stagflation. He discusses problems with the measured rate of unemployment, and the inadvisability of an incomes policy. The essays cover the following topics: monetary and fiscal policy, the labor market, the employment ratio, exchange-rate flexibility, the tax system and inflation, institutional rigidities, and trends in food production, by such authors as Fellner, Stein, v.N. Whitman, Haberler and Weidenbaum.

Contemporary Economic Problems 1977. Washington, D.C.: American Enterprise Institute, 1977.

In his guide to this volume, Fellner sounds a familiar warning in his elabora-tion on the dangers inherent in the use of ambitious expansionary policies to achieve an arbitrarily defined state of full employment. The common theme of this edition is the dependence of the sustainable level of macroeconomic activity in the United States on the existence of a host of structural and insti-tutional rigidities. Topics covered by the various essays include inflation and unemployment, the composition of fiscal expenditures, demand-management policies, the lessons of 1973-76, recent wage and price developments, Ameri-can agriculture, the international monetary system, international economic coordination, and the income transfer system, by Stein, Fellner, Haberler, v.N. Whitman, Chiswick and others.

Contemporary Economic Problems 1978. Washington, D.C.: American Enterprise Institute, 1978.

With this volume, Fellner's title changed from Editor to Project Director of the annual *Contemporary Economic Problems* series. A very brief prefatory note replaces the more lengthy introductions of the two previous editions, since each essay in this volume begins with a summary. The common theme of the essays is the link between the macroeconomic problems involved in the return to a sustainable growth path and underlying microeconomic, struc-tural problems. Topics include inflation, the international business cycle, problems with the measured unemployment rate, price controls, wage trends, recent agricultural legislation, the U.S. trade deficit with a floating dollar, sustainability of the world recovery, immigration policy, and health care pol-icy, by Fellner, Stein, Haberler, v.N. Whitman, Chiswick and others.

Contemporary Economic Problems 1979. Washington, D.C.: American Enterprise Institute, 1979.

In a brief preface, Fellner notes that this volume's common theme remains the same as preceding editions, namely the macroeconomic implications of certain, key structural problems. This volume is divided into three parts: American productivity trends, the inflationary environment, and special problems. Essays cover topics on productivity issues, the erosion of monetary control due to financial developments, the impact of inflation on household wealth, a balanced budget, the structure of wages, current problems, agricul-ture, recent natural gas legislation, the economic progress of immigrants, and a retrospective on the system of leading economic indicators, authored by

Fellner, Stein, Kendrick, Denison, Cagan, Perlman, Haberler, Chiswick and others. Each essay is preceded by a summary.

Contemporary Economic Problems 1980. Washington, D.C.: American Enterprise Institute, 1980.

These essays center around the continuing problem of inflation, although some address questions that would figure importantly even in an environment of price stability. Topics include policy alternatives for the achievement of disinflation should gradualism fail, new monetary policy operating procedures, achieving policy credibility, corporate financial policies, the growth in government budgets, the international role of the dollar, problems with price indexes, wages trends under the Carter Administration's guidelines, American health care, a review of a major government labor force study, and the world food situation, by Fellner, Stein, Cagan, Penner, Haberler, Perlman, Chiswick and others. Each essay is preceded by a summary.

Contemporary Economic Problems: Demand, Productivity, and Population. Washington, D.C.: American Enterprise Institute, 1981.

This volume has three parts: demand restraint in an inflationary era, international productivity and supply comparisons, and demographic problems. Topics include anti-inflation policy, the American president as chief economist, statistical problems in the measurement of inflation, the gold standard, international comparisons of recent productivity trends, agriculture in centrally planned economies, the economic malaise of the 1980's, new patterns of population growth, the exploding cost of social security, and immigration policy reform, by Fellner, Stein, Kendrick, Haberler, Perlman, Chiswick and others. Each essay is preceded by a summary.

Contemporary Economic Problems: Disinflation. Washington, D.C.: American Enterprise Institute, 1984.

This volume opens with a foreword by the president of the American Enterprise Institute, William J. Baroody, Jr., in which he notes the death of William J. Fellner and praises his enormous contributions to economic thought, policymaking, and the AEI. A longer memorial tribute by Gottfried Haberler, a long-time Fellner colleague, follows. Fellner states in his introduction that this 1983-1984 edition covers various aspects of the disinflationary process. Essays by Fellner, Cagan, Haberler, Perlman and others cover such topics as the economic costs of disinflationary policy, and the effects of disinflation on financial markets, Federal deficits, international finance, the housing market, business liquidity, labor markets, and industrial relations. A summary precedes each essay.

4. PUBLIC REMARKS BY FELLNER

Nomination of William John Fellner, Hearing before the Committee on Banking, Housing and Urban Affairs, United States Senate, 93rd Congress, 1st Session, October 11, 1973, Washington, D.C.: U.S. Government Printing Office, 1973.

> These confirmation hearings, which lasted for less than one hour, consisted mainly of exchanges between Fellner and Wisconsin Senator William Proxmire, who is unsure of Fellner's recent recommendation that a 5% target for the unemployment rate should be substituted for the current 4% target. Proxmire points to the 1966-69 time period as one in which unemployment was below 4% yet inflation was not serious, and believes the current problem with inflation to be associated with supply shortages rather than a low level of unemployment or excessively stimulative demand policies. Fellner says that inflation has been accelerating. To control it with a 4% jobless target requires periodic restraint which will lead to an unemployment rate averaging more than his suggested target of 5%. He also explains the demographic shifts in the labor force, greater entry by women and teenagers, which make 5% a more appropriate target, and elaborates on a subsidized jobs program to ease the burden on those disemployed by his 5% target.

The Nature and Causes of Accelerating Inflation: A Late Hour Reminder, Remarks by William Fellner at the Ninth Annual Financial Conference of The Conference Board, held in New York, February 20, 1974, unpublished.

> This is one of many speeches given by Fellner in his capacity as CEA member. The temptation to follow the politically popular short-run path must be resisted if a more regimented long-run is to be avoided. Inflation has accelerated as a result of demand policies which pursue employment targets that are inappropriate given the changes in the composition of the labor force. A more disciplined monetary-fiscal stance must be adopted which imposes costs on those market participants who continue to behave in a way inconsistent with price stability. A credible policy which makes clear the willingness of policymakers to risk recession in order to end inflation is needed.

Remarks by William Fellner, made at the Business and Manufacturing Conference on Inflation, held in Pittsburgh, Pa., September 16, 1974, News Release of the United States Department of Commerce, Office of the Secretary.

Inflation in the U.S. and abroad has developed as a result of excessive concern with short-run employment objectives. A return to normalcy will require an uncomfortable period of adjustment, though nothing resembling a crisis should be expected if serious policy errors are avoided. Once the effects of raw materials price increases work their way through the price structure, the rate of inflation can begin to decelerate. Responsible decision-makers should refrain from behavior that would cause an escalation of wages and prices. Tighter fiscal policy would ease strains in the credit markets by reducing government borrowing.

"What's Needed Is to Adjust for the Impact of Inflation," *U.S. News & World Report,* July 25, 1977, p. 38.

In this question and answer interview, Fellner outlines a tax indexation plan to prevent inflation from causing tax revenues to increase. Tax laws should be rewritten to allow for adjustments to tax brackets, exemptions and the standard deduction for individual taxpayers, and adjustments to the tax treatment of depreciation and inventories for corporations. Tax cuts since 1965 have not been sufficient to offset inflation, and have redistributed the tax burden.

The Dollar Abroad, Inflation at Home, an AEI Forum held August 31, 1978, Washington, D.C.: American Enterprise Institute, 1978.

Fellner joined Robert Solomon, Herbert Stein, and Henry Wallich in a panel discussion moderated by John Charles Daly concerning the dollar and inflation. Fellner sees the declining dollar to be a result of the inflationary policies pursued in the U.S. He rejects the idea that inflation differentials are reflections of the growth differentials among economies. Whatever added growth the American economy is enjoying will be transitory, since it is based on inflationary policies. While gold sales may temporarily prop up the dollar, its decline will continue until the inflation rate is reduced.

Remarks by William Fellner on the Occasion of His Receipt of the Commander's Cross of the German Order of Merit, January 8, 1979, unpublished.

Fellner praised the West German postwar recovery in remarks addressed to the Ambassador at a ceremony held at the Embassy of the Federal Republic of Germany in Washington. He comments on the perception of many West

Germans that their revival has stressed materialistic values at the expense of cultural values. With time, he believes strong economic performance will in fact foster new cultural achievements, not displace them.

"Time to Return to the Gold Standard?," *U.S. News & World Report,* September 7, 1981, pp. 71-72.

Fellner debates Lewis E. Lehrman in a question and answer format on the desirability of a return to the gold standard. Fellner opposes a return based on his belief that the price of gold will prove too unstable. A successful return requires that the price of gold change very little relative to prices for other goods. Given supply conditions in the gold market, Fellner does not believe this stable relationship would hold.

CHAPTER III
Works About Fellner and His Ideas

Rowen, Hobart, "Fellner Weighed for CEA," *The Washington Post*, August 14, 1973, p. D11.

> This is perhaps the first press account to report that Fellner was under consideration for the CEA. Fellner is the object of high praise, described as "one of the most distinguished American economists." Observers characterized him as "an intellectual giant" and the "most distinguished name ever" proposed for the CEA. His career and conservative orientation are detailed, including his faith in markets, distaste for controls, and skeptical attitude towards the concepts of the full employment budget and potential output. He believes that an unemployment rate target below 5% pursued with expansionary monetary and fiscal policy will quicken the pace of inflation. Employment objectives could be achieved without risking more rapid inflation through a government-subsidized employment program.

Holsendolph, Ernest, "People and Business," *The New York Times*, September 25, 1973, p. 57.

> Fellner's nomination by President Nixon to succeed Marina von Neumann Whitman on the Council of Economic Advisers is reported. Described as a distinguished conservative, he is thought unlikely to encounter any serious opposition during his confirmation.

"Fellner Named to President's Council," *Yale Daily News*, September 25, 1973, p. 3.

> Fellner will become the fifth Yale economist to serve on the CEA in the last fifteen years. Merton Peck and James Tobin, faculty colleagues and both

veterans of the CEA, offer a generous assessment. Fellner is a "humane economist" who has enjoyed the advantage of a European scholarly education. His "wisdom and good judgment" will "elevate the stature of the Council." He will bring "charm and wit" to the job.

Grant, James, "Fellner Opposes 4% Jobless Goal," *The Baltimore Sun*, September 28, 1973, p. 21.

At a press conference held at the AEI to announce the publication of a study he directed, Fellner expresses his support for a balanced budget, monetary restraint and a quick end to controls. Controls will turn out to be both bad economics and bad politics. The use of inflationary demand policies to reduce unemployment to 4% is ill-advised, since certain labor shortages will arise at a 5% rate. A program of subsidized public employment could bring the overall jobless rate down to 4.5% through the creation of 400,000 jobs at a cost of between $2 and $3 billion, financed largely through the elimination of existing job programs. Fellner reveals that he voted for Nixon in both 1968 and 1972, but is registered as an independent.

Milius, Peter, "Nixon Nominee Blames Government for Inflation," *The Washington Post*, September 28, 1973, p. A16.

Fellner held a press conference at the AEI to announce the publication of *A New Look at Inflation: Economic Policy in the Early 1970's*. An essay by Fellner in this volume is critical of some of the policies of the Nixon Administration, including its 4% unemployment rate target, the latest round of wage-price controls, and the overstimulation of the economy during the prior election year. According to Fellner, a price freeze is not good economics, but may seem at first to be good politics. But a freeze only suppresses the symptoms of inflation, and will eventually make for bad politics.

Shanahan, Eileen, "Nixon Economic Nominee Urges 5% Instead of 4% Jobless Target," *The New York Times*, September 28, 1973, p. 17.

This major news story reports Fellner's support of a 5% target unemployment rate instead of the administration target of 4%, which he considers inflationary. These views were expressed at an AEI news conference called to make public the results of a study by Fellner, the conclusions of which were critical of current policy. This is described as an unusual forum for a nominee who still faces confirmation. Speculation is offered concerning the effect of his remarks on his chances for confirmation, which had seemed virtually assured. His plan for a government-subsidized jobs program to ease the hardship resulting from his recommended 5% target is detailed. Fellner made known his lack of enthusiasm for Melvin Laird's proposed tax increase.

"Nixon Controls, Monetary Policy Assailed by His New Nominee for Economic Adviser," *The Wall Street Journal*, September 28, 1973, p. 5.

This account covers the same ground as those in *The New York Times* and *The Washington Post*, but also mentions Fellner's support of Nixon's veto of an increase in the minimum wage, and his belief that a 4.5% jobless rate could be achieved with a subsidized employment program financed by the elimination of unsuccessful manpower programs.

"Phase 4 to Fail: New Nixon Aide," *The Chicago Tribune*, September 28, 1973, p. 31.

An Associated Press story, complete with a photograph of Fellner gesticulating with raised arm at his press conference, appeared in this and many other newspapers across the country, including *Detroit Free Press*, *The Plain Dealer* (Cleveland), *Redwood City* (California) *Tribune*, *San Francisco Chronicle*, and *Washington Star-News*. In addition to many of the same details carried in other reports of Fellner's press conference, this account and variations in other newspapers mention the following concerning his views: controls can suppress inflationary symptoms only if enforced ruthlessly and supplemented by allocations and rationing; the dislike of other top administration advisers for controls falls short of his call for their immediate abolition; an end to controls will result in a very moderate price rise which should correct some economic distortions; and any large scale interference with the price structure is to be avoided.

"Washington Wire," *The Wall Street Journal*, September 28, 1973, p. 1.

Fellner is reported to be the likely successor to his friend Herbert Stein as CEA chair. While described as less articulate than Stein, it is hoped that his age will add some needed maturity to the Council.

"A Surprising Conservative for the CEA," *Business Week*, September 29, 1973, p. 86.

In this full page article, the hope is expressed that Fellner's nomination will restore the CEA to its rightful place in the policymaking process, and end its role in partisan politics. Fellner's views and disagreements with current policy are mentioned. He is willing to risk a mild recession to tame inflation, but his support for a public service jobs program to ease the burden on the unemployed demonstrates his aversion to dogma. He has been able to combine his conservatism with a social conscience.

Cray, Douglas W., "A Real Hawk on Inflation," *The New York Times*, September 30, 1973, Section 3, p. 8.

Fellner is expected to be blunt on matters officials are usually reticent to discuss. Colleagues call him a man of wisdom, good judgment and Old-World charm, and a "real hawk on inflation." Described as conservative, he is not doctrinaire and has incorporated Keynesian thinking into his own work. An opponent of wage-price controls, he views a policy of demand restraint as the only way to bring inflation under control. His support of a public jobs program is said to show a sensitivity to the plight of those who might lose jobs as a result of his policy recommendations.

"Fellner Favors Restrained Policy to Reverse Inflation," *Yale Daily News*, October 3, 1973, p. 4.

A posture of restraint for monetary and fiscal policy is needed to slow inflation, even at the expense of impeding economic growth. Fellner's distaste for wage and price controls, a key component of recent Nixon policy, is reported. He opposes a recent proposal for a tax increase combined with a refund at a later date.

"Text of the President's News Conference on Foreign and Domestic Matters," *The New York Times*, October 4, 1973, p. 30.

Nixon is asked if he agrees with Fellner's position that the target unemployment rate should be 5%, not 4%. Nixon is aware of his nominee's "outspoken comments" on both this matter and the question of an early end to wage and price controls. He finds "economists are the most independent breed of the human species except for members of the press." His "economic advisers are not always right but they are always sure." The important point is to keep unemployment as low as possible, and assure a job for every

American who wants to work. The exact numerical target is of less significance. These comments were widely reported in the press, by *The Wall Street Journal*, *Journal of Commerce*, major newspapers and news services.

Milius, Peter, "Stein Sees More Inflation, Urges Labor to Be Patient," *The Washington Post*, October 6, 1973, p. A2.

While being quizzed by reporters about wage and price controls, CEA chair Herbert Stein was told that Fellner thought controls to be bad economics, and perhaps even bad politics. Stein's rejoinder was that Fellner "was not selected for his mastery of politics."

"Economist's Economist," *The Economist*, October 6, 1973, p. 57.

Fellner's CEA nomination is reported enthusiastically. He is said to be a respected academic economist whose appointment is reassuring to those disturbed by the increasingly political role of the CEA and the growing policy influence of non-economists such as Melvin Laird and John Connally. Fellner is called a non-doctrinaire conservative, who is independent and outspoken. His economic views are briefly described.

"Prof. Fellner's Complaint," *Newsweek*, October 8, 1973, p. 83.

A study by Fellner was published shortly after he was nominated to the Council of Economic Advisers in which he criticizes President Nixon's economic policies. The study describes policy during the previous presidential election year as excessively expansionary, and the 4% target rate for unemployment as too ambitious. A 5% target rate is seen more likely to avoid inflationary pressure. Fellner is mentioned as likely successor to Herbert Stein as chair of the CEA.

"Fellner Approved as CEA Member by Senate Panel," *International Herald Tribune*, October 12, 1973, p. 7.

This Reuters news story reports that the Senate Banking Committee voted to recommend the approval of Fellner's nomination to the full Senate. The nominee's views on unemployment targets, monetary policy and wage-price controls are reported, along with Senator Proxmire's description of Fellner as a "tremendously competent economist."

Shanahan, Eileen, "The Economist's Dilemma," *The New York Times*, October 14, 1973, Section 3, p. 8.

> Shanahan reports on the growing perception that the Nixon Administration was using the CEA for political purposes. CEA chair Herbert Stein is thought to have contributed to this politicization with his uniformly cheery pronouncements in the face of difficult economic news. Fellner, the new CEA member-designate and likely successor to his long-time colleague Stein, is said to support more public honesty on the part of CEA members.

"Outspoken Adviser," *Time*, October 15, 1973, p. 99.

> President Nixon's comments on the "outspoken" views of his CEA member-designate are recounted. Fellner's criticism of the administration's 4% unemployment rate target and overly stimulative policies of the previous year are mentioned. Fellner is characterized as a hard-liner on inflation, and likely successor to Stein.

Samuelson, Paul A., "Policy for Stagflation," *Newsweek*, October 15, 1973, p. 99.

> In his weekly column, Samuelson mentions Fellner's recent appointment to the CEA. Fellner is a old and admired friend, but they have often disagreed on the appropriate degree of tightness for monetary and fiscal policy. Samuelson attributes these differences with Fellner to value judgments. Fellner's concern for inflation is influenced his vivid memories of the terrible Continental hyper-inflations of the 1920's. Samuelson's most haunting memories are of the Great Depression, explaining his concern for those who become unemployed by policies aimed at inflation.

Rowen, Hobart, "Advisers' Report Forecasts a Mild Recession," *The Washington Post*, February 2, 1974, p. A14.

> In a briefing to reporters at the time of the release of the annual economic report, Fellner said the CEA was reluctant to recommend that the formal 4% unemployment rate target be abandoned. In lieu of a redefinition, the CEA had published two full employment budgets, one using the 4% rate and another one for a 4.6% rate that assumes no changes in the jobless rate for the major age-sex categories of the labor force. Fellner stated that no one was

presently calling for a 4% goal, and it was "in abeyance" for the current year, though adding that it had not yet been permanently discarded.

Golden, Soma, "'74 Held Critical for Curbing Inflation: Economic Panel Member Urges U.S. Restraint," *The New York Times*, February 21, 1974, pp. 45 and 48.

Fellner's speech to The Conference Board is reported. He urges government to resist pressures to pump up the economy, and attempt instead to bring inflation under control. If inflation of 8% or more persists, controls with regimentation exceeding any heretofore experienced will be instituted. Government is held responsible for inflation, caused by the pursuit of employment goals that were too ambitious. Described as a "conservative with a conscience" for his support of a jobs program for those hurt by the restrictive policies needed to end inflation, Fellner urges Congress and the Federal Reserve to join with the administration in convincing business and labor that continued inflation will no longer be accommodated. He hints that President Nixon erred by saying in his State of the Union address that there would be no recession. Such assurances can make anti-inflation policy less convincing.

"Inflation: The Big Squeeze," *Newsweek*, March 4, 1974, p. 62.

Fellner urges policymakers to resist the temptation to stimulate the weakening economy, but rather to see the situation as an opportunity to make progress against inflation. If the effort is not made, he warns that a long-term inflation may bring "regimentation" and "loss of personal freedom."

Silk, Leonard, "Climbing Interest Rates," *The New York Times*, July 10, 1974, p. 57.

Silk examines whether higher interest rates brought on by tight monetary policy can slow inflation and make possible lower interest rates over the longer-term. Fellner's views are reported. He sees policy lacking credibility. The needed demand restraint must be adopted without any wavering in order to convince the public of the steadfastness of government in restoring price stability. A continuation of past vascillation does not bode well for the future of our political and social institutions.

Golden, Soma, "Economists, Seeking Inflation Policy, Are Skeptical on Value of Budget Cuts: Meeting Today Meant to Find Consensus," *The New York Times*, September 23, 1974, p. 57.

In advance of the Ford Administration's summit on inflation, several leading economists met to develop policy options. Many of them feel that budget cuts would not be helpful, but Fellner is of the opposite opinion. He believes that a reduction in government spending, while having a neutral effect on employment, will ease borrowing pressures in the credit markets and lower interest rates. This will promote investment in new capital stock. Expansion of capacity in sectors experiencing bottlenecks will ease price pressures.

Cray, Douglas W., "People and Business," *The New York Times*, September 25, 1974, p. 57.

Fellner confirms his plans to leave the CEA in February after the Council completes its annual economic report to the president. He claims policy disagreements or disenchantment with government service played no role in his decision. He found his service to be exciting, interesting and educational, yet wished to return to his research on inflation and productivity at the AEI.

"Noted Economists Discuss Indexing, Inflation," *The AEI Memorandum,* Fall, 1974, p. 5.

According to Fellner's remarks in a panel discussion, indexation could simplify the readjustment process if inflation were easing. He sees indexation spreading, and though it may have some good effects, it is not likely to make the current situation easier. Fellner is mentioned elsewhere in this same issue: his essay in the recent AEI publication, *Essays on Inflation and Indexation*, is cited (p. 7), in which he says indexing would accelerate inflation under current conditions in the U.S. economy; and the announcement in September of his intention to leave the CEA and return to the AEI (p. 12) is noted.

Rowen, Hobart, "Economy Picture Worsens: Auto Collapse, Coal Strike Hurting GNP," *The Washington Post*, November 20, 1974, pp. A1 and A25.

Fellner notes that auto production rates are well below the normal replacement rate, indicating an upturn in the auto industry at some point in the future. This suggests that the developing recession may begin with a sharp decline, followed by a rapid recovery.

Lackman, Conway L., and Jos. L. Craycraft, "Sales Maximization and Oligopoly: A Case Study," *Journal of Industrial Economics*, December, 1974, pp. 81-95.

This article demonstrates the ongoing significance of Fellner's *Competition Among the Few* to the oligopoly literature. The corrugated specialties industry is examined to compare observed prices with the predicted prices of various oligopoly theories. The best price predictions were obtained by integrating the expanded Fellner pricing-band model (which stipulates equal cost firms, product differentiation, and no coordination) with the assumption that the objective of the firm is to maximize sales revenue.

"Fellner Wants Tax Cut Applied to Business and Capital Gains," *The New York Times*, December 4, 1974, p. 68.

Fellner followed a speech by CEA chair Alan Greenspan before the National Economists Club, suggesting that any tax relief to fight the recession should apply to corporate taxes and capital gains taxes as well as to individuals. Both Fellner and Greenspan agree that if additional economic stimulus is warranted it should come in the form of a tax cut, not increased government spending. Fellner, while recognizing that inflation has raised the tax burden of individuals, believes the distortions brought to the corporate tax base and the capital gains tax have been even more severe.

Gannon, James P., "Ford Aides Talk Tentatively of Tax Cuts, But White House Reaffirms Policy Aims," *The Wall Street Journal*, December 4, 1974, p. 5.

Official Ford Administration policy still called for a tax increase to fight inflation despite indications of a deepening recession. But in speeches to the National Economists Club, both Fellner and Greenspan opened the possibility of tax cuts. If a cut is needed, Fellner favors a tax revision that would undo the distortions caused by inflation. He predicts that the recession will push the unemployment rate above 7% in 1975, and the "period of pronounced decline" will last at least through March of the following year.

"Getting a Break," *Newsweek*, February 3, 1975, p. 53.

Though fearful of speaking too soon, Fellner is quoted expressing his belief that "we have turned a corner" in the effort to control inflation.

Rowen, Hobart, "Indexed Tax Structure Advocated by Fellner," *The Washington Post*, February 14, 1975, pp. D11 and D12.

In a speech before a Civil Service audience during his last month as a member of the CEA, Fellner called for a revised tax system indexed to inflation. He blamed "inflationary distortions" for a $30 billion increase in tax payments by individuals and corporations for 1974. The annual Economic Report of the President, written by the CEA and published days earlier, examined bracket creep, but had made no formal commitment to an indexed tax system. Fellner stated that indexation must be a part of any future tax considerations.

"Policy: Tempest in the CEA," *Time*, February 24, 1975, p. 25.

The departure of Fellner and Gary L. Seevers from the CEA is reported. Both are said to be resentful of CEA chair Alan Greenspan's failure to consult with them in the formulation of Ford Administration economic policy to combat the 1974-75 recession. CEA staff economists are also disgruntled over Greenspan's unwillingness to present their views to the White House favoring added economic stimulus.

Golden, Soma, "More Jobless Aid Seen Raising Rate," *The New York Times*, February 25, 1975, p. 51.

In December, 1974 Congress liberalized the unemployment insurance laws by extending coverage to thousands of previously ineligible workers and by increasing the maximum period over which benefits can be paid to one full year. A study completed for the Department of Labor concluded that these changes would boost the measured unemployment rate by nearly one percent, since the protection of the unemployment insurance program would now cover more people and also allow longer job searches. Fellner is quoted stating his agreement with the general findings of the study, but he believes the full impact of the expanded coverage might go far beyond what the study estimates.

Shanahan, Eileen, "Recession Analysis," *The New York Times*, March 9, 1975, Section 3, p. 11.

There was a debate concerning the date of the start of the current recession. The National Bureau of Economic Research had established November, 1973 as the starting date, while others believed it to be the late summer of 1974. Fellner finds the evidence for a late summer or early fall date convincing. Uncertainty over official government statistics for the first three quarters of 1974 opened the possibility that economic performance in that period was stronger than what was reported.

Jones, Brendan, "People and Business," *The New York Times*, May 13, 1975, pp. 47 and 51.

President Ford's nomination of Paul W. MacAvoy of M.I.T. to fill the CEA vacancy created by Fellner's departure the previous February is reported.

"Automatic Tax Cut Tied to Inflation Rate Is Urged In Study Led by Ex-Aide to Ford," *The Wall Street Journal*, June 27, 1975, p. 4.

This article reports on the conclusions of an AEI study headed by Fellner which recommends the indexation of the Federal tax system to remove the distortions caused by inflation. The study proposes such changes as the indexation of the personal exemption and the standard deduction for individuals, and revised tax treatment of depreciation and inventories for corporations. It is estimated that tax revenue would have been $16 billion less in 1974 had the study's tax plan been in effect. Congressional consideration of indexation during the current year is thought unlikely by Fellner, though he believes that such a system will eventually be adopted.

Rowen, Hobart, "Indexing Plan Urged to Cut Over-Taxing," *The Washington Post*, June 27, 1975, pp. D9 and D11.

The same details as those in *The Wall Street Journal* of the same day (see previous annotation) are reported in this article. It is noted that inflation can move low income households paying no tax into taxable brackets. For business, inflation causes distortions constituting an unlegislated tax on capital. At a press conference called to announce this AEI tax study, Fellner states, in response to a question, that his indexing system is not regressive, but neutral, and it is lower income groups that are harmed most by inflationary distortions of the tax system.

"A Break for the Taxpayer?," *Forbes*, August 1, 1975, p. 42.

The bracket creep that results when inflation interacts with a progressive income tax is described. Fellner is quoted stating the impact this creep has on government tax revenues, and recommending that tax brackets, the standard deduction and depreciation charges be adjusted to eliminate these revenue effects. It is improper for politicians to rely on inflation to increase revenues instead of an explicitly legislated tax increase.

Golden, Soma, "Johnson Administration Exonerated by New Study of Blame for Inflation," *The New York Times*, December 30, 1975, p. 36.

Could the Johnson and Nixon Administrations conducted a more effective policy against inflation? At the 1975 annual meeting of the American Economic Association, two economists, Albert Hirsch and Harold Shapiro, use optimal control theory to answer no. They claim that even if policymakers had been aware of the unforeseen circumstances of the past decade no feasible policy mix could have been devised to assure a smooth path for the American economy. Fellner dismisses the methodology of this study and the validity of its findings. Policy would have been more successful had government acted to reduce inflationary expectations, a possibility not taken into account in the models used in this study.

"Tax-cut Therapy for a Stutter," *Business Week*, January 12, 1976, p. 22.

Fellner agrees with other leading economists on the need for additional tax cuts. While others take this position in hopes of sustaining the recovery from recession, Fellner's support is based on the belief that tax rates are in need of adjustment due to the bracket creep caused by inflation.

"Hunting New Remedies," *Newsweek*, May 17, 1976, p. 78.

Several economists give their views on the scourge of stagflation and possible cures. Fellner expresses the belief that the marketplace has come to expect very high inflation, and policy has begun to recondition those expectations to a lower level.

Law, Peter J., "The Illyrian Firm and Fellner's Union-Management Model," *Journal of Economic Studies*, May, 1977, pp. 29-37.

This article is representative of many in the economics literature which have drawn their inspiration from the work of Fellner. His classic analysis of bilateral monopoly is used to examine the Illyrian firm, a firm which seeks to maximize income per worker and has as its empirical counterpart the labor-managed enterprise. Viewed as a special case of Fellner's general model in which labor bargains for its wage rate and the amount of employment, this analysis indicates a response by the Illyrian firm to changes in demand and fixed costs quite different from that suggested by previous work.

Moore, Basil J., Review of *Contemporary Economic Problems 1976*, edited by William Fellner, Washington, D.C.: American Enterprise Institute, 1976, *Journal of Economic Literature*, June, 1977, pp. 540-42.

Fellner's works were widely reviewed in the very best journals. While most reviews were favorable, this one takes Fellner to task for the recommendations made in his essay "Criteria for Demand Management Policy in View of Past Failures." Moore sees Fellner's policy as forcing government to use unemployment and depression in order to discipline unions and firms in their wage and price behavior. This policy would do harm to those innocent of any damaging wage or price practices, while leaving the guilty but powerful, like OPEC, unscathed.

Balassa, Bela, and Richard Nelson, Eds. *Economic Progress, Private Values, and Public Policy: Essays in Honor of William Fellner.* Amsterdam: North-Holland, 1977.

This festschrift was published to honor Fellner on the occasion of his seventieth birthday. The essays are organized into three parts: long-run economic progress, consistency of private market equilibrium with public values, and macroeconomic policies. Themes figuring importantly in Fellner's work are emphasized. Topics include a Schumpeterian analysis of competition and growth, the evolution of the reaction function, and stagflation. Contributors include Reynolds, Dorfman, Schelling, Phelps, Balassa, Tobin, Brainard, Klein, Wallich, Triffin and Haberler.

Rowen, Hobart, "The Tax-Cut Dilemma," *The Washington Post*, May 11, 1978, p. A19.

The Carter Administration is faced with a difficult choice. Subsequent to its proposal for a $25 billion tax cut, unemployment declined substantially. Fellner is quoted calling for a much smaller tax cut, no more than $7 billion. With an unemployment rate of 6%, he believes inflation to be the main threat, and deficit reduction more appropriate than a large tax cut.

"The Inflation Surge," *Newsweek,* May 29, 1978, pp. 68-69.

> Fellner is quoted saying that people have learned that government cheats them by the excessive creation of money. In terms that are characterized as Calvinist, he states his belief that a recession is unavoidable, since it offers the only means by which government can reassert its credibility in combatting inflation.

Shabecoff, Philip, "Jobless Rate up as Work Force Tops 100 Million," *The New York Times,* June 3, 1978, p. 34.

> Fellner is quoted expressing the belief that attempts to lower unemployment below its current level will cause inflation to flare up. Unless policy focuses on the gradual reduction in money growth, a new recession is inevitable.

Clark, Lindley H., Jr., "Speaking of Business: Economic Ups and Downs," *The Wall Street Journal,* September 12, 1978, p. 36.

> Clark cites the policy views contained in Fellner's introduction to *Contemporary Economic Problems 1978*, in which he says that the public has lost faith in the government's anti-inflation policies. Credibility can restored only if government announces and consistently pursues a policy of monetary-fiscal restraint. Such a policy might restore price stability within three years without severe economic dislocation.

"Review and Outlook: Rose Garden Platitudes," *The Wall Street Journal,* March 9, 1979, p. 22.

> In castigating Carter Administration tax policy, this editorial cites Fellner's estimate that if the current 9% inflation rate persists individual taxes will rise by 15% due to bracket creep.

Silk, Leonard, "Economic Scene: Ex-Advisers Advise Again," *The New York Times,* October 23, 1981, Section D, p. 2.

> Seven former members of the President's Council of Economic Advisers, and all former or present economists at Yale University, met to exchange policy views and experiences. Fellner's response to William Nordhaus' assertion that bringing inflation down to 3% would necessitate 8% unemployment or

higher for at least five years is reported. In a strong rebuke, Fellner dismisses this unemployment prediction as unprovable, saying the economy would respond well if a credible policy for stopping inflation were demonstrated.

Smith, J.Y., "William Fellner, Ex-Economic Adviser, Dies," *The Washington Post*, September 16, 1983, p. B6.

> This obituary goes well beyond a simple recitation of the major events in Fellner's life by describing the economic and political context of the 1970's and early 1980's during which Fellner's policy influence was at its peak. The failure of demand-management policies to keep the unemployment rate low and achieve reasonable price stability at the same time is discussed. It is to the resolution of this policy dilemma that Fellner devoted his energies. The Federal Reserve policy begun in 1979 restrained inflation but only at the cost of a very deep recession. Fellner argued for a policy which set careful limits on money growth to inhibit inflation but would do so without severe unemployment. In the aftermath of the 1981-82 recession, he believed Federal Reserve actions exceeded those limits. Fellner's role in bringing indexation into the tax codes is discussed.

Waggoner, Walter H., "William J. Fellner Dies at 77; Economics Professor at Yale," *The New York Times*, September 16, 1983, Section A, p. 15.

> The main details of Fellner's life are related. An influential and traditional conservative economist, he is credited with assisting the Reagan Administration in the preparation of legislation to index income taxes to inflation. He was instrumental in fostering the notion within policymaking circles that policies which are excessively expansionary bring inflation without any long-lasting improvements in real terms.

"Died. William Fellner, 78," *Time,* September 26, 1983, p. 75.

> Fellner is described as an influential conservative economist whose work on inflation was instrumental in leading to eventual indexation of Federal income taxes.

"William Fellner: 'Giant among Economists'," *The AEI Memorandum,* Fall, 1983, p. 2.

The passing of Dr. Fellner is noted, and a brief review of the main details of his life is provided. His role at the AEI is mentioned, and the eulogies delivered by his colleagues at his memorial service are quoted.

Clark, Lindley H., Jr., "Speaking of Business, Thatcher and Reagan: The Failure Ratio Is High," *The Wall Street Journal*, November 29, 1983, p. 33.

Clark reports on a paper on the U.S. economy by Fellner which was delivered posthumously at the tenth annual Carnegie-Rochester Conference. Fellner perceives the American political climate to be more conducive to the private enterprise system, but still worries about the tendency of policymakers to take a short-run view. He sees the reduction in the underlying rate of inflation as the major achievement of the Reagan Administration. Pursuing monetary targets is the best way to assure continued progress, with the understanding that these targets may require adjustment from time to time.

Tobin, James, "William John Fellner, 1905-1983," *Brookings Papers on Economic Activity*, No. 2, 1983, pp. vi-vii.

Fellner's very active participation in the Brookings Panel conferences is remembered, along with his focus on the essential issues and meticulous fairness. Noted as a scholar of integrity and independence, he "defies classification" into any particular school of thought.

William Fellner: May 31, 1905-September 15, 1983, Washington, D.C.: American Enterprise Institute, 1983.

This is a collection of the eulogies delivered at a memorial service for Fellner held on October 1, 1983 at American University in Washington, D.C. Tributes were presented by Gottfried Haberler, Herbert Stein, James Tobin, Henry C. Wallich, and Bela Balassa.

Clark, Lindley H., Jr., "Speaking of Business: A Word About the International Debt Problem," *The Wall Street Journal*, January 10, 1984, p. 33.

Fellner's work with the *Contemporary Economic Problems* series published annually by the AEI is praised. Clark notes the recent publication of the latest volume in the series, and the last under Fellner's direction. Its theme is disinflation, a process which Fellner had hoped would be gradual, but in

Clark's view was abrupt and severe. The bulk of the article is devoted to a discussion of Gottfried Haberler's remarks on the international debt problem in his contribution to the latest edition of *Contemporary Economic Problems*.

Baroody, William J., Jr., Foreword to *Contemporary Economic Problems: Disinflation*. Washington, D.C.: American Enterprise Institute, 1984.

> Fellner is credited with conceiving the annual AEI *Contemporary Economic Problems* series. Under his guidance, the AEI's research program in economics had achieved prominence in the public discourse on policy. This volume on disinflation was the product of a group of scholars who worked under Fellner's direction.

Haberler, Gottfried, "William Fellner in Memoriam," in *Contemporary Economic Problems: Disinflation*. Washington, D.C.: American Enterprise Institute, 1984, pp. 1 4.

> Haberler's reflections are those of a very close and admiring colleague who was instrumental in bringing Fellner to the AEI. His friend "Willy" is portrayed as a man whose ideas were far ahead of his time. In the aftermath of the Keynesian Revolution, Fellner called for the restoration of money to its rightful place in macro theory long before the rise of monetarism. He recognized the role of expectations and institutional rigidities in macroeconomic behavior well in advance of the current interest in rational expectations and micro foundations. Fellner's important influence on policy through his scholarship, government service and activities as a consultant is noted.

Adelman, Irma, "Fellner, William John (1905-1983)," in *The New Palgrave: A Dictionary of Economics, Volume 2*, edited by John Eatwell, Murray Milgate and Peter Newman, New York: Stockton Press, 1987, p. 301.

> The inclusion of an entry on Fellner in this venerable tome attests to the enduring importance of his work. In this admiring sketch, Fellner is described as noble, profound and humble, a liberal of the old school who had been deeply affected by the events of the interwar period in his native Europe. His *Monetary Policies and Full Employment* is said to reflect a limited kind of Keynesianism that acknowledged government's role in ending deep depressions but counseled against a rigid full employment guarantee. His credibility hypothesis represents an amplification of this earlier work.

Marshall, James N., "Fellner, William J.," in *Biographical Directory of the Council of Economic Advisers,* edited by Robert Sobel and Bernard S. Katz, New York: Greenwood Press, 1988, pp. 67-75.

> This essay provides a reasonably detailed account of Fellner's life. It also assesses his major works, his economic views and his lasting contribution to economic thought. The circumstances surrounding his nomination and confirmation as a member of the CEA are given special emphasis.

Name Index

Subject Index

acceleration principle, 71-3

Accelerationist View, Phillips Curve and the, 22, 89, 101

Acta Oeconomica, Fellner's article on debate between neo-Keynesians and monetarists, 47, 96; Fellner's article on Phillips Curve trade-off, 90

AEI Economist, The, Fellner's work in, 105, 108

AEI Memorandum, The, Fellner on inflation indexation in, 126; note of Fellner's death in, 133-34

Alfred Marshall Lecturer, Fellner as, 13

American Economic Association, Fellner as president of, 1, 19, 130; Fellner's 1969 presidential address on technological progress to, 20, 87; Schumpeter's "March into Socialism" speech at 1949 meeting of, 53

American Economic Review, 9; Fellner's work in, 66-67, 69, 72, 75, 78, 83, 85, 87-88, 93-94, 106

American Enterprise Association, forerunner to AEI, 41

American Enterprise Institute (AEI), 1-2, 8, 11, 20-21, 28, 30, 36, 41-42, 45, 120, 129, 134-35; brief history of, 41-42; Fellner as Adjunct Scholar at, 41; Fellner as Resident Scholar at, 27, 41, 126

American Hungarian Foundation, its Abraham Lincoln Award to Fellner, 22

American University, 58

Annual Economic Review, of January, 1950 by CEA, 73

anti-Semitism, 2

anti-trust, 32, 60, 69-70, 79; extension to labor unions, 78

Associated Press, photo of Fellner carried by, 29, 121

automatic stabilizers, 74; effect of inflation on, 43-44

average-cost pricing, and uncertainty, 68-69

balanced budget, 113, 120; encouragement of capital formation through, 49; restoration of price stability with, 28; supply-side economics as means to achieve, 49

balanced budget amendment, Fellner's view of, 57

Baltimore Sun, The, Fellner's AEI press conference in, 120

Bellagio Group, its formation and purpose, 18-19

Berkeley, 5-6, 10-11; University of California at, 5; Fellner's reasons for leaving, 10

Berlin 3, 48; University of, 3; Fellner Ph.D. earned at, 3-4; Leontief Ph.D. earned at, 3, 53

Bernhard-Harms Prize, Fellner's receipt of, 53; his lecture, 106

bilateral monopoly, 6, 10, 60, 67-68, 70-71; article based on Fellner's work on, 130-31

biographical essay, and sketch, of Fellner, 135-36

Bretton Woods Agreement, 18, 84, 87

Brookings Institution, 2, 11-12, 21, 41, 101

Brookings Panel on Economic Activity, Fellner's participation on, 55, 108

Brookings Papers on Economic Activity, Fellner article on the Phillips Curve inflation-unemployment trade-off, 21-22; Fellner's work in, 89, 95-96, 99, 101-2, 108; note of Fellner's death in, 134

Budapest, 2-4, 23-24, 47; ancient cities of Buda and Pest, 4, 23; Public Library of, 4; University of, 3, and Fellner's lecture at, 23-24

budget deficits, and policy, 25, 49, 52, 55, 57, 93-94, 96, 105, 107, 110

Bureau of Business and Economic Research (at Berkeley), 6-7, 59

Business Behavior, Value and Growth, Fellner's review of, 78

business cycle, 73-74; theory of, 69

Business Week, Fellner CEA nomination in,

economic growth, 75-76, 78-80, 85; land in model of, 88; methodology for long-range projection of, 73

Economic Journal, Fellner's work in, 76, 79

Economic Planning Agency, of Japan, 34-35

Economic Policy and Full Employment, Fellner's review of, 67

Economic Policy and Inflation in the Sixties, a policy critique, 20, 45

Economic Progress, Private Values, and Public Policy: Essays in Honor of William Fellner, 47, 131

Economic Report of the President, Fellner's contribution to, 32; Fellner's press briefing on 1974 edition of, 33-34; review of effect of inflation on tax system in, 40; statutory provision for, 24, 32

Economic Stabilization Program, Nixon's, 32

"Economic Theory Amidst Political Currents: The Spreading Interest in Monetarism and in the Theory of Market Expectations," abridged version of Fellner's Bernhard-Harms Lecture, 53, 106

economic thought, history of, 61, 108, 111; Fellner's contributions to, 114, 135-36

economics curriculum, Fellner's views on, 13, 61

Economist, The, Fellner's CEA nomination in, 123

elasticities, cross-elasticities and market structure, 72

Emergence and Content of Modern Economic Analysis, 14, 61; genesis of, 13; rationale for, 14

employment, theory of, 69

Employment Act of 1946, its provisions, 24, 32, 74-75

entrepreneurial activity, 109

equilibrium, timeless, and period analysis, 66-67

eulogies and memorials, of Fellner, 133-35; of Okun by Fellner, 101

exchange-rates, fixed, 18-19, 84; flexible, 19; introduction of controlled floating of, 19, 92; limited flexibility in, 88, 92; role of dollar in system of flexible, 90-91; shiftable-parity and band-and-crawl to achieve greater flexibility in, 19, 85, 87; trade deficit and, 94; transitional problems in a shift from fixed to flexible, 19, 84-85

expectations, inflationary, 43, 45-46, 50, 53-54, 62, 89, 93, 98, 102, 106, 130, 135

external economies and diseconomies, 66

Federal Institute of Technology (at Zurich), 3

Federal Republic of Germany, 53; award of Commander's Cross of the German Order of Merit to Fellner by, 48, 53; diplomatic corps of, 53; Fellner's view of economic miracle of,

48; Washington Embassy of, 48

Federal Reserve System, and its policies, 28, 37, 55, 96, 99; Board of Governors of, 2, 11; Fellner's views on policies of, 47-48, 110-11, 125, 133

festschrift, in Fellner's honor, see *Economic Progress, Private Values, and Public Policy*

fiat money, 19, 51, 104-5, 109-10

fine-tuning, 8, 47, 60, 74, 96-97, 106

fiscal policy, 82-83, 98-99;compensatory, 67, 69, 73-74, 79-80; Fellner on the automatic (or built-in) stabilizers of, 57, 101

Forbes, 44; Fellner on tax indexation in, 129-30

Ford Administration, 44, 47; CEA chair in, 35; inflation summits of, 36-37, 125; reversal of tax policy in 1974, 38-39, 41; tax increases and budget proposed by, 38; Treasury Secretary in, 39

foreign exchange, and the dollar, 102-3

full employment guarantee, 7, 59-60, 67, 69, 135

full structural econometric models, neo-Keynesians reliance on, 54, 56

General Theory of Employment, Interest and Money, The, 46, 72; Fellner's view of, 46, 108; quote on practical men and ideas from, 14; interest rate theory in, 64

Germany, Fellner's views on German people, culture, Nazism and Third Reich, 48, 117-18

gold convertibility, 90, 103; suspension of, 19, 91

Gold, Money, Inflation and Deflation, series on, 59

gold standard, 19, 51, 88, 104-5, 109-10, 118

government expenditures, explanation of growth in, 108-9

Great Depression, 36, 124; effectiveness of monetary policy during, 8; diversion of attention of economics profession during, 12; public policy impact of, 24

Gypsy music, 23

Harvard University, 5, 10-11, 22, 53

high-employment budget, Fellner's criticism of concept of, 52, 107

historical orientation, of Fellner's work, 57-58

Hungarian Academy of Sciences, its Institute of Economics, 23

Hungarian, art, 4; authorities takeover of a Fellner family business, 4; colleague, B. Belassa, 47; Embassy in Washington, 22; Fellner's views on the people and their standard of living, 23; friends of Fellner, 3; interest in Western economic debates, 24, 47; ministry official who arranged Fellner's return visit to Hungary, 22; Parliament, 4; poetry and literature, 4; politics, 4

Hungarian Economic Association, 47

U.S. News & World Report, 44; Fellner debates the gold standard in, 118; Fellner's article on inflation in, 99-100; Fellner's views on tax indexation in, 117
utility, 15-18, 62, 81-83; operational, 85-86

"Valid Core of Rationality Hypotheses in the Theory of Expectations, The," Fellner on rational expectations, 50, 102
Value and Capital, theory of interest rate in, 64
value judgments, in economic debate, 52, 124
velocity of money, erratic behavior of, 110-11; stability of, 54-56, 95-96, 107
Viet Nam war, 25, 29

wage and price controls, 28-29, 33, 54; Fellner's call for the abolition of, 29, 31; Fellner's characterization as "bad economics" and "bad politics," 28; Fellner's opposition to, 11, 20-21, 31, 62, 78, 91; in Nixon Administration's New Economic Policy, 25-26
wage-push inflation, 78
Waldorf-Astoria, inflation summit held at, 37
Wall Street Journal, The, 44; article about Fellner tax indexation plan in, 42; article by Fellner on tax indexation in, 42, 94; article contesting validity of Fellner's credibility effect in, 52; Fellner erred, disinflation viewed as abrupt and severe in, 134; Fellner on inflation policy in, 134; Fellner urges tax cut in, 127; Fellner's AEI press conference in, 121; Fellner's policy of credible demand restraint in, 132; Fellner's tax indexation study in, 129; Fellner's views on Carter Administration tax policy cited in editorial in, 48, 132; report on Fellner as possible successor to Stein as CEA chair in, 121
war inflation, prevention of, 6, 59; tax policy to avoid, 67
Washington Desk page, Fellner's forecasts for *Dun's* on its, 44
Washington Post, The, 44; article about Fellner tax indexation plan in, 42; article on likely Fellner nomination to CEA in, 26, 119; Fellner briefing on CEA annual economic report in, 124; Fellner obituary in, 133; Fellner on auto sales in, 126; Fellner on Carter's proposed tax cut in, 131; Fellner's AEI press conference in, 121; Fellner's tax indexation plan in, 127-28; Fellner's tax indexation study in, 129; Stein's comments on Fellner political mastery in, 123
Watergate scandal, 26-27, 29, 35
welfare state, 53
Weltwirtschaftliches Archiv, Fellner's Bernhard-Harms Lecture published in, 53, 106; other Fellner work in, 87
West Germany, see Federal Republic of Germany

Whip Inflation Now (WIN) button, 36
William Fellner: May 31, 1905-September 15, 1983, collection of eulogies of Fellner, 134
World War II, diversion of attention of economics profession during, 12; end to price controls following, 36; relief of Great Depression by, 24; resettlement of Fellner brothers after, 4, 22
writing syle, of Fellner, 6-7

Yale Daily News, Fellner nomination to CEA in, 119-20; Fellner's views in, 122
Yale Review, The, Fellner article in, 77
Yale University, 2, 13-14, 18-20, 35, 41, 47, 58; Fellner as economics department chair at, 15; Fellner's move to, 10-11; Fellner's role in undergraduate program at, 13-14, 61; Fellner's uncertainty experiments with undergraduates at, 16; meeting of former CEA members from, 51, 132-33

Zeitschrift fur National-okonomie, 5
Zurich, 3

About the Author

JAMES N. MARSHALL is Professor of Economics in the Department of Economics at Muhlenberg College in Allentown, Pennsylvania and holds the Ph.D in economics. He has earned degrees from the Massachusetts Institute of Technology, the Wharton School at the University of Pennsylvania, and Lehigh University. In addition to this book, he has authored several papers, essays and book reviews in the fields of economics and finance.

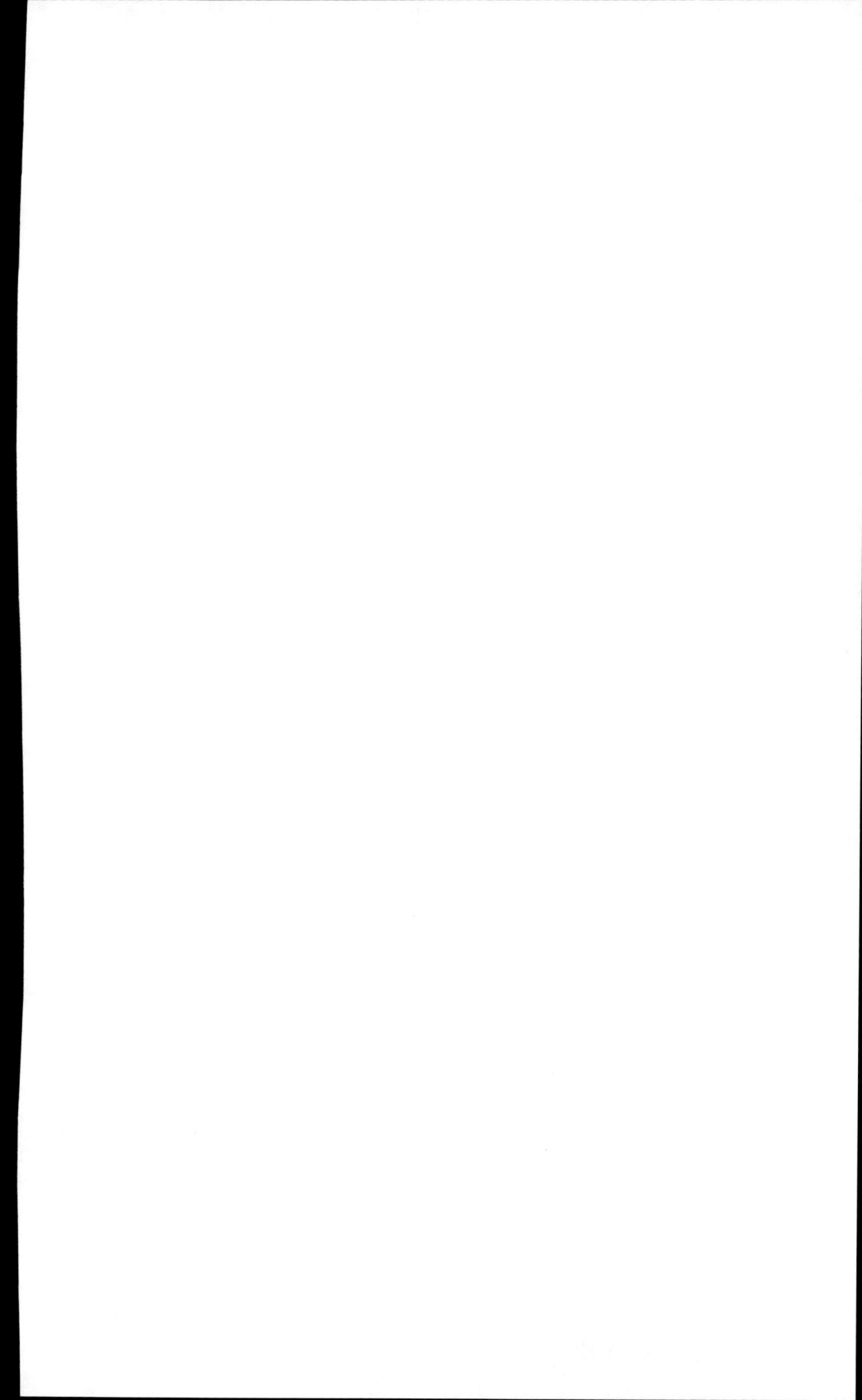

www.ingramcontent.com/pod-product-compliance
Lightning Source LLC
Chambersburg PA
CBHW070442100426
42812CB00004B/1189